HAPPY BIRTH

CW00539988

GRACE O'MALLEY

THE BIOGRAPHY OF IRELAND'S PIRATE QUEEN 1530–1603

Anne Chambers

ANNE CHAMBERS

GILL BOOKS

In memory of my grandfather
James Cruise

Gill Books
Hume Avenue, Park West, Dublin 12
www.gillbooks.ie
Gill Books is an imprint of M.H. Gill and Co.

© Anne Chambers 1998, 2003, 2009, 2018, 2019
978 07171 8577 1

First edition published in hard cover 1979
First paperback edition 1983. Reprinted 1986
Second paperback edition 1988. Reprinted 1991, 1994
Third paperback edition 1998. Reprinted 2002
Fourth paperback edition 2003
Fifth paperback edition 2009
Hardback anniversary edition published 2018
This paperback anniversary edition published 2019

Index compiled by Cover to Cover
Print origination by O'K Graphic Design, Dublin
Printed by GraphyCems, Spain

Photographs courtesy of the individuals, institutions and agencies
noted beneath each picture.

This book is typeset in 11/14 pt Minion.

The paper used in this book comes from the wood pulp of
managed forests. For every tree felled, at least one tree is planted,
thereby renewing natural resources.

A CIP catalogue record for this book is available from the British
Library.

5 4 3 2

CONTENTS

AUTHOR'S NOTE   V
FOREWORD   VII

INTRODUCTION   1
1. Powerful by Land and Sea   5
2. The World of Granuaile   18
3. *Fortuna Favet Fortibus*   33
4. The Pirate Queen   49
5. 'A Most Famous Feminine Sea Captain'   60
6. 'Nurse to All Rebellions'   77
7. 'A Notable Traitoress'   92
8. The Meeting of the Two Queens   106
9. End of an Era   125
10. The Descendants of Granuaile   137

APPENDICES
1. MANUSCRIPT DECIPHERMENTS
   I.   Petition of Richard Bourke,
         22 April 1580   146
   II.   Letter Patent Queen Elizabeth I,
         14 April 1581   147
   III. Milly Mac Evilly, Deed of Kinturk,
         1582   149
   IV.   Granuaile's Petition to Queen Elizabeth I,
         July 1593   151
   V.   The Eighteen 'Articles of Interrogatory',
         July 1593   153

VI.   Sir Richard Bingham to the Lord
        Treasurer of England, July 1593   160
VII.   Granuaile's Petition to the Lord Treasurer
        of England, September 1593   164
VIII.   Queen Elizabeth I to Sir Richard Bingham,
        September 1593   165
IX.   Granuaile's Petition to the Lord
        Treasurer of England, April 1595   167
X.   Granuaile's Petition to the Lord
        Treasurer of England, May 1595   169
XI.   Court of Chancery Deposition, 1626   170
XII.   Last Will and Testament:
        Murrough-na-Maor O'Flaherty, 1626   172
XIII.   Viscount Mayo: Letters Patent, 1627   174
2. POEMS AND SONGS   176
3. GENEOLOGY   197

REFERENCES   199
BIBLIOGRAPHY   204
INDEX   209

AUTHOR'S NOTE

Since first published in December 1979 the endurance and popularity of this biography reflects the magnetism of its subject. Grace O'Malley (*Granuaile*) continues to enthral, inspire and capture the imagination of new devotees worldwide as she undoubtedly captured mine.

While her life is well documented in Elizabethan state correspondence and her name is enshrined as a political leader in the famous Boazio map of Ireland (1599) her absence in Irish historical records, which initially motivated my own interest, has since been rectified. Grace O'Malley's place and contribution to the political, social and maritime history of Ireland is now acknowledged and celebrated.

She has inspired new generations of artists, sculptures, fiction writers, documentary makers, musicians and composers, most notably Irish composer Shaun Davey, whose Granuaile Suite is an evocative musical interpretation of her factual life. Her story has been documented for radio and television worldwide and her place in history is now part of schools' curricula in many countries.

My own journey over the past forty years in the company of this pioneering feminist and trailblazer has lead me to many countries and introduced me to many people whose own lives or careers have been inspired and shaped by this extraordinary woman.

International focus on gender equality, the 'Me Too' movement and other feminist campaigns, makes Grace O'Malley's life, albeit lived over four hundred years ago, resonate even more today. She shines as an inspirational beacon to what women everywhere can achieve, even in the most demanding and difficult environments.

As ageism in society, particularly attitudes to older women, comes under greater scrutiny today, that she retained her status as a woman of power and remained actively involved right to the end of her long life undoubtedly makes Grace O'Malley a symbol of positive ageing and through her example the realisation that age need not be a terminus – merely another port-of-call.

ANNE CHAMBERS

By the same author

Shadow Lord: Theobold Bourke—Tibbott-ne-Long: Son of the Pirate Queen, 1567–1629
At Arm's Length: Aristocrats in the Republic of Ireland
La Sheridan: Adorable Diva, 1889–1958
Eleanor Countess of Desmond, 1545–1638
Ranji: Maharajah of Connemara
Pirate Queen of Ireland (children)
The Geraldine Conspiracy (novel)
Finding Tom Cruise (short stories)
T.K. Whitaker: Portrait of a Patriot
The Great Leviathan: Howe Peter Browne, 2nd Marguess of Sligo, 1788–1845

Further information about the author and her published work is available from
www.graceomalley-annechambers.com
www.gillbooks.ie
www.newisland.ie
www.collinspress.com
www.transworldireland.ie

FOREWORD

The courage of the suffragettes astounds us. The forces ranged against them confound us. It was all such a very short time ago as the centenary commemorations remind us.

But go back even further to a different time in Ireland, half a millennium ago, when Ireland's first recorded pioneering feminist Grace O'Malley ruled the waves and introduced England's Queen Elizabeth I to the language of the Gael. Granuaile's story is told here and what a dramatic narrative it is. By land and by sea, against the background of political and social upheaval and disintegration, Grace O'Malley proved herself to be the original female trailblazer and mouldbreaker.

Gender discrimination against women is long established and rooted in history, tradition and culture. The primacy of patriarchy, often cultivated by religious doctrines, has negatively impacted women's lives in almost every country and culture over the centuries – and still does today. Anne Chambers pointedly reminds us however, that this was not always the case. Grace O'Malley's life testifies to a time when things were very different. She was the inheritor of the Mother Goddess and Warrior Queen attributes of her more remote Bronze Age ancestors, a time when the matriarchy held sway. That society ruled by powerful women gave way to the more familiar structure of second-class citizenship for women, their voicelessness, lack of legal status and dependency on men. Grace O'Malley was one of the few women in modern history to break that mould.

Anne Chambers deserves our thanks for bringing this extraordinary woman out of the shadows of history and elevating her to her rightful place not only in the annals of political, social and maritime history, but in the story of the liberation of women everywhere. Even now, five centuries later, Granuaile stands out as a shining example of the unyielding grit and determination needed to overcome the man-made and natural obstacles life plants squarely in the path of women.

Today, the battle for gender equality goes on, for our world mostly continues to fly badly on one wing instead of two. In almost every sphere of life and on every continent, embedded discrimination and discriminatory attitudes prevent women from fulfilling their true potential and humanity from fully flourishing. The loss of momentum, the sheer waste of talent is scandalous, but it is not the end of the story.

There is, in our world, a vast reservoir of female potential, talent, experience and knowledge just waiting to change the face of the Earth and make it smile. Granuaile's story, with its tragedies and its comedies, its triumphs and disasters pushed through and transcended, can in the end make us smile, knowing that for women – and for civilisation – the best is yet to come, if we follow her star.

MARY MCALEESE
FORMER PRESIDENT OF IRELAND.

INTRODUCTION

There came to me also a most famous feminine sea captain called Granny Imallye and offered her services unto me, wheresoever I would command her, with three galleys and two hundred fighting men, either in Scotland or in Ireland. She brought with her her husband for she was as well by sea as by land well more than Mrs Mate with him ... This was a notorious woman in all the coasts of Ireland.

SIR HENRY SIDNEY, LORD DEPUTY OF IRELAND, 1577

For centuries the life of the iconic sixteenth-century warrior leader by land and sea, Gráinne Ní Mháille (Grace O'Malley) or Granuaile, as she is more familiarly known in Ireland, was abandoned to the vagaries of myth, fiction and folklore. Why this should have happened says more about the negative side of being an icon than it does about being Granuaile. Icons are sometimes dissident, subversive, mould-breaking, radical and, at times, heretical too, often resulting in their banishment instead of their commemoration. Since Granuaile subscribed to all the above traits she thereby paid the penalty of omission.

Like many of her sisters, Granuaile was also a victim of the mainly male orientation of history. But in her particular case more than mere male chauvinism ensured her dismissal from historical record. Irish heroines were required to fit a specific mould, suitably adorned in the green cloak of patriotism, their personal lives untainted, their religious beliefs Roman Catholic. Granuaile, as one of her male detractors wrote of her, 'a woman who overstepped the part of womanhood', who allowed neither social, political nor religious convention to deter her, did not readily conform to the patriotic, untainted, God-fearing and dutiful

1

picture of Gaelic womanhood promoted by later generations of Irish historians.

There are many aspects of Granuaile's life that qualified her as *persona non grata* in the roll-call of Irish heroes. Born c. 1530, the daughter of a Gaelic chieftain, she already excelled in the traditional seafaring attributes of her family—sea-trading in Ireland, Scotland and Spain, with some piracy and plundering on the side—before she assumed the more traditional role of wife and mother in a politically-arranged marriage. As a wife, however, convention did not deter her from superseding her more reckless first husband in his role as chieftain, or from avenging his death. Neither did it deter her from divorcing her second husband, from taking a lover, from reuniting with her husband who, from Sidney's observation above, would seem to have been content to walk in her shadow. As a mother, much to Queen Elizabeth's amazement, she did not hesitate to 'chastise' one son by attacking his castle and driving off his cattle herds when he foolishly allied with her sworn enemy, or from saving the life of her youngest son when her ship was attacked by North African pirates.

When Gaelic law spurned her as a female chieftain, leading by example, both by land and by sea, she endured the same danger and hardship as her followers. Her ability and success rendered the *salic* code, which debarred female clan leaders, redundant. Contrary to law, custom and social mores, her daring and charisma made her leader of an army of two hundred men and captain of a fleet of 'galleys'—the versatile cargo-cum-plunder-cum-warship of the period.

On the military front she personally led her army on the battlefield against individual English military generals who tried to curb her power, eventually becoming a matriarch, not merely of her own followers and extended family, but of neighbouring clansmen, whose chieftains had either died in the numerous conflicts of the period, or who had abandoned their obligations to protect their dependent followers. And her maritime skills gave her role a double edge. It took immense skill and courage to ply the dangerous Irish coastline and the seas beyond.

When the expansionary and colonisation policies of Granuaile's great contemporary Queen Elizabeth i of England impacted on

Ireland in the last decades of the sixteenth century, Granuaile's leadership qualities in the political arena came into play. Skilfully negotiating her way through the Machiavellian web of Elizabethan court politics, she outmanoeuvred many of the most prominent English statesmen of her day. Her correspondence and meetings with such Elizabethan movers and shakers as Lord Burghley, Sir Henry Sidney, Sir John Perrot, the Earl of Ormond, the Earl of Tyrone, Sir Richard Bingham, Sir Nicolas Malby, Robert Cecil and eventually Queen Elizabeth, is evidence of Granuaile's political acumen. The inclusion of her name on the famous Boazio's map of Ireland of the period confirms her status as a figure of political significance.

Her personal struggle for political prominence, however, mirrored the final struggle for survival of the archaic world that bred and bore her. Sixteenth-century Gaelic Ireland was fragmented and politically outmoded. Inter-clan feuding and divided loyalties against a determined enemy, unified and strong under their female monarch, left every Irish leader to fend for himself. Granuaile's principal motivation was to ensure the survival of herself and her extended family in the political and economic chaos precipitated by the Tudor conquest of Ireland.

In 1593, with a lengthy catalogue of rebellion, piracy and other 'disloyal' activities registered against her at the English Court, bearing the tags 'nurse to all rebellions for forty years', 'a director of thieves and murderers at sea', 'a most notable traitoress', she boldly sailed her galley from her castle on Clew Bay on the west coast of Ireland to Greenwich Palace to negotiate face-to-face with her perceived enemy Queen Elizabeth I. The correspondence emanating from the meeting of these two remarkable women, by then elderly and experienced in the ways of the world, is testimony to the audacity of Granuaile in persuading the English queen to fly in the face of the advice of her own military men in Ireland. Granuaile not only kept her head but ensured her family's future security and her own freedom until her death in 1603.

Yet her role in the history of the sixteenth century was allowed lapse into the realm of folklore and fiction. The *Annals of the Four Masters*, that seminal source of Irish history compiled a few years after her death and in a place where memories of her activities were still verdant, do not even mention her name. The English State Papers, on the other hand, contain references to her as late as 1627, some twenty-four years after her death. Such bias erased from the pages of Irish history one of the most remarkable women and, in so doing, diminished our understanding of the past. However, it is a measure of her greatness that her memory was preserved by folklore. Legends are not created about insignificant people. To be remembered in folk memory is as much a tribute to, and validation of her status, as any academic treatise.

As to the factual evidence relating to Granuaile, it was left to the English administrators and generals who had come to conquer her country, to write her into historical record. And this is where I found her. These Elizabethan artefacts, held in both public and private institutions, are now faded and brittle, their age-darkened, spider-like handwriting evidence of the passage of four hundred years since their authors first put quill to parchment. From the swirls and flourishes of these sixteenth-century relics the story of Granuaile springs to life. And when analysed within the historical context of the traumatic epoch in which she lived, she emerges as a fearless leader, by land and by sea, a political pragmatist and tactician, a ruthless plunderer, a mercenary, a rebel, a shrewd and able negotiator, the protective matriarch of her family and tribe, a genuine inheritor of the Mother Goddess and Warrior Queen attributes of her remote ancestors. Above all else, she emerges as a woman who broke the mould and thereby played a unique role in history.

It is, forty years since my biography first helped write Granuaile back into history—she had more than created her own legend. Since then through music, song, dance, drama, TV documentaries, and her inclusion in schools curricula, her story has reached the public domain and now seems certain to endure.

My own voyage in the company of this iconic woman seems destined to continue as Granuaile captures the imagination of new generations of admirers as she most surely captured mine.

CHAPTER 1
POWERFUL BY LAND AND SEA

Duine maith riamh ní raibh
D'iabh Máille acht 'n a mharaidhe,
Fáidhe ne síne sibh-sí,
Dine báidhe is bhráithirrí.

A good man never was there
Of the O'Malleys but a mariner,
The prophets of the weather are ye,
A hospitable and brotherly clan.

O'DUGAN (d.1372)

G ranuaile was born into the clan Uí Mháille, a hardy, seafaring people on the west coast of Ireland. According to the ancient genealogies of Ireland, the O'Malleys were descended from the eldest son of a high king of Ireland, Brian Orbsen, who was killed at the battle of Dam Chluain, near Tuam, county Galway, circa 388 A.D. They were hereditary lords of the region called the Umhalls (*umhall* meaning territory), later anglicised as the 'Owles', a territory comprising the baronies of Murrisk on the south shore of Clew Bay and Burrishoole on the north. The barony of Murrisk, called *Umhall Uachtarach* or Upper Owl, included the islands of Clare, Inishturk, Caher, Inishbofin, Inishark and a multitude of smaller islands in Clew Bay. The barony of Burrishoole was called *Umhall Íochtarach* or Lower Owl and originally included the island of Achill. The two baronies were generally referred to as *Umhall Uí Mháille* (territory of the O'Malleys) or the 'Owles of O'Malley'.

5

In 1235 the Anglo-Norman de Burgos invaded Connaught and in a demonstration of military power swept aside the fragmented Gaelic opposition. In the transition of land and power that followed, the invading Butlers were granted some of the O'Malley territory in *Umhall Iochtaracht*—the barony of Burrishoole, known as *Leath Fherghuis* (Fergus's half), Fergus being head of one of the three O'Malley septs. The Butlers built a castle known as Tyrenmore close to Burrishoole Abbey. They, in turn, were later dispossessed of the barony of Burrishoole by the sept of Ulick de Burgo, with the exception of Achill, which reverted back to the O'Malleys. This remote connection between the O'Malleys and the Butlers was to be effectively evoked 400 years later by Granuaile in her efforts to obtain an audience with Queen Elizabeth I.

The O'Malleys lived in relative harmony with their de Burgo neighbours, becoming their allies in war and related through intermarriage. In 1342, the de Burgos, like many of their fellow Normans, renounced their allegiance to the English crown and adopted Gaelic names and customs. They became divided into two branches. The Mayo Bourkes adopted the title MacWilliam *Iochtarach* (i.e the Lower MacWilliam) and the Galway Burkes became known as the MacWilliam *Uachtarach* (the Upper MacWilliam). The O'Malley chieftain gave his daughter Sabina in marriage to the new MacWilliam of Mayo. Unlike the other sub-chieftains who held under the MacWilliam, the O'Malley chieftain paid no rent or tribute to his powerful overlord but merely, as stipulated, a 'rising out of six score bands to be maintained by himself, but they have maintenance for the first night from MacWilliam'.[1]

The earliest written reference to the O'Malley territory of Umhall is in the fifth century with the ascent by St Patrick of the spectacular conical mountain then known as *Cruachan Aigle* (Eagle Mountain). In Tireacháin's notes on the life of the saint contained in the *Book of Armagh*, it was written:

> And Patrick went to Mount Egli to fast on it for forty days and forty nights, keeping the discipline of Moses, Elias and

Christ. And his charioteer died in Muirisc Aigli, that is the plain between the sea and Aicill and he buried the charioteer, Totmael, and piled stones as a sepulchre ...[2]

Patrick's pilgrimage in 441 A.D. has been commemorated since by pilgrims from all over the world who each year walk in his footsteps to the summit of the mountain that now bears his name.

The rugged, scenic splendour of the Umhalls moved William Makepeace Thackeray to write in 1842: 'It forms an event in one's life to have seen that place, so beautiful is it and so unlike all other beauties that I know of'.[3] The territory is encompassed by the peak of Croagh Patrick to the south, Mweelrea, Croaghmore on Clare Island and Slievemore on Achill to the west and the Nephin range to the north. At its heart is the broad expanse of the island-strewn Clew Bay, that 'miracle of beauty', with Clare Island at its mouth, a sphinx-like bulwark against the surge of the mighty Atlantic ocean that stretches away towards the western horizon. The Umhalls comprised some fertile land around Belclare and Murrisk and wide tracts of bog, marsh, lake, rivers, rough mountain grazing and extensive woodland. Apart from its scenic beauty, this sea-washed territory of the Umhalls was an appropriate base for a seafaring clan.

Although an island, Ireland has produced few seafaring families of note. The O'Malleys differed from the majority of Irish clans in that they derived their living mainly from the sea. Their clan motto, *terra marique potens* (powerful by land and sea), proclaimed them lords of the seas along the west coast of Ireland. In the ancient Book of Rights (*Leabhar na gCeart*) which lists the rights and tributes to be paid to the king of Connaught, it is thus recorded: 'the command of the fleet to O'Flaherti and O'Mali, whenever he [the king] goes on sea or on the high sea'.[4] O'Malley paid the king at his residence at Cruachan a yearly tribute of 'one hundred milch cows, one hundred hogs and one hundred casks of beer'. The king, in return for O'Malley's service, tributes and loyalty, presented him with the substantial annual gift of 'five ships, five horses, five swords and five corselets'.[5]

Like many coastal families, the O'Malleys claimed a traditional overlordship of their immediate sea territory, including the right to levy tolls for safe passage and to sell fishing rights to foreign fleets. Writing in 1579, an English administrator seeking to abolish this custom recorded:

> Towards the sea coast there lieth many fair islands, rich and plentiful of all commodities, there cometh hither every year likely about fifty English ships for fishing. They have been compelled to pay a great tribute to the O'Malleys ...[6]

The O'Malleys were themselves intrepid seafarers, whose seafaring was not merely confined to Ireland. A fifteenth-century poem confirms what tradition has always maintained—that they regularly traded and plundered as far as Spain and Scotland:

> *Leomhain an oirir uaine*
> *eolaigh oirír na Spáinne*
> *ag buain chruidh do Ceann Tíre*
> *gearr míle ar muir d'ibh Máille.*

> They are the lions of the green sea
> men acquainted with the land of Spain
> when seizing cattle from Kintyre
> a mile by sea is short to the O'Malleys.[7]

One of the earliest references to the name Uí Máille appears in 1123, in the *Annals of the Four Masters* recording that 'Tadhg Ua Máille lord of Umhall was drowned with his ship at Aran.'[8] From then the name appears frequently in various historical records. In 1413 the annals record how Tuathal O'Malley returned home from mercenary service in Ulster

> ... with seven ships and their crews ... a storm arose on the western sea, which drove them to the right towards Scotland,

where six of the ships with all their crews were sunk ... Tuathal
himself with much difficulty effected a landing in Scotland.[9]

The annals further state that 244 of Tuathal's crewmen were
drowned in this tragedy, an indication of his substantial seapower.
It was this Tuathal O'Malley who, on being wounded in a quarrel
with a poet, instead of claiming an *eric* (the legal payment for
bloodshed by Brehon Law), chose instead to have the poet
compose a poem for him in atonement—an interesting insight
into the cultural obverse of a warlike Gaelic chief, as well as an
acknowledgement of the significance of poetry in the Gaelic world.
In his bardic verses the poet eulogised Tuathal and praised him for
his choice:

> You did not claim a pledge for your wound
> You ignored the loss of the best blood
> Here to requite you for it is a melodious poem
> You deserved from me the price of your healing.[10]

It required a special measure of skill and daring to extract a living
from the sea along the formidable Atlantic seaboard. The sea
routes north to Scotland and south to the Continent, along the
indented western coastline, were hazardous. Impediments such as
basic navigational aids, inaccurate charts, wooden-hulled ships and
the ever-present threat of piracy, added to the danger. But their
mobility by sea gave the O'Malleys distinct advantages over their
land-bound neighbours. It provided them with an escape route
from their enemies in time of attack, an advantage much availed of
by Granuaile and her sons. It allowed them access to foreign markets
to sell their produce in exchange for goods unavailable at home. It is
reasonable to assume that over the centuries O'Malley castles were
bedecked with more exotic furnishings than their neighbours and
their tables replenished with the wines of France and Spain.

Less tangible, but nonetheless advantageous, was the
opportunity denied most of their land-bound contemporaries—
to mingle with other peoples and cultures, to observe, to learn, to

glean knowledge of events in the wider world outside of Ireland. To seafaring folk like the O'Malleys the sea was ever a highway, while landlubbers saw it merely as a barrier. Recent research on trade links between Ireland and the Continent has confirmed what tradition has always held, that from the Middle Ages, Irish-owned ships, manned by Irish crews, regularly crossed the sea to ports in England, France and Spain. The ports along the west coast of Ireland tended to trade with Bristol in England and with those on the west coast of France and on the north coast of Spain.

For a sea-going clan like the O'Malleys, there was another incentive to trade their produce in foreign markets. Galway city was the centre of trade on the west coast. By the early sixteenth century it was considered 'one of the first emporia of trade, not only in Ireland but, with few exceptions, in the British Isles as well'.[11] But the wealthy merchant families who ruled the city had enacted a series of restrictive bye-laws which prohibited non-residents, particularly the Gaelic clans living outside the city walls, from trading there. Trade in wool, the mainstay of the Gaelic clans, was prohibited. In 1460, the Corporation of the city enacted:

> … that ne merchent, ne maryner, ne shipman, should unlode, ne transport over the seas, unfremans goods, but only fremans, upon paine to lesse the said goods or the just value therof and to forfoyte 100 shillings.[12]

This restriction, coupled with the racist sentiment of a later 1518 bye-law, which fined citizens who entertained their Gaelic neighbours within the city without licence of the mayor and council on any feast day, so 'that neither O' ne Mac shall strutte ne swagger thru the streets of Galway',[13] made it imperative that the O'Malleys trade their produce in foreign markets, free from such taxes and impediments.

Fishing was an important source of the clan's income. The fishing grounds off the coast of O'Malley's lordship were considered one of the most fertile in Ireland. Herring, hake, cod, ling, turbot, salmon and shellfish were the main species caught.

The fish was usually salted or smoked and packed in wooden barrels for export. Hides, tallow, frieze cloth, deer and sheepskins, furs such as pinemarten (considered a highly fashionable accessory in the sixteenth century), coney, fox and otter were other commodities from the west of Ireland which found a ready market abroad.

As in most coastal communities plundering and piracy supplemented the O'Malley income from earliest times. The ancient annals record with regular monotony O'Malley raids on outlying coastal settlements from Kerry to Donegal: 'Eogan O'Máille went with the crews of three ships against Cille bega [Killybegs, county Donegal] in the night … They raid and burn the town and take many prisoners'.[14] Granuaile, who indulged in the profession with more success than most of her ancestors, was accused of being 'a chief director and commander of thieves and murderers at sea',[15] and is recorded as raiding from the Scottish isles to the south coast of Ireland.

Piracy has been in existence for over five thousand years. From ancient Persia to modern-day China, every known civilisation throughout the ages has produced a pirate community. Depending on political and, to a lesser degree, cultural considerations, piracy has been viewed pragmatically by rulers down through the centuries. 'The Ancient Greeks and Carthaginians had no qualms about piracy being proper conduct'.[16] The Vikings used it as a means to establish footholds in Ireland, Britain and the Continent. In the Red Sea, the Persian Gulf and along the north African coast, piracy flourished throughout history. In the Far East it was undertaken on a massive scale and still exists today as it does off the coast of Somalia. Granuaile's contemporary Queen Elizabeth I gave her letters of marque to the pirate turned privateer Sir Francis Drake, when it seemed likely that his unlawful activities on the high seas would substantially supplement her state coffers. Granuaile's career predated by a hundred and fifty years the careers of Caribbean female pirates—Irish-born Ann Bonny and her companion, Mary Read.

The struggle for power and profit at sea no more than mirrored a similiar struggle on land, but perhaps with more romance and notoriety. Piracy is often a symptom of political chaos on land and in Ireland in the sixteenth century, as the old Gaelic world faced the ultimate assault by a more powerful neighbour and slowly disintegrated, such was the case. This period saw Granuaile's career at sea reach its zenith. Her strongholds, situated deep within the inlets of Clew Bay, accessible only to those with local knowledge of its dangerous channels, tides, currents, reefs and sandbanks, made capture or reprisal, as it had for her ancestors, virtually impossible. It was not until the end of the sixteenth century when cartographers began to more accurately map the remoter havens of the west coast that time and the English navy caught up with her and her family's activities at sea.

There was another string to the O'Malleys' maritime bow. The employment of mercenary fighters was a common feature of Gaelic warfare. The most renowned were the *gallóglaigh* (foreign warriors), the gallowglass who came from the isles and highlands of Scotland. They were hired annually, usually from May to October, by individual Gaelic chieftains or gaelicised Anglo-Norman lords, to fight in their armies. The Clan Donnell was the gallowglass family most associated with the west of Ireland and O'Malley ships ferried them to and from their Scottish homeland. A branch of the Clan Donnell eventually settled permanently in Umhall as sub-chieftains of the O'Malleys.

If the gallowglass were the mercenaries of the land, the O'Malleys might well be termed the mercenaries of the sea. O'Malley ships and crews were much sought after for hire by warring chieftains and, to judge from the many references in the annals to their involvement in various battles and skirmishes throughout Ireland, there was no scarcity of work. This mercenary tradition was continued by Granuaile and her sons until the early years of the seventeenth century.

The number and size of the O'Malley fleet has never been precisely quantified. Irish-built trading vessels of the sixteenth century resembled a version of the clinker-built wooden cog of late medieval times. There are, however, many references to the number of ships under the direction of individual members of the O'Malley clan. Tuathal O'Malley was recorded as having seven ships under his command in Ulster in 1413, while in 1513 Eoghan O'Malley attacked Killybegs with three ships. Granuaile is recorded as commanding from three to twenty ships at various times during her career.

The 'galley' was the ship most associated with the O'Malleys and particularly with Granuaile. Wooden-hulled and clinker-built, it had a shallow draught which allowed it to manoeuvre in low water. Powered by as many as thirty oars and a single sail, it was a speedy and versatile craft. The galley is thought to have evolved from the long ships, *langskips* of the Vikings, the intrepid seafarers from Scandinavia. The typical Viking ship had a keel, a mast of pine or ash measuring up to 11 metres, a square sail, a single row of oars on either side, a side rudder affixed to the starboard quarter and could attain a speed of up to ten knots. Major developments in boat-building practices subsequently occurred, particularly in the fifteenth century. The single-masted ship, difficult to steer and to sail only with the wind, gave way to lateen rigged two- and three-masted ships such as the carrack, galleon, galleas and galley. The Mediterranean-type galley had evolved from the ancient trireme but by the sixteenth century its once three-tiered oar power had given way to a row of single oars, each oar manned by several rowers. Long and narrow, these galleys often had as many as three masts, small decks fore and aft and could accommodate as many as three hundred men. Four of these galleys formed part of the attempted invasion of England by the Spanish Armada in 1588 but proved ill-suited to the northern seas.

Experts appear reluctant to accept that the O'Malley galleys were a far more substantial craft than the smaller Hebridean galleys, commonly depicted on stone slabs and tombstone carvings. Descriptions of the galleys commanded by Granuaile in the sixteenth century show that they differ substantially in size from these. In 1576 Granuaile could offer Sir Henry Sidney 'three galleys and two hundred fighting men' capable of sailing anywhere in Ireland or in Scotland. The State Papers further record in 1599:

There are three very good galleys with Tibbott ne Long, son to Grany O'Malley … that will carry 300 men apiece … There are no galleys in Ireland but these.[17]

In 1601 an English sea captain on patrol off the Mayo coast describes a skirmish with one of Granuaile's galleys which, as he recorded, was 'rowed with thirty oars and had on board ready to defend her 100 good shot'.[18] All the extant descriptions of Granuaile's galleys point to vessels of considerable size, perhaps a cross between the Hebridean galleys of the North and the more substantial galleys of the Mediterranean. What we do know for certain is that they were of such strength, versatility and capability that for the space of fifty years they carried Granuaile and her army of 'two hundred fighting men', plus the plunder she accumulated en route, safely in dangerous and unpredictable seas off the coasts of Ireland, Spain and Scotland.

In 1991 a re-enactment took place of the 400-mile (640-km) voyage from Clew Bay to the Scottish isle of Stornoway, in memory of both Granuaile and Somerled, Lord of the Isles. The replica galley used had sixteen oars, less than half the number recorded on the galleys operated by Granuaile. From descriptions in the State Papers, it would appear that the galleys under Granuaile's command were not only substantial but were also unique in Ireland. As Colin Mudie, designer of the *Brendan* and *Argo* vessels for Tim Severin's epic voyages, as well as Granuaile's replica galley mentioned above, warns:

> … we … have to look at historic craft not from any vantage point of technological superiority but from a much more humble station, appreciating how little we may know and how much there may be to learn.[19]

For a seafaring clan, part of whose income was derived from plunder and piracy, it was essential that O'Malley land bases were strategically situated—secure from retaliation as much as sheltered from the elements. The ring of O'Malley castles strung around the shoreline of Clew Bay adequately fulfilled these requirements. The seat of the O'Malley chieftain was at Belclare Castle—the Fort at the Mouth (*Béal*) of the Plain (*Chláir*), i.e. the plain of Murrisk. It was situated at the mouth of the Owenwee river on the site of an ancient *dún* (fort). Inland from Belclare and to the southeast was a lake dwelling (*crannóg*) on the island in Moher lake, a place of refuge for the chieftain, his family and their valuables in time of danger. The family also possessed a castle at Cathair-na-Mart (Fort of the Beeves), situated near the present Westport House, a castle at Murrisk, Carrowmore, west of the present town of Louisburgh, Kildawnet on Achill Island and the castle on Clare Island.

Clare Island and Achill are the only O'Malley castles extant. Although not the main residences of the O'Malley chieftain, they afford some insight into the living conditions of a Gaelic leader from about the twelfth century. Both castles are strategically situated, with commanding views of the sea, yet undetectable by passing sea traffic. The castle on Clare Island is situated on a low, rocky headland looking eastwards into the broad expanse of Clew Bay. It overlooks a fine crescent-shaped sandy beach, suitable for mooring ships of shallow draught. Directly below is a sheltered creek which has deep water at high tide. The castle is three storeys high and once possessed battlements which gave an uninterrupted view of the open sea beyond the island. The three floor levels were connected by a stone stairway, straight rather than spiral, the more usual defensive access.

The strong rectangular castle of Kildawnet is situated on a slight promontory on the west shore of Achill Sound. The Sound, with its strong and unpredictable currents, is a sea-passage which connects Clew Bay with Blacksod Bay to the north. With local knowledge, it provided a swift access or escape north or south between Achill Island and the mainland. The entrance to the Sound at the southern end is protected by the island of Achill Beg. The castle itself is quite hidden from view from the outer sea and is surrounded by mountains and seascapes of the wildest splendour.

Like other Gaelic clans before the Reformation, the O'Malleys sustained orders of monks on their lands. The abbey at Murrisk was built by the O'Malleys in 1457 for the Augustinian friars on land granted by the chieftain Thady O'Malley. It is beautifully situated on a quiet inlet of Clew Bay, beneath the towering peak of Croagh Patrick. Built in late Gothic style, its single-aisle church and a range of domestic buildings are now in semi-ruin. One of its best preserved features is the delicate east window with its interlacing bar tracery and five trefoil parts. A striking feature of the abbey is its turreted south wall. At the western end of the church a partly vaulted tower once stood. Ironically, after the initial account of its foundation, nothing more was recorded about the abbey until notice of its proposed suppression on 27 March 1574, when Sir Peter Carew, in a despatch to the English Lord Deputy in Ireland, mentioned 'the abbey of Moyriske possessed by Friars or rebels so as her Majestie hath no commoditie in the same'.[20] In 1578 the queen leased the lands of the abbey to James Garvey. The friars, however, continued to reside in the abbey buildings. In 1635 a chalice, bearing the inscription: 'Pray for the souls of Theobald, Lord Viscount Mayo and his wife Maeve Ne Cnochoure who had me made for the monestary of Mureske in the year of our lord 1635', was presented to the abbey. (Theobald or Tibbott-ne-Long Bourke was the son of Granuaile.) Murrisk Abbey would have featured largely in the lives of the O'Malley chieftains situated as it was close to Belclare castle. It is perhaps likely that Granuaile was baptised and married there and many of her kinsmen and women lie buried beneath its now roofless walls.

The abbey on Clare Island was built in 1224 by the O'Malleys two centuries before Murrisk. Originally a Carmelite cell, it was later attached to the famous Cistercian house at Knockmoy. The later fifteenth-century church consisted of a nave, chancel and sacristy, as well as a range of domestic buildings to the north, which no longer exist. In the chancel, and thought to date from the fourteenth century, mural paintings, which once covered the entire ceiling in a kaleidoscope of colour, depict mythical, human and animal figures, including dragons, a cockerel, stags, men on foot and on horseback, a harper, birds and trees. On the north wall of the chancel is a well-cut, undated, limestone slab showing a stallion salient on a wreath above a Norman-style helmet, a wild boar trippant in the centre, with three bows, arrows affixed, pointing at the boar. At the right-hand base is a replica galley, with furled sail and five oars on a side, with the name 'O'Maille' and the O'Malley motto *Terra Mariq Potens* in smaller lettering above. The entire shield and crest is surrounded by mantling and is thought to date from the early seventeenth century. Beside the slab is a tomb canopy, with elegant cusped tracery which, although recent research suggests dates from the fourteenth century, tradition has always held to be the burial place of Granuaile. The Norman-style helmet on the stone slab could possibly have relevance to Granuaile's second husband, Richard Bourke, the Mayo MacWilliam (1581–1583). The memorial and slab seem somewhat incongruous in such a remote setting and, if tradition is to be believed, is indeed a fitting resting place for Granuaile.

After the initial setback at the hands of the de Burgos in the twelfth century, by which the jurisdiction of the O'Malley chieftains became restricted to Umhall Uachtarach and Achill, the O'Malleys continued their seafaring activities with renewed vigour. By the sixteenth century they were, as the English State Papers acknowledge, 'much feared everywhere by sea'.[21] Politically they continued as an independent clan, the O'Malley chieftain being the only Gaelic chieftain in Mayo to retain his rank until the extinction of the title in the seventeenth century.

CHAPTER 2
THE WORLD
OF GRANUAILE

... men of sense
Hand down that Muireasc surely has its name,
From lovely Muirisc of the snowy hands,
The daughter of great Hugony the King,
She was a downright beauty, daring, bold,
And fixed her habitation near this bay,
Beneath the base of Cruachan Aigli, where
She ruled o'er hardy sailors and great men.[1]

The lines of this ancient poem eulogise a legendary woman leader called Muireasc, from whom the O'Malley Barony of Murrisk is said to have taken its name. Nothing more is known about her, but in a prophetic way her life presaged that of her sixteenth-century descendant Granuaile, acknowledged leader also 'o'er hardy sailors and great men' one thousand years later.

This connection between two women from the same remote lordship, more than a millennium apart, is not as strange as it may appear. The warrior woman Muireasc lived in a time when Ireland was part of a Bronze-Age matriarchal culture in which the dominant deities were women. The name of Ireland itself is that of the mother-goddess Eriú or Éire, said to be one of the three legendary goddesses who ruled the country at the time of the invasion by the Milesians. The mystical Tuatha de Danaan, worshipped by the pagan Irish, had the all-powerful goddess Dana as their deity. In early Irish mythology the sovereignty of Ireland (*Flaitheas Éireann*) was epitomised by a woman, invariably dressed in a blue cloak. Later still, during the Celtic culture of the late Iron Age, which gave rise to the heroic legends of Fionn mac Cúmhal, the Fianna and the Red Branch Knights of Ulster, the dominance of the woman warrior class was still much in evidence. The prime hero of the Red Branch cycle, Cúchulainn, learned his battle prowess under the tutelage of the woman warrior Scathach. In combat he overcame the warrior princess Aoife only by resorting to trickery. Classical writers testified to the fighting skills of Celtic women. The Roman historian Tacitus confirmed that the Celts of Britain made no distinction as to sex in the choice of their military commanders, as in the case of Boudica. The warrior queen Maeve of Connaught was a powerful and fearless woman who was prepared to go to war to achieve her ambition. Many of the warriors of the heroic legends of the Fenian and Ulster cycles used their mother's name in place of a patronymic, such as the king of Ulster, Conor Mac (son of) Nessa, reinforcing the idea that in Ireland, in earlier times, descent was accomplished through the female line.

The demise in Ireland of a society ruled by powerful warrior women coincided with the advent of Christianity and the influence of Roman law which accompanied it. Roman society was male-dominated, the male having ultimate power over the lives of his dependent household, including women, and also over his slaves. Descent was exclusively patrilineal and inheritance confined to the legitimate male heir. Christianity both inherited and defended this system. The writings of the early Christian saints such as Paul, John, Ambrose, Jerome and Augustine reflected the degraded position of women in Roman society. Augustine wrote of the 'horrible beastliness of women', that they were not born in God's image and should be tolerated on sufferance, debarred from holding any position of authority. As Roman law and Christian ethos began to dominate society, this negative attitude towards women became enshrined in state and religious laws across Europe. By the sixteenth century male historians and commentators, often clerical, perpetuated this attitude to women. However, amidst their reassertion of women's inferiority, their alleged weakness and unsuitability for high office in either church or state, often lurked a fear which inadvertently revealed man's acknowledgement of women's true potential. In his condemnation of women's role in politics, in which he accuses them of being 'the cause of many troubles, have done great harm to those that govern cities, and have caused in them many divisions … '², the sixteenth-century political analyst Niccolo Machiavelli involuntarily acknowledges women's potential.

The Romans overcame Celtic nations from Asia Minor to Britain. Only Ireland remained outside Roman influence. Patrick brought Christianity to Ireland in the fifth century, and with it Roman law which found itself in direct conflict with the indigenous law of Ireland known as Brehon law. On few other issues did Brehon and Roman laws differ so fundamentally as on that of the status of women. Gradually, as Christianity infiltrated native Irish law, women's role in the power stakes in Ireland became diluted. Roman salic law, which debarred women from leadership, eventually became part of Brehon law. The role of women became confined to childbearing, charitable deeds (for which they were occasionally lauded in the Irish annals), and subservience to their husbands. In succeeding centuries, while individual women such as Gormflaith, Dervogilla O'Rourke, Margaret FitzGerald Butler, Countess of Ormond, Eleanor Butler, Countess of Desmond and Fionnula Mac Donnell (*Iníon Dubh*), managed to come to political prominence, it tended to be within the orbit of their husbands' or lovers' power struggles. By the time of Granuaile in the sixteenth century, an analogy for an independent woman ruler could be found only in myth and legend. In turn, this caused the life of Granuaile herself to be relegated to myth, rather than acknowledge that a woman could usurp what had by then come to be accepted as the exclusive role of men.

While Granuaile's career as a political and military leader by land can be said to mirror that of her female Celtic ancestors, no such analogy can be found to explain her role as leader by sea. From the beginning of time, seafaring has been considered a male preserve and piracy a male bastion. From the legendary odysseys of Jason, Ulysses and Sinbad, to the explorative voyages of Columbus, Da Gama and Magellan to the New Worlds, down to

in Latin means 'apple'. The Irish word *Umhall,* meaning territory, is similar in pronounciation to the Irish word for apple, *úll.* Thus O'Malley of Umhall became O'Malley of Pomo in the English State Papers.

The landscape of Ireland at the time of Granuaile's birth was virtually unchanged since the Anglo-Norman invasion of the twelfth century. The population numbered no more than 700,000 people. Great primeval forests of oak, birch, ash, scots fir, hazel, willow, alder and holly, as well as dense woodlands, covered a sizeable part of the country. There were large tracts of marsh and boglands interspaced by arable and open pasture lands. There were few roads and even fewer bridges. Most of the towns were situated on the coast or on the navigable rivers. Because of the absence of roads and bridges, travel was extremely difficult and there was much recourse to travel by water—on river, lake and sea. The mountain pass, the forest pathway and the river ford were the all-important keys to communication and their control was often the cause of warfare.

Behind a natural screen of forest, water and mountain the Gaelic world flourished. Since there were no accurate maps of the country, successive English kings, who claimed lordship over Ireland since the twelfth century, knew as much about the country as they did about the far-off Americas. The actual mapping of Ireland towards the very end of the sixteenth century was a major contributory factor to the eventual overthrow of the Gaelic world at the beginning of the seventeenth century. These maps were in themselves potent symbols of the extension of English control in Ireland.

Granuaile was born at the beginning of an era that was to prove a milestone in the history of Ireland. The effects of the Anglo-Norman invasion of the twelfth century were by then scarcely evident. English power was confined to Dublin and the Pale, a small area stretching north, south and west of the city. The native Irish held all Ulster, with the exception of parts of Down and Antrim, most of Connaught, the north and west of Munster, the midlands and west Leinster. The native customs, laws and language, which had received a reversal at the time of the Anglo-Norman invasion, flourished. Even the descendants of the Anglo-Norman dynasties, such as the earls of Kildare, Desmond and Ormond and the de Burgos in Connaught, had become gaelicised, becoming 'more Irish than the Irish themselves' to varying degrees, depending on their political and geographical proximity to Dublin, the centre of English power. At the time of Granuaile's birth, it was recorded that Ireland was divided into as many as

> ... sixty counties ... where reigneth sixty chief captains ... that liveth only by the sword and obeyeth to no other temporal person but only to himself that is strong. And every of the said captains maketh war and peace for himself and holdeth by the sword and hath imperial jurisdiction within his room and obeyeth to no other person, English or Irish, except only to such persons as may subdue him by the sword.[6]

A few decades earlier, the Tudors had succeeded in bringing to heel the powerful feudal magnates in England, claiming a divine right to rule over them. In Ireland, however, no similar central authority had emerged to mould the regained power of individual chieftains and gaelicised Anglo-Norman lords into a viable, strong, centralised government. Instead, inter-clan warfare, which was to be the Achilles heel of Gaelic resistence to England later in the century, prevailed.

Granuaile's father, as one of the 'sixty captains' referred to above, ruled the lordship of Umhall, according to native Brehon law. The Gaelic legal system was distinct to Ireland and had evolved over the centuries from its Celtic origins, absorbing some aspects of the two main incursions into Ireland—Christianity in the fifth century and the Anglo-Normans in the twelfth century. The very nature of Gaelic society and its capacity to assimilate foreign influences made it resilient. Gaelic society was comprised of clans or extended family groupings. The chieftain did not inherit by feudal primogeniture but was elected by members of the ruling sept (family) within the clan. By Gaelic law a brother could succeed a brother, a nephew an uncle, a younger son a father to the chieftaincy. A custom known as 'tanistry' had been introduced whereby the elected successor (*tánaiste*) was chosen during the chieftain's lifetime. By the sixteenth century Salic law was an established part of the system. The laws regarding Gaelic land tenure also differed from the feudal system and involved a complex method of land distribution which differed from region to region. On the death of a chieftain or a co-heir, or in some areas on an annual basis, each May Day, the clan lands were redistributed among the landholding members of the clan. The chieftain enjoyed a life interest only in the lands pertaining to the chieftaincy. The fosterage of the sons of an overlord with a sub-lord was a common practice among the Gaelic Aristocracy and further strengthened the links of dependency between clans. Sons born outside wedlock were not discriminated against either socially or legally. They were eligible for election to the chieftaincy and enjoyed the same inheritance rights as sons born within wedlock.

The chieftain's power was based on a system of clientship (*célsine*), whereby he strove to have as many sub-lords (*úir-rí*) as possible under his control. In lieu of his protection, sub-lords were forced to pay their overlord dues and tributes, such as cattle, sheep, grain, flour, honey or candles, and the provision of lodging and entertainment, known as cuddy (*cuid oíche*), to the chieftain and his retinue. They were also obliged to fulfil specific duties, including the provision of a 'rising out', an agreed number of armed men, to assist the overlord in war. The O'Malley chieftain provided this duty to his overlord, the MacWilliam Bourke of Mayo. Likewise the O'Malley chieftain was in receipt of 'the chief rents of barley, butter and money as well as all fines for bloodshed, all skins of animals killed or to be killed … with all customs and other casualties'[7] from his sub-lords, the MacGibbons and Clandonnells, within the lordship of Umhall.

Debarred from the chieftaincy and thereby from political power, Gaelic women, as the annals confirm, were rarely acknowledged other than as wives of chieftains, doers of charitable works, donors of bequests to abbeys and monasteries and occasionally as patrons of educational establishments. Politically some featured in the historical records as disruptive or negative influences or as mistresses of powerful men, such as the infamous Dervogilla O'Rourke whose amorous entanglements inadvertently led to the Anglo-Norman invasion of Ireland in 1169. Some, like Eleanor Butler FitzGerald, Countess of Desmond and Margaret FitzGerald Butler, Countess of Ormond, ably filled the vacuum caused by their husband's political inadequacies but received little official acknowledgement in the process.

While Gaelic law may have mitigated against women in the political sense, in other respects, particularly in the area of marriage and divorce, it accorded them more protection and many more rights than those enjoyed by their English or European counterparts. Gaelic women could retain their maiden name during their marriage(s). Granuaile was never referred to by her married names. She herself testified to the fact (see Appendix 1. v) that the dowry, or marriage portion, which women brought with them to their marriage was protected by law and was refundable on death of, or divorce from, their husbands. However, as she also complained, such dowries were refundable to women only on a first marriage. Twice married herself, she circumvented this impediment by simply sequestering her second husband's castle in lieu. Irish law also permitted women, like Granuaile and her mother, to own and administer their own land and property, a practice which contrasted with English law, where the husband enjoyed absolute control over the property of his wife. In a late sixteenth-century poem composed in honour of Granuaile's youngest son, Tibbott-ne-Long Bourke, it is significant that he is referred to by the poet as 'the ruddy-cheeked heir of Gráinne'[8], rather than of his father—testimony to the fact that Granuaile was a proprietor in her own right.

As well as the ruling class, Gaelic society was comprised of freemen and landless labourers, referred to alternatively as betagh (*biatach*) or churls. The betagh were the backbone of Gaelic society. They worked from dawn to dusk for their chieftain and received few privileges in return. There was also the learned class (*aos dána*) which included the poets (*filí*), the most revered of all classes, the bards and the dispensers of law, the brehons (*breitheamh*) or judges. There were two classes of military men, the gallowglass and the kerne (*ceithearn*). Mercenary soldiers from the Scottish isles and highlands the gallowglass were men of great strength and stature, dressed from neck to heel in chain mail, with conical iron helmets and were armed with great swords and the infamous battleaxe. The kerne were the light infantry of the chieftain's army. Armed with bows and arrows, javelins and darts, their speed and agility were of special advantage on marshy land where they could outrun and outmanoeuvre even enemy horsemen. Gaelic forces seldom fought in military formation. They attacked by making rapid and irregular forays before withdrawing using their knowledge of the terrain, the woodland, forest, marsh and bog to their advantage. Prior to the Elizabethan conquest, clan rivalry, disputes over succession, land and cattle-raiding were the principal causes of inter-clan warfare.

Despite the Reformation in England, Ireland still adhered to the old religion. Gaelic Catholicism, however, differed from that of the church of Rome. The sweeping reforms of previous centuries had failed to make much impression on its structure and ethos and the Gaelic church adhered to many practices of its Celtic pagan roots. A chieftain's coronation ceremony was not conducted in a church but at the pagan rath of his remote ancestors. A pattern of hereditary clergy had evolved where members of a particular family, often non-clerical, were invested with abbacies and bishoprics. Some of the clergy, including bishops and abbots, were either married or maintained concubines. Many of the aristocratic families sought and were given licence to marry within the prohibited degrees of consanguinity. A form of Celtic secular marriage prevailed. Trial marriages were common and divorce was a legal right of both men and women. Granuaile is traditionally said to have availed of both a trial marriage and a divorce. The sacraments were celebrated haphazardly and many of the Gaelic clergy were illiterate.

The living conditions of Gaelic chieftains were geared to a predominantly agrarian and military lifestyle, a feature reflected in the construction of their 'castles', which were built primarily for shelter and defence rather than for comfort. Before the advent of cannon, such structures were virtually impossible to capture. Dubhdara O'Malley lived in the stone fortress of Belclare, a larger edition of the surviving O'Malley castles of Clare Island and Kildawnet. These castles or towers were four or five storeys high with a bawn enclosed by high walls, often with a small barbican protecting the entrance. The castle was lit by narrow slit windows called loops and had turrets and crenellations below the roof, which was usually made of thatch, occasionally of lead. The castle was dark and damp inside, especially the lower floors which were used mainly for storage. The chieftain and his family lived in the upper apartments which were brighter and had a large fireplace. The walls were whitewashed and decorated with antlers, skins and green-leaved branches. Furniture was minimal and basic: wooden tables, benches, presses and bedsteads. Around the outskirts of the castle nestled the beehive-shaped dwellings of the chieftain's followers. While remains of the stone fortresses of the chieftains dot the Irish landscape, few if any examples of the dwellings of his followers have survived. Writing at the turn of the last century, a visitor to Achill Island, saw however, one of the last surviving examples of these ancient dwellings which, as he recorded, comprised:

> ... a low circular room, thatched outside but within ceiled with stout rafters; a massive bog pine pillar in the centre holds up the roof. There is a low door, no window and a small hole in the roof to let out the smoke ... one or two little sleeping berths close to the fire, a stone ledge for a candle end, a bag of meal within reach for the stirabout and an iron pot which cooks food for man and beast ... The stone walls of the building are several feet thick.[9]

Accounts of the lifestyle of sixteenth-century Gaelic chieftains were recorded mainly by English military commanders during the turbulent decades of the second half of the century. Their portrayal of the customs of the country and people they came to conquer, and which differed from those obtaining to England at the time, is, not suprisingly, unflattering and biased. Some non-military English travellers, however, were somewhat more objective in their observations. Recording a visit to a chieftain's castle, one wrote:

> The lady of the house meets you with her train … Salutations past, you shall be presented with all the drinks in the house, first the ordinary beer, then aquavitae, then sack, then old ale … The fire is prepared in the middle of the hall … the table is spread and plentifully furnished with [a] variety of meats, but ill cooked and without sauce … They feast together with great jollity and healths around … the harper begins to tune and singeth Irish rhymes of ancient making.[10]

The main meal of the day was taken at evening. For the majority, porridge made of oatmeal and milk, flavoured with butter or honey, and oaten griddle cakes was the staple diet. For the noble classes the diet was varied. Beef, mutton, venison, poultry and game were widely consumed with vegetables such as cabbage, onions, wild garlic, watercress and leeks. Salmon, herring and shellfish were an additional luxury for those with access to rivers and the sea. Dillisk eaten with butter was considered a delicacy. Meat was generally boiled or roasted on a spit (*bir*). Buttermilk was a favourite drink of all classes and was 'wonderfully cold and pleaseing',[11] according to one description. Native *uisce beatha* (whiskey), ale and great quantities of wine from France and Spain were plentiful. Mead, a honey-based drink, was considered a special beverage and the area that produced it praiseworthy. O'Malley's territory of Umhall, particularly in the vicinity of Murrisk, was notable for the production of mead, as the old laudatory expression, 'mead-abounding Murrisk', acknowledges. Meals were served in the chieftain's house on low, wooden trestle tables. Meat was placed on large wooden or pewter platters from which everyone helped themselves by cutting slivers with a knife. Food was eaten with knife and hands; forks were still a rarity both in Ireland and in England.

In summer, like his contemporaries, Dubhdara O'Malley and his household left Belclare to go '*booleying*'—to graze the clan cattle herds in the mountain uplands. This custom had its origins in the Celtic past and survived in O'Malley territory until recent times when in the last century it was recorded that 'grazing in common was lately found by the Congested Districts Board, in full operation on Clare island, and in re-arranging the land there they wisely left the old custom undisturbed'.[12]

In the seventeenth century an English traveller, John Dunton, during a visit to the territory of Granuaile's grandson, Murrough-na-Mart O'Flaherty, in Connemara, described the temporary living conditions of a Gaelic chieftain during a booley.

> The house was one entire long roome without any partition. In the middle of it was the fireplace with a large wood fire which was no way unpleaseing tho in summer time. It had no chimney but a vent hole for the smoake at the ridge.

Dunton was told by O'Flaherty:

> ... that they had newly put up this for a 'booley' or summer habitation, the proper dwelling or mansion house being some miles farther neare the sea, and such a one they commonly built everie yeare in some one place or other and thatched it with rushes. I had sheets and soft white blankets ... and they assur'd me no man ever gott cold lyeing on the green rushes, which indeed are sweet and cleane, being changed everie day if rain hinders not.

Dunton was entertained by O'Flaherty during his stay:

> We had at dinner no less than a whole beef boyl'd and roasted, and what mutton I know not so profewsly did they lay it on the

table. At the end where the lady sate was placed an heap of oaten cakes above a foot high, such another in the middle and the like at the lower end, at each side of the middle heap were placed two large vessels filled with Troandor or the whey with buttermilk and sweet milk … We had such ale … and bulcaan, and after dinner myn host ordered his doggs to be gotten ready to hunt the stagg. He had his horse saddled and one for me too … Eighteen long greyhounds and above thirty footemen made up the company.[13]

Such a lifestyle was redolent of the ancient sagas of the Celtic world from whence it emanated.

Cattle were the principal source of wealth of the Gaelic clans and the hides of cattle a major export. Fishing was another lucrative income for the O'Malleys and the building and maintenance of the fleet of fishing and trading vessels, nets and other fishing equipment was essential to the clan's survival. Leisure time was devoted to hunting red deer, which abounded in the Umhalls, and also the ferocious wild boar, the emblem on the O'Malley shield. Falconry was another favourite activity of the Gaelic chieftains and the best falconries were to be found in west Connaught. Travelling storytellers and musicians entertained the chieftain's household during the winter months. These itinerant entertainers were also an essential source of news and gossip. Chess, dice and card-playing were popular pastimes and professional gamblers, known as 'carrows' (*gearbhach*), toured the countryside and were eagerly received in the houses of the Gaelic and gaelicised aristocracy.

Such was the state of Ireland at the time of Granuaile's birth. The prevailing ethos, language, laws, customs and dress were Gaelic. The power of Gaelic chieftains and of gaelicised Anglo-Norman lords was at its highest. England's authority, with the exception of Dublin and the Pale, had long ceased to have any effect on the daily lives of the majority of the people. Yet the reversal of English power had not been translated into political gain by the Gaelic chieftains. For the greater part of the century

Ireland remained devoid of any unifying ideological stimulus. A state of disunity and fragmented loyalties prevailed and energy and intellect was wasted on petty power struggles. In sixteenth-century Ireland, tribal warfare, cattle-raiding and blood money were as much part of daily life as they had been in the time of Queen Maeve and Cúchulainn. The situation contrasted sharply with most of Europe and more latterly with Ireland's nearest neighbour, England. There the yearning for change, discovery, knowledge and the achievements of the Renaissance and the Reformation held sway and one centralised authority, the monarchy, demanded and received the allegiance of every subject.

Such was the antique society that bore and bred Granuaile, a society which, unless it adapted to the fundamental changes that had occurred in the world outside its own narrow orbit, was destined to perish.

Like her society, Granuaile, in her role as a woman warrior leader, was also a product of the past. To survive she too would have to adapt or pay the price of infexibility.

CHAPTER 3
FORTUNA FAVET FORTIBUS

G ranuaile's childhood, like that of Gaelic children generally, is undocumented. From the meagre information relating to the lives of children in Ireland in the sixteenth century it is clear that the period of childhood was short-lived. The custom of fosterage, widespread among the Gaelic aristocracy, dictated that sons were sent to foster parents from as early as six years of age. Since succession to the chieftaincy was by the selection of the fittest, their education centred, like their Celtic forebears, on mastering the skills and techniques of warfare and weaponry, riding stirrupless on horseback and proving their mettle as potential chieftains by raiding their neighbours.

Concentration on physical prowess might well have been at the expense of learning. Judging by the crosses made, in lieu of signatures, on English state documents of the period, it is clear that many chieftains, including Granuaile's second husband, Richard Bourke (see Appendix 1. 1) may have been illiterate. This likelihood, however, must be balanced by two relevant observations: the existence in most chieftains' household of scribes, lawyers and *filí*, whose function was to provide the chieftain with the necessary written and verbal skills and advice on the legal administration of his lordship; as well as the reluctance of chieftains to put their names to documents drafted by English officials whom they distrusted and which were written in a language they did not understand.

While knowledge of the rearing and education of boys in sixteenth-century Gaelic Ireland is vague, that of the daughters of the aristocracy is virtually unknown. Together with accession to political power, women's access to the bardic ranks was greatly restricted. The days of the female bard and poetess, of the fabled Liadán and Feídelm, were no more. The honoured ranks of the *filí* had become confined to men. The male-administered bardic, monastic, and secular post-Norman schools had no place for female pupils. The scant records of the few nunneries established in Ireland provide little evidence of any significant female scholarship. Yet some Gaelic women, usually the daughters, wives or concubines of chieftains, Anglo-Norman lords and the learned classes—despite the educational bias and oftentimes derogatory denunciations of their male counterparts—managed to circumvent the system and become more learned than their menfolk. The letters of such contemporary Irish noblewomen as Eleanor Butler, Countess of Desmond and Joan Butler, Countess of Ormond, the handwriting, the extensive vocabulary, the well-turned phrases, display a shrewd and consummate knowledge of the prevailing political ethos, along with an ability to skilfully negotiate with the most prominent and astute political minds of the time, and is testimony to some degree of a formal education.

In terms of such political acumen and negotiating skill it is clear from her correspondence that Granuaile was on par with her Anglo-Norman sisters. Her extant correspondence, numbering some five petitions to Queen Elizabeth and her Lord Treasurer, Lord Burgley, and her fascinating autobiographical answers in 1593 to the Lord Treasurer's set of eighteen questions (see Appendix 1.v) reveal an equally shrewd and knowledgeable mind. From the penmanship of her correspondence, however, it seems unlikely that Granuaile was the actual scribe, but from the evasiveness and political cunning displayed therein, she was undoubtedly their author.

Education in Ireland during the sixteenth century was dispensed in a somewhat haphazard fashion, confined, as in most European countries, to the religious, aristocratic and merchant classes. The Renaissance influence and the aspirations of Christian Humanists such as Erasmus and Thomas More towards making education available to all levels of the laity, and particularly their commitment to the education of women, scarcely touched Ireland. Where it did it was confined to the lordships of the Anglo-Norman magnates, the cities and the Pale. Other than Granuaile and a handful of her sisters, in the main, the wives of Gaelic chieftains, immersed themselves in rearing their families and managing their households.

By the mid-1500s Ireland had long abandoned her claim to be the 'island of saints and scholars'. The great monastic schools of the golden era of learning and enlightenment in the 7th and 8th centuries, which had attracted scholars from all over Europe, were no more. While a few religious schools, mainly teaching canon law and Latin, continued in existence, a university system had failed to emerge. Even poetic craft was mainly expended on eulogising and elegising Gaelic chieftains and Anglo-Norman lords. In the few schools maintained by Gaelic bards the intricate metres of Gaelic verse continued to be taught to members of hereditary bardic families. Much of this teaching was verbally rather than literally transmitted, as were the tenants of Brehon law handed down by the Gaelic judges. These bardic schools also taught Latin (which in the sixteenth century would seem to have been in use by both laity and clergy) the Greek and Roman classics, philosophy, mathematics, reading and writing in both Gaelic and Latin. Students mainly comprised the sons of the Gaelic and Anglo-Norman aristocracy who had not the means (or the desire) to seek their education in the universities of Europe or England.

Grace O'Malley's educational ability and training is evident from her correspondence, from her negotiations with administrators and military personnel in the English service in Ireland and from the written statements and records of others relating to her preserved in the Elizabethan state papers. Her own correspondence demonstrates a shrewd and able ability and an understanding of the European political realities of the period. That she understood and spoke English as well as Gaelic is evidenced from her face-to-face meetings with notable statesmen of the period including, William Cecil (Lord Burghley), Sir John Perrott, Lord Henry Sidney, his son, the famous poet-courtier-soldier, Sir Philip Sidney and with Queen Elizabeth

I whom she met in Greenwich in 1593. The contacts made outside Ireland by virtue of the advantages emanating from her maritime career undoubtedly also made her conversant with the languages of the countries and communities she connected with in her travels.

Given the wholly unorthodox role she adopted, contrary both to law and social convention, in her later life and to her ability and success as a leader by land and by sea for over forty years, it is more likely that Granuaile's education was geared to where her interest lay, in her father's world of ships, trade, politics and power. To achieve even part of what she was later accused of by English administrators in Ireland, she had to be accomplished in the skills of seafaring. Her ability to sail her ships to Scotland, England and Spain rank her with the best mariners of her time. Doubly endowed with O'Malley blood, seafaring was in her genes.

This aptitude for and affinity with the sea, her clan's benefactor in war and in peace, undoubtedly shaped Granuaile's character and outlook. As a young girl, as she later testified, she accompanied her father on many of his fishing and trading voyages and absorbed his knowledge and skills. And there was much to learn: the tides and currents, the moods of the sea, to become, as O'Dugan wrote, 'a prophet of the weather' like her ancestors, to know when to set sail and when to stay ashore; to know the capability of the ships she sailed, about canvas and hawser, ballast and anchor; to navigate by star and by compass; to learn about the perils of the treacherous Irish coastline, the protruding rocky headlands and hidden reefs and shallows. Later the threat of English warships out to capture her, or competitors in the piracy trade out to relieve her of her cargo and her life, augmented the hazards. Judging by the success and lengthy duration of her career by sea, Dubhdara O'Malley taught his daughter well. It was perhaps her father's character, authority, even his physical attributes, that drew Granuaile to emulate him in later life, to dress like him, to adopt his lifestyle and, in effect, to become more like a son than a daughter.

Her choice of career, notwithstanding her family background, for a woman was unique. Seafaring was and has always tended to be the exclusive domain of men. The nature of the environment, both from a physical and decorous point of view, tended to exclude women. Male moral values pervaded ship life. Swearing, basic hygiene, carousing, violence, as well as the sexual difficulty posed by the presence of a female among an all-male crew, made seafaring a demanding and dangerous option for a woman. Seafaring in the sixteenth century was not for the faint-hearted. Conditions on board were primitive, privacy non-existent. For a women's physique it must have been intolerable. Skin toughened under the barrage of wind and spray, hands hardened and nails split by hawser and canvas, bare feet chafed from the roughly-hewn, swaying decks, sodden woollen trews and linen shirts clinging uncomfortably, cold, unappetising food, the discharge of natural bodily functions lacking any privacy. To give birth on a galley on the high seas, as Granuaile did, seems unimaginable. Life on ship, on lengthy trade and fishing voyages, was monotonous with little but singing and gaming to help to relieve the tediousness of long days and nights at sea.

Piracy and plunder was part of seafaring life in every coastal community as it was for the O'Malleys on the west coast of Ireland. In any clime piracy was a grim and dangerous occupation, the penalty for which was death by hanging. Many of Granuaile's English contemporaries were 'seen off at Wapping Old Stairs' the execution site for pirates on the river Thames. For pirates in the West Indies who dared to go 'on the account' on capture they breathed their last at Gallow's point, east of the old pirate city of Port Royal in Jamaica. Two of the most notorious female pirates who followed in the wake of Granuaile, Irish-born Ann Bonny and her companion Mary Read, 'pleaded their bellies' at their trial to escape the hangman's noose.

To be a female commander of pirates, engaging in the trade of 'maintenance by sea' over the space of forty years, like Granuaile, required a stern but fair hand. To keep her all-male crews under her control, she had to lead from the front and to be as daring and courageous as those she commanded. Above all else, however, she had to be successful at her 'trade' and fulfil the basic requirement of piracy everywhere: 'no prey – no pay'.

Grace O'Malley is known in Irish folklore as 'Granuaile' pronounced Grainne Mhaol. As the Irish word 'maol' denotes 'bald' so, it was assumed, that she had little or no hair. This gave rise to many fanciful stories as to how she shaved her head to look like a boy in order to be allowed sail with her father. It is, however, more reasonable to assume that the name Granuaile is a corruption of her family original name 'Melia' of which 'O'Malley' is the more modern anglicised version. Many anglicised versions of her name appear in the English State Papers, including Grany O'Maly, Grany Imallye, Granny Nye Male, Grany O'Mayle, Granie ny Maille, Granny ni Maille, Grany Maillye, Grany O'Mally, Grayn Ny Mayle, Grane ne Male, Grainy O'Maly, Granee O'Maillie.

Granuaile's childhood was spent at the family castles of Belclare and Clare Island. During this time there was little to disturb the traditional way of life pursued by her family. The seasons and the sea dictated the ebb and flow of life in the O'Malley household as it had done for generations. Fishing and trading voyages, storms, occasional shipwrecks (welcomed, as in all coastal communities, as reward from the sea), summer booleying and deer hunting, the yearly visit to and by O'Malley's overlord the MacWilliam Bourke, the excitement at the arrival of strolling musicians, mummers, and particularly the carrows, were the annual highlights. To judge by contemporary reports, Gaelic chieftains seemed addicted to gambling which, according to one observer, 'so infected the public meetings of the people and the private houses of the lords ...'[1] Grace clearly became as 'infected' as her peers, and her gambling skills were later commemorated in a sixteenth-century poem:

> *Gráinne na gcearbhach do creach*
> (Grace of the gamblers he plundered)[2]

The way of life followed by her clan for centuries, however, was about to face its ultimate challenge. Remote from Dublin, the centre of English power in Ireland, hidden behind a protective screen of wood, forest, bog and the river Shannon, the O'Malleys, like most western clans, were little concerned about the schemes and plots being hatched far away by an English king and which were to be carried to a decisive and bloody conclusion by a daughter he had once spurned. A woman who was destined to become England's greatest monarch, Ireland's most determined conqueror and Granuaile's unlikely benefactor.

The winds of change between Ireland and her powerful neighbour began to blow more fiercely towards the last decade of the reign of England's turbulent monarch Henry VIII. From 1529 to 1536, religious and matrimonial problems commanded Henry's attention. The revolt and ruthless extinction of the House of Kildare in 1537, however, directed the King's gaze across the Irish Sea to his neglected lordship. Rather than resort to costly warfare, Henry instituted a policy of 'surrender and re-grant' in an attempt to gain control of Ireland. To implement this policy, Henry had himself confirmed 'King of Ireland' instead of 'Lord of Ireland', the title held by previous English monarchs. Thus began the new 'Kingdom of Ireland' which was to last until 1800.

The surrender and regrant policy was based on the theory that all Irish lands held by both Gaelic and Anglo-Norman lords depended on the crown of England. On submission, the chieftain or lord would receive back his lands, in the king's name, provided he agreed to rule by English law and custom and attend the king's parliament in Dublin. In return each Irish lord would receive an English title equivalent to his Gaelic status. Throughout 1541 some of the most prominent chieftains and lords submitted to the king's deputy in Dublin. Murrough, chieftain of the great O'Brien clan in Munster, was created Earl of Thomond. In Ulster O'Neill, regarded by many as the hereditary king of Ireland, submitted and accepted the title Earl of Tyrone. In Connaught, Ulick Burke, the Upper MacWilliam of Galway, was created the Earl of Clanrickard.

Thus started the Tudor conquest of Ireland by means of a policy of subtle effectiveness. As the chieftains and lords accepted the terms and titles of the English king, so they became obligated to abandon the Irish laws and customs that had endowed them with their positions as chieftains in the first place. Their acceptance of the English terms ran contrary to the Gaelic principles governing election and land tenure. Some chieftains felt coerced into acceptance, others did so out of greed or disillusionment with the impermanency of the Gaelic system which allowed for little continuity, but most accepted only for as long as it suited their own purpose. It was a triumph for Henry who at his death in 1547, by a relatively peaceful, inexpensive yet effective policy, had extended his authority, nominally at least, over Leinster and parts of Ulster, Munster and Connaught. In the remainder of the country, suppression of the native laws and customs, as well as the anglicisation of the native aristocracy, would take longer but the machinery had been firmly set in motion.

Mayo, as yet, remained untouched by these political changes. The affairs of the country, even within Connaught, were of little consequence to the O'Malley chieftain or to his neighbours, provided they remained free to rule their territories unhindered from either Irish or English interference. In Umhall the fishing was good and O'Malley could afford to thumb his nose at the avaricious merchants of Galway and choose his own markets. The only blip on the scene may have been that his daughter looked set to become the sailor her half-brother Donal never was and, in the male-oriented society of Gaelic Ireland, that was something that could not be countenanced, beyond childhood. There was little future for a woman inclined towards male pursuits. The only career move for a woman was to the marriage bed and, for the daughter of a chieftain, marriage had to pay political dividends.

Grace was about sixteen years old when she was married to Donal O'Flaherty, son of Gilledubh O'Flaherty, chieftain of the Ballinahinch sept, the senior ruling branch of the extensive O'Flaherty clan. The O'Flahertys were rulers of the vast, rugged territory of Iar-Chonnacht, an area roughly equivalent to modern-day Connemara. They were a warlike clan, as their motto 'fortune favours the brave' implies. They co-existed in relative harmony with their neighbours the O'Malleys, however, and were their allies in war. For Dubhdara O'Malley, the match between his daughter and the O'Flaherty chieftain was especially satisfactory. By Gaelic custom, Donal was the elected *tánaiste* to the chieftaincy of all the O'Flaherty septs and future ruler of all Iar-Chonnacht. At the time of his marriage to Granuaile he was chieftain of the Barony of Ballinahinch. His chief castle was on the coast at Bunowen, some three kilometres south of Slyne Head, the most westerly point on the coast of Connaught. It had a deep harbour with good anchorage and was sheltered from the west by the Hill of Doon. Granuaile's new home was separated from Umhall by the deep fiord of Killary and by some of the most spectacular scenery in the country. It was bounded to the north west by the Twelve Bens, in the distance south-eastwards were the extensive island-strewn waters of Lough Corrib, while all around lay the stones, moors and lakelets of Connemara.

As the daughter of a chieftain, Granuaile did not go empty-handed to her marriage. As was customary she brought a substantial dowry (*spréidh*) to her husband in the form of cattle, horses, sheep and household goods. Special 'sureties for the restitution of the same', according to her own testimony, 'in manner and in form as she hath delivered it', were an integral and important part of the matrimomial contract, in the event of the death of her husband or in case, as she later testified, 'they are divorced.'[3] Since divorce was prevalent among the Gaelic aristocracy, marriage contracts thereby made provisions for such an eventuality. On the death of her husband or upon divorce, the wife was entitled to receive in full the dowry she had brought with her to the marriage. In some parts of Gaelic Ireland a special tax or imposition (*cáin beag*) was raised within the lordship for the maintenance of the chieftain's wife. On the death of the chieftain, the widow did not normally receive any part of his property. As Granuaile later stated, 'the countries of Connaught among the

Irishry never yeilded any thirds to any woman surviving the chieftain.'[4] This made the imposition of sureties for the restitution of a woman's dowry a vital part of the marriage contract.

As a young bride, separated from her family and the familiar surroundings of Umhall, Granuaile may well have experienced a sense of isolation and homesickness. The role expected of her now was that of wife, homemaker and potential mother. To be at the command of her husband, submissive to him in all things, must surely have been anathema to Granuaile. Her upbringing was in an environment of equality; the sea made no distinction between female and male sailors. By the later evidence of her relationship with her second husband, with whom, as the records testify, 'she was ... well more than Mrs Mate with him,'[5] it is difficult to imagine that she adapted easily to playing the role of dutiful wife.

Her young husband, as his sobriquet *Dónal-an-Chogaidh* (Donal of the Battles) suggests, was a reckless and truculent chieftain, hardly the type to allow his authority be usurped by his wife. A clash of personalities seemed inevitable. But for a time at least Granuaile fulfilled what society, her father and her husband deemed to be her role. She bore Donal two sons, Owen and Murrough, and a daughter, Margaret, named after her own mother, of whom nothing but her name and ancestry and the fact that she inherited land in her own right in Umhall, was recorded.

While for a time marriage may have altered Granuaile's way of life it did little to change her husband. In 1549 Donal was implicated in the murder of Walter *Fada* (Tall) Bourke, son of David Bourke, *tánaiste* to the MacWilliam of Mayo. The murder was committed at the O'Flaherty castle of Invernan in Moycullen to the west of Galway city. It is recorded that Donal murdered Walter at the instigation of his sister Finola, stepmother of Walter. By eliminating her step-son, Finola sought to enhance the political future of her own son, Richard Bourke, as a candidate for the MacWilliamship, the most powerful and prestigious chieftaincy in Connaught. Donal's likely gain from the murder is less clear. The promise of an alliance between himself and Richard, when as the

O'Flaherty and the MacWilliam respectively, together they would control Mayo and Iar-Chonnacht, might well have been an incentive. However, only part of the plot was realised while the remainder turned out in a way that neither Donal, Finola or Granuaile could have anticipated.

While her husband continued to play the role of warlord, constantly feuding with his neighbours, particularly the Joyce clan, over the disputed ownership of a castle in Lough Corrib, Granuaile was not content to be a stay-at-home wife. Judging by later records which accuse her of being in action for over forty years, it is clear that what Gaelic law denied her she simply seized for herself. It was during her marriage to Dónal-an-Chogaidh that, whether through his inadequacies as a chieftain or simply by her own inclination, Granuaile superseded him in his authority over his clan and, more incredibly still, was accepted by his clansmen, many of whom later chose to leave Iar-Chonnacht and to live under her rule in Mayo.

Bunowen castle was an ideal base from which to launch a new seafaring career. Around this time the first reports of attacks on ships sailing into the busy port of Galway were recorded. Galway city was hostile to the O'Flahertys, about whom the citizens had inscribed over the west gate of the city: 'From the ferocious O'Flahertys, Good Lord deliver Us.' Just as the city imposed taxes on the Gaelic clans who wished to trade there, Grace and her followers sought to do the same on the seas off their territory. Out of the cover of the coastal islands and bays their galleys swooped on the lumbering merchantmen. Negotiations for safe passage into Galway were usually rewarded with a toll or part of the cargo. Laden with the agreed or extracted spoil, Granuaile and her men disappeared into one or other of the numerous uncharted bays along the indented coastline. The merchants of Galway city were powerless against such attacks and conveyed their frustration to the English Council in Dublin:

The continuing roads used by the O'Malleys and O'Flaherties with their galleys along our coasts, where there have been taken sundry ships … bound for this poor town, which they have not only rifled to the utter overthrow of the owners and merchants, but also have most wickedly murdered divers of young men to the great terror of such as would willingly traffic …[6]

Whether such leadership was forced on Granuaile out of necessity or by inclination, there had to be some receptive, ambitious need within her that drove her to take on such a role at a time and in a society that sought to consign women to a life of domesticity and dependence. Gaelic society demanded that their leaders were strong of will and body, able to protect those who gave them allegiance and defend their domain. Any sign of weakness or frailty on the part of a chieftain was certain to unleash the ambitions of his competitors. To retain control of her crewmen, to enforce her will, it was essential that Granuaile led by example, enduring and outdoing the men she led, by land and by sea, as a later poem testifies regarding her attack on the castle of Renvyle:

> No braver seaman took a deck in hurricane or squalls
> Since Grace O'Malley battered down old Currath castle
> walls.[7]

It was undoubtedly her strength of character, her charisma, absolute courage, adaptability and self-belief that propelled Granuaile into a position of leadership in what was an exclusively male role and environment. Across the Irish Sea another woman was preparing to assume the role of leadership in a man's world. She was to excel and be immortalised as the greatest of England's monarchs. Her impact on Ireland would leave an indelible mark and destroy forever the way of life that nurtured and sustained Granuaile.

Elizabeth i assumed the throne in November 1558 and commenced her long and powerful reign which was to end with Ireland brought to heel, the might of Spain shattered and the security of England, the yardstick of all her policies, achieved. It was a time of dangerous uncertainty for the young queen who ascended the throne in the knowledge that many of her own subjects, because of her father's divorce and the fact that she was a woman, had reservations about her right to rule. The implementation of the provisions of the Reformation became imperative to copper fasten her position, since Catholicism regarded her as illegitimate and a usurper. Her rival for the throne of England, Mary Queen of Scots, had married the Dauphin of Catholic France. The prospect of France and Scotland allied against her, although Elizabeth was never a religious bigot, meant that fidelity to Catholicism became synonymous with disloyalty and, as her reign progressed, in Ireland, it equated to rebellion against her rule.

Initially Elizabeth sought to continue her father's policy of surrender and regrant in a bid to conquer Ireland by civil rather than more expensive military means. A parliament was assembled in Dublin in 1560 to establish the new queen's title and to reverse her dead sister's attempt to re-establish the old religion. In Ulster, the new chieftain of the O'Neills, Shane O'Neill, resisted any English interference in Ulster affairs. Because of his strength and the remoteness of his country, Elizabeth had little option but to make peace, acknowledge him as the O'Neill and withdraw the newly-established English garrison at Armagh. In Connaught, the Earl of Clanrickard, a loyal supporter of the crown, maintained a watching brief on his 'unloyal' neighbours, the Mayo Bourkes. One of the Bourke Chieftains, Finola's son, Richard Bourke, leading an army of one thousand Scottish mercenaries, marched into Galway and plundered the lands of MacMaurice and Lord Athenry. Clanrickard hastened to the defence of his fellow countrymen and defeated the Mayo 'invaders', killing seven hundred of their number. With some difficulty Richard escaped to the safety of Mayo where English law had, as yet, to obtain a foothold.

In Iar-Chonnacht, however, the first effects of the expansionary policies of the new queen became apparent. In 1564 a minor chieftain of the O'Flaheties, Murrough-na-dTuadh (Murrough of the Battle Axes), chieftain of Gnomore, in the northern part of the Barony of Moycullen, commenced a military campaign to extend his power in the traditional way. He firstly attacked the Earl of Thomond, then the Earl of Clanrickard, whom he defeated decisively at Trá Bán (the White Strand), two miles west of Galway city. This incident was too serious to be overlooked by the English authorities. Given his undoubted strength and the remoteness of his territory, to overcome Murrough by force would prove costly. If, however, he could be persuaded to become loyal to the crown, it would help spread Elizabeth's anglicisation policy into the remote west. Consequently the queen pardoned Murrough and appointed him lord of all Iar-Chonnacht. In return, Murrough promised 'to observe the Queen's peace, to appear and answer at all sessions within the province ... to satisfy the demands of all the Queen's subjects ...'[8] The appointment of Murrough as chieftain of Iar-Chonnacht was a direct challenge and a repudiation of Brehon law. Murrough was a minor chieftain in the O'Flaherty hierarchy. There was already a legitimate chieftain and Granuaile's husband, Dónal-an-Chogaidh, was his elected *tánaiste*.

This example of English divide-and-conquer policy, which was to be used effectively throughout the second half of the century, had the desired effect. It set Gaelic and English law on a collision course from which only one side could emerge victorious. The peace of Iar-Chonnacht was shattered by inter-tribal warfare, intrigue and double-dealing, as each sept attempted to take advantage of the situation. Granuaile's husband, as *tánaist*-elect to the chieftain by right of Gaelic law, had most to lose. His status as future chieftain was usurped by an outside force which appeared more powerful than the native law that had created him *tánaiste*. As the scramble for power spread among the O'Flaherty septs, it became clear that right by Gaelic law was no longer a guarantee of power. Unless legal right was reinforced by military power it could simply be set aside.

Dónal-an-Chogaidh died soon after these developments. According to tradition he met his end, inevitably, at the hands of his enemies, the Joyces, while defending the disputed castle on Lough Corrib. Because of the courage he displayed in defending the castle, the Joyces had nicknamed him *An Cullagh* (The

Cock). On his death, with much anticipation, the Joyces descended on 'Cock's castle' to re-claim it for themselves. They reckoned without Granuaile who, leading her husband's clansmen, defended the castle with a display of such skill and bravery that it was quickly renamed Hen's Castle (*Caisleán-an-Circa*), the name it retains to this day.

Tradition also holds that some time later, a strong force of English soldiers out of Galway city besieged Granuaile and a few followers in Hen's Castle. Conditions within grew desperate but Granuaile was determined not to surrender. Instead she had the lead roof of the castle stripped, melted down and the molten liquid tipped over the parapets onto the besiegers beneath, who beat a hasty retreat to the mainland to continue the siege from a safer distance, impounding Granuaile's boats in the process. Without the means of escape Granuaile despatched one of her men under cover of darkness to the nearby Hill of Doon, to light a beacon to alert her followers to her predicament and the siege of Hen's Castle was subsequently lifted.

Following the death of her husband, Granauile experienced the discriminatory dictates of Gaelic law. Despite her competence, bravery and success as *de facto* chieftain, Gaelic law would not countenance a woman chieftain. Her husband's cousin was elected to succeed him. Her young sons, Owen and Murrough, then in fosterage, stood to inherit, as Granuaile later testified, 'the fourth part of the Barony of Ballinahinse'.[9] Their inheritance was immediately thrown into the cauldron of unrest that the queen's appointment of Murrough-na-Tuadh had provoked in the region, when Murrough-na-Tuadh 'entered into Ballynehinsey … there did build a strong castle and the same with the demain lands thereof kept many years'.[10] Granuaile's second son, Murrough, by adopting the same tactics as his adversary Murrough-na-Tuadh, eventually recovered his father's lands as well as the newly built castle of Ballinahinch.

Now a widow, Granuaile returned to her father's territory of Umhall, taking with her the O'Flaherty men who wished to continue to serve under her command. She settled on Clare

Island and from there, with a flotilla of three galleys and a number of smaller 'baggage' boats, launched herself on a career of trade piracy and plunder which she later euphemistically described to Queen Elizabeth as 'maintenance by land and sea',[11] a career that was to establish her as the legendary Pirate Queen of Ireland.

CHAPTER 4
THE PIRATE QUEEN

There stands a tower by the Atlantic side,
A grey old tower by storm and sea-waves beat.
Perch'd on a cliff, beneath it yawneth wide,
A lofty cavern of yore a fit retreat
For pirates galleys, altho' now you'll meet
Nought but the seal and wild gull. From that cave
A hundred steps do upwards lead your feet
Unto a lonely chamber. Bold and brave
Is he who climbs the stair, all slippery from the wave.

IRISH PEDIGREES, VOL. II

A s the widow of a Gaelic chieftain, Granuaile was entitled by law to the return of her dowry, as well as to her widow's 'thirds', a percentage of her late husband's property. Because of his clan's inability to pay, most likely because of the expense incurred by Donal in his constant warring, this, as she later testified, was denied her; 'the countries of Connaught among the Irishry never yielded any thirds to any woman surviving the chieftain, whose rent was uncertain, for the most part extorted.'[1] In view, however, of the restitution she took on the death of her second husband for the non-payment of her 'thirds', it seems unlikely that Granuaile left Ballinahinch without securing some compensation from the O'Flahertys in lieu.

By early 1560 she had returned to her father's territory of Umhall. As her father's only daughter and, more particularly, as sole heir to the lands of her mother, Margaret, her return there made sense. Clare Island with its strategic tower-castle was an ideal base for an aspiring sea-trader and pirate. The castle afforded an encompassing view of Clew Bay, while its sheltered location made it virtually indiscernible to passing shipping. Little in the way of sea traffic could move in or out of the bay without being observed by the inhabitants of Clare Island Castle.

While there is little recorded detail relating to Granuaile's activities during this period of her life, it is clear from her later correspondence to the English Court that she was actively establishing her authority in the area. In a petition to Queen Elizabeth in 1593 Granuaile maintained that 'circumstances', on which she did not then choose to elaborate,

> forced her to make head against her neighbours who in like manner constrained your highness fond subject to take arms and by force to maintain herself and her people by sea and land the space of forty years past.[2]

In 1593 she was also accused by an English military governor of being a 'nurse to all rebellions in the province for forty years,'[3] which implied that from as early as 1550 Granuaile was operating as an independent warrior chieftain, competing for power in the whirlpool of Gaelic tribal disorder, as later she did when faced with English military aggression.

It is during this period of her life that Granuaile assembled the force of 'two hundred fighting men' referred to by Sir Henry Sidney, capable of fighting under her leadership anywhere in 'Ireland and Scotland'. Her 'business' links with Scotland centred on plundering raids on the outer islands and the lucrative importation of the 'gallowglass' Scottish fighters hired by the Irish chieftains, usually on a seasonal basis from May until September. Throughout the later decades of the sixteenth century Granuaile's galleys provided the transport to convey them to and from Ireland.

Her army comprised men from various local clans: O'Malley, Bourke, O'Flaherty, MacCormack, MacNally, Conroy and Clandonnell. That these clansmen were prepared to abandon their own clan, with its inherent obligations and allegiances, pocket the ingrained suspicion and animosity that bedevilled the Irish clan system and, strangest of all, accept the leadership of a woman, contrary to male pride and native mores, is, given the time, a unique tribute to her leadership. In an age in Ireland where loyalty was transient, especially when England began to undermine the foundations of the indigenous clan structure, the loyalty of Grace O'Malley's disparate group of followers endured. That she was successful undoubtedly helped as did the fact that she was willing to lead by example. Long after her death her memory as a warrior leader survived. As late as 1623, an English lord deputy recalled her military prowess and the fact that she had 'borne arms ... was famous and is yet renowned by them [the people] ...'[4]

She is said to have been immensely proud of her followers and to have declared 'go mhfearr léi lán loinge de cloinn Conroí agus cloinn MicAnallaidh ná lán loinge d'ór'[5] (that she would rather have a shipful of Conroys and MacNallys than a shipful of gold). Her men looked to her to lead them successfully and safely by land and especially by sea. To enjoy the loyalty and trust of her mixed bunch of hardy clansmen and mariners, she had to possess a special charisma. Granuaile undoubtedly enjoyed the company of men, of being 'a man's woman', living in close proximity with them, unaffected by female reticence or false modesty. She indulged in at least one male pursuit—gambling—while folklore also maintains that her sexual exploits were in keeping with her uninhibited seafaring life. It is hinted in the English State Papers of the period that she may have borne at least one son out of wedlock. Sir Henry Sidney's description of her in 1576 as being 'notorious in all the coasts of Ireland', perhaps is testimony to this aspect of her life. However, sexual promiscuity was often an insidious charge made against women who stepped outside of what was deemed a woman's role and especially so in the case of women who went to sea. Like her contemporary Queen Elizabeth it was also said that she was given to angry outbursts and to swearing.

After her father's death the O'Malley fleet came under Granuaile's direct leadership from her stronghold on Clare Island.

Her O'Malley relatives were established at the castles of Kildawnet, Carrowmore, Cathair-na-Mart, Murrisk and Belclare. With Doona Castle also in her hands, she commanded the sea passage north towards Erris and Tirawley. From Donegal to Waterford, along the Irish coastline, her attacks by sea were numerous and widespread. Her fame grew. Stories of her exploits were peddled from port to port. On land she began to accumulate extensive cattle and horse herds, which by 1593 numbered, by her own admission, over one thousand head, making her a very wealthy woman indeed.

There are many traditional stories relating to her activities by sea including attacks on various castles along the coast. She demolished part of Curradh Castle at Renvyle, supposedly with a cannonball shot from the deck of her ship. Whenever she alighted on nearby Inishbofin she impounded the islanders' boats for the duration of her stay and ran an iron chain across the mouth of the harbour to prevent access to the island. On the Aran Islands she was more feared than welcomed and, according to one account, when she came with 'her people in ships to Port Mhurbhe [Kilmurvey Bay] the battle raged east to Cill Éinne.'[6] In Burtonport, Killybegs and Lough Swilly, the O'Boyle and MacSweeney clans were subjected to her raids, while her attack on the castle of O'Loughlin in the Burren in County Clare has passed into legend. Her plundering attack on the lands of the powerful Earl of Desmond in Thomond resulted in her capture and imprisonment for almost two years.

Her seizure of the lonely castle of Doona on the coast of Erris was traditionally said to have been in reprisal for the murder of her lover by a sept of the MacMahon clan who resided there. According to legend, Granuaile was on a pilgrimage at the holy well on Clare Island on St Brigid's Day when news was brought to her that a ship had foundered near Achill Head. The chance of salvage proving stronger than religious observance or foul weather, in the teeth of a gale Granuaile set sail across the storm-tossed stretch of water that divides Clare Island from Achill.

Almost four hundred years later the eminent scientist Robert Lloyd Praeger, who organised the unique scientific survey of the island in 1909, wrote of the experience:

> Away we went under one scrap of sail, over great waves roaring in from the west. The boat rushed down into deep troughs where there was no breath of wind and only water all round and up again over high crests where the wind half choked us, and we got a momentary wide glimpse over far-stretching angry seas to distant black foam-rimmed cliffs ...[7]

Granuaile found the ship broken up off Achill Head. Amidst the wreckage she rescued a young man from the rocks, and brought him back with the salvage to Clare Island. Hugh de Lacy, the son of a wealthy merchant from Wexford became her lover. Their joy, however, was short-lived. While hunting deer on Achill Island, Hugh was killed by the MacMahons of Doona Castle. Heartbroken, Granuaile plotted her revenge. When the MacMahons came on pilgrimage to the nearby holy island of Caher, high on the ramparts of her castle on Clare Island, Granuaile watched and waited until they landed on the island. Like an eagle she swooped on their boats, cutting off their means of escape and killed those responsible for Hugh's death. Her revenge still not assuaged, she sailed for Doona, routed the garrison and took the castle for herself.

Granuaile's determination to avenge a wrong was further demonstrated in a folktale about a neighbouring chieftain who tried to steal her property. Fearing reprisal, the chieftain hid in a church on a small island whose only inhabitant was a holy hermit. Granuaile surrounded the church and vowed to starve the chieftain into submission. With the help of the hermit, the chieftain dug a tunnel to the cliff-face, from which he lowered himself with a rope onto a boat, and made good his escape. Breaking his vow of silence, the hermit informed Granuaile that her quarry had escaped and cursed her for trying to harm someone who had sought sanctuary in his church. Granuaile's reply was, unfortunately, not recorded.

Granuaile's association with Howth Castle in county Dublin that best demonstrates her boldness and daring. Situated in the English Pale, some fifteen kilometres from Dublin, Howth was then the principal port for the city. Returning from a voyage, Granuaile's ship was forced to put in at the port to take on water and provisions for the journey back to Mayo. As was the Gaelic custom while in port, Granuaile sought hospitality at the castle of the local lord, St Lawrence, the Earl of Howth. She found the gates of the castle locked against her and was told that the Earl was at dinner and would not be disturbed. Indignant at such inhospitable treatment, Granuaile set out to return to her ship. On the beach before the castle she encountered the grandson and heir of the Earl. She kidnapped the young boy and sailed for Clew Bay. In great trepidation St Lawrence set off for Mayo, to secure the release of his heir from the clutches of the notorious pirate by payment of whatever ransom she demanded. Scorning his offer of gold and silver, Granuaile made St Lawrence revise his definition of hospitality by extracting a promise that the gates of Howth Castle would never again be closed and that an extra place would henceforth be set at his table for anyone seeking his hospitality. Relieved at the simplicity of her demand, St Lawrence readily agreed and departed from Mayo safely with his grandson.

The abduction of the heir of Howth has traditionally been ascribed to Granuaile. However, the seventeenth-century historian and genealogist Duald MacFirbis, in his *Great Book of Genealogies*, maintained that the perpetrator of the deed was Richard Bourke, the MacWilliam of Mayo from 1469 to 1479:

This was the very same Richard who took the Lord of Beann Edair [Howth] and brought him with him to Tirawley, and there was nought else required of him for his ransom but to keep the door of his court open at dinner time.[8]

But MacFirbis's statement must be examined in the light of the treatment and attitude of Irish annalists and historians in general to Granuaile. While the English State Papers and associated manuscripts of the period include numerous references to her and her extraordinary career, her exclusion from contemporary Irish annals and histories shows a remarkable bias. To later generations of Irish historians and annalists, Granuaile simply did not fit the required mould as a patriot and as a woman and so to eliminate rather than to acknowledge her existence was the easier course.

Tradition however is steadfast in its assertion that she abducted the heir of Howth. Moreover Grace O'Malley's name is commemorated on many street signs in Howth village to this day. At Howth Castle today, which still in the ownership of the St Lawrence family, to honour her agreement made with their sixteenth-century ancestor, an extra place continues to be set at the table and the old castle gates remain open.

Records in the keeping of the St Lawrence family further testify to her association with the incident.

Lord Howth gave a ring to Grace O'Malley as a pledge on the agreement … it was preserved in the O'Malley family until 1795 when an Elizabeth O'Malley married John Irwin of Camlin, county Roscommon, when the ring moved to the Irwin family. An Irwin son emigrated to America taking the ring with him. He was a solicitor and married and later his grandson, John Vesberg, a New York solicitor, had it mounted into a brooch.[9]

The abduction incident is much in keeping with Granuaile's style and character that, as E. Ball recorded in his book *Howth and its Owners*, 'the possibility that an incident such as tradition relates may have occurred is beyond dispute.'[10]

While Granuaile received short shrift from Irish historians and annalists, tradition and folklore more than compensated in keeping her memory alive. Many of the stories relating to her have been preserved by word of mouth, handed down from one generation to the next. In 1838 the scholar John O'Donovan, while collecting information for the Ordnance Survey letters relating to county Mayo, found that Granuaile was then

> … most vividly remembered by tradition and people were living in the last generation who conversed with people who knew her personally. Charles Cormick of Erris, now 74 years and six weeks old, saw and conversed with Elizabeth O'Donnell of Newton within the Mullet, who died about 65 years ago who had seen and intimately known a Mr Walsh who remembered Gráinne. Walsh died at the age of 107 and his father was the same age as Gráinne.[11]

These folk stories and legends are in themselves a tribute to Granuaile, an acknowledgement of the impact she made on her time and on the community in which she lived.

As Granuaile continued to pursue her trade by land and sea from her base on Clare Island, political events outside Ireland began to impinge on the freedom both she and her Gaelic world enjoyed. Religious polarisation between Catholicism and Protestantism erupted in France into a fierce and bloody struggle for religious supremacy. While King Philip of Spain, the powerful self-appointed defender of the old religion, was determined that Protestantism would not gain a foothold in Spanish-controlled Netherlands, the Protestants of the Netherlands looked to Queen Elizabeth for help, thus setting England on a collision course with Spain.

In Ireland an ongoing feud between two powerful Anglo-Norman magnates, the earls of Desmond and Ormond, exploded into war. In a pitched battle at Affane in 1565, Ormond defeated Desmond. The incident brought into focus the unstable and divided political situation in Ireland and its potential as a base against England for her enemy Spain. But despite the danger that Ireland posed to England's security, money or the lack of it once again stayed England's resolve to embark on all-out military conquest. When Sir Henry Sidney, the queen's deputy in Ireland, raised the possibility of colonisation as a means of extending England's hold over its neighbouring island, however, it presented an effective and less expensive method of bringing the country to heel. It was a prospect that was to have a profound effect on the Gaelic world of Granuaile, the repercussions of which have lasted to the present day.

The colonisation prospect was greeted in England with enthusiasm. Younger sons of English landed gentry, with little prospects under the law of primogeniture, as well as enterprising adventurers from the West Country, saw it as a means to a fortune. First into the fray came Sir Peter Carew, armed with a spurious claim to lands in Meath and Carlow and to Desmond-held lands in Kerry and Cork. His claim originated in the dim and distant Anglo-Norman conquest four hundred years previously. However, in his enthusiasm to endow himself with the lands and property of Irish chiefs and lords, Carew also laid claim to lands owned by the brothers of the loyal Earl of Ormond, and cousin of the queen. This resulted for a time in an unlikely alliance between the rival houses of Desmond and Ormond, who rose in arms to protect their properties. On the strength of Carew's initial success, however, scores of his fellow countrymen followed in his wake on a mission of land-grabbing on a grand scale.

In the manner and language of the coloniser, to these English pirate-adventurers Ireland was as remote and unknown as the far-off Americas, peopled by a race as alien as the red-skinned Indians, governed by 'barbarous' chieftains and uncouth brehons and bards—a race and country that, as they asserted, would benefit from the 'civilising' hand of a superior conqueror. The Elizabethan conquest of Ireland had commenced.

In Connaught, English authority was further extended throughout the Province in 1569 by the appointment of Sir Edward Fitton as military governor and by the establishment of a council consisting of a justice, a provost-marshal, attorneys and sheriffs. The powers of the governor, who was also president of the council, were extensive. He, in effect, exercised the power of the lord deputy within his own designated area. At this time Sir John Perrot was appointed President of Munster. The presidencies of Connaught and Munster provided the English government with an institutionalised vehicle from where all legislative policies and military strategies, formulated to undermine the foundation and institutions of native Irish law and society, as well as to further the colonisation process, would in future emanate. Although the English presidencies would meet stiff native opposition by the very institutional aspect of their power they had the in-built ability to survive the challenge of the divided and individualistic native society they sought to abolish.

In Mayo native opposition to the newly established English presidency did not take long to materialise. Governor Fitton and his ally the Earl of Clanrickard clashed with the MacWilliam of Mayo and his allies, including the O'Flahertys and Richard Bourke, his *tánaiste*, at Shrule on the borders of Mayo and Galway. Both sides claimed victory but, later in the same year, the MacWilliam submitted to Fitton and agreed to pay the crown a yearly rent of 200 marks. His death at the end of 1570 marked a milestone in the history of Mayo. During his reign as the MacWilliam, English authority had gained a foothold in his territory that had hitherto been a bastion of Gaelic law and custom. It was the start of a turbulent transfer of power from the Connacht chieftains to the English crown which was to continue for a period of some thirty years. Since the chieftains saw their ancient privileges threatened by the establishment and extension of the new administration, they sought either to oppose the English, if they were strong enough, or to ally with them in order to retain their power.

Granuaile's emergence as a leader in her own right, contrary to both native and English law, coincided with these radical developments. In many ways there is a curious analogy between Granuaile's struggle, in both the political and personal sense, and the struggle of Gaelic Ireland against Elizabethan England. At first both are boldly defiant in the face of English encroachment. Eventually, however, the relentless pressure exerted by the English administration in Ireland, and the inability of the Gaelic leaders to formulate a cohesive campaign of opposition, Granuaile's efforts to maintain her power becomes, like that of the Gaelic world into which she was born, a struggle for survival.

CHAPTER 5
'A MOST FAMOUS FEMININE SEA CAPTAIN'

By 1567 Granuaile relinquished widowhood to marry again. Life expectancy for sixteenth-century women was as little as forty years. Then in her late thirties, and given the dangerous career path she had chosen, she was lucky to have survived for so long. Traditionally it was held that her second marriage was motivated more by material than by emotional needs: possession of her husband's strategically situated castle of Carraigahowley (Rockfleet) being her principal objective. No doubt her choice of mate was also influenced by the fact that her second husband's lands had access to many sheltered harbours including Burrishoole where, according to one contemporary account, 'a shypp of 500 tonnes may lye at ancure at loe water'.[1]

It is likely that this time round Granuaile choose her own husband. Richard-an-Iarainn Bourke, chieftain of the sept of Ulick of Burrishoole and Carra, a senior branch of the Mayo Bourke dynasty caught her eye. His father, David, had been the MacWilliam until his death in 1558. (Richard was the stepbrother of Walter Fada Bourke, murdered by Granuaile's first husband, Dónal-an-Chogaidh O'Flaherty.) As chieftain of the sept Ulick, and as the son of a previous MacWilliam, Richard was eligible for election to the MacWilliamship, the most powerful and coveted title in Connaught. His territory in Umhall Iochtarach stretched along the northern shore of Clew Bay, from Achill to Westport.

This was not the first O'Malley–Bourke marriage. In the fifteenth century, Granuaile's namesake, Gráinne Uí Máille, had married Thomas Bourke from Burrishoole. Their commemorative silver-gilt chalice is preserved in the National Museum of Ireland.

Richard's nickname *an iarainn* [in iron] was traditionally said to have originated from his habit of wearing an outdated suit of armour inherited from his remote de Burgo Anglo-Norman ancestors. It is more likely, however, that his name derived from the iron works situated on his lands at Furnace in Burrishoole.

From extant records it appears that Richard-an-Iarainn had been married previously or was the father of illegitimate sons. Besides the son he had with Granuaile, three other sons, Edmund, Walter and John, and a daughter, Catherine, are referred to in the English State Papers. In her correspondence with the English authorities, Granuaile mentions having three sons and later, in a Bill of Chancery, her son by Richard-an-Iarainn claimed to be his mother's sole heir. However, Edmund Bourke in particular was often mistakenly referred to by the English authorities as being Granuaile's natural son by Richard. (There are many references as well as some extant documents relating to him in both the English State Papers and the Westport House manuscript collection (see appendices)).

Richard Bourke was a worthy consort for Granuaile. In the mould of a Gaelic warrior, he was well-connected, wealthy and brave, if somewhat impetuous. In 1553 he was involved in a tribal dispute with the Bourkes of Gallen who, on that occasion, defeated him, took him prisoner, and killed 150 of his men. In 1558, when his father was the MacWilliam, in an ongoing feud with the Earl of Clanrickard, commanding a huge army of over 1,000 Scots mercenaries, Richard plundered the lands of MacMaurice and Lord Athenry, allies of Clanrickard, in county Galway. Later, in a fixed battle with Clanrickard, he was defeated with the loss of over 700 of his Scottish mercenaries. By the time of his marriage to Granuaile, politically Richard-an-Iarainn had established himself by birthright, influence and might as a future contender for the powerful MacWilliamship title.

Tradition holds that Granuaile married her second husband strictly on her own terms, opting for a trial marriage for a period of one year. If either she or Richard wished to withdraw from the arrangement after that time, they were free to do so. Trial marriages were common among the Gaelic aristocracy, and divorce by the Brehon legal system was availed of by both women and men.

> In no field of life was Ireland's apartness from the mainstream of European society so marked as in that of marriage ... Down to the end of the old order in 1603, what could be called Celtic secular marriage remained the norm in Ireland ... Christian matrimony was no more than the rare exception, grafted onto this system.[2]

Tradition further holds that when the marriage had reached the stipulated year's duration, and when Granuaile had installed herself and her followers in her husband's castle of Carraigahowley, she locked him out, and from the ramparts shouted down the words of divorce—'Richard Bourke, I dismiss you'—in one fell swoop acquiring a castle and ridding herself of a husband. Their divorce was, however, a temporary aberration, as Granuaile and Richard-an-Iarainn featured together as a powerful partnership for almost twenty years.

Richard-an-Iarainn's principal castle was at Burrishoole, with secondary castles near the present town of Newport and Carraigahowley (Rockfleet), the castle most associated with Granuaile. Situated on a quiet inlet of Clew Bay, Carraigahowley is a typical square tower keep of the period. In the time of Granuaile the entrance was protected by a small barbican. It stands some 20 metres high, comprising four storeys, linked from the first-floor level by a spiral stairway, and is surmounted by ramparts and a wall walk. The lower internal levels are dimly lit by loop windows and include some curious features still extant, such as a stone privy with an outflow to the sea, which at high tide encircles the castle on three sides. The main apartment on the fourth floor was inhabited by Granuaile on an almost continuous basis until her death in 1603. It has a bright and airy aspect and commands a fine view towards the sea. It has a stone-flagged floor, a fireplace, recessed windows and a curious arched doorway on the east wall leading out to a fifty-foot drop to the ground below. This has a less sinister use than one might expect, being a loading bay through which objects, too bulky to be carried via the spiral stairway, were hauled up by a pulley. In the south-facing wall there is a loophole through which traditionally it was said the hawser of Granuaile's favourite galley was attached to her bedpost at night. A small stairway leads from this chamber to the ramparts above. The castle has been partly restored and, even in its present stark state, it is not difficult to imagine the bare chambers transformed into a comfortable and strategic stronghold.

That Granuaile was the dominant partner in her marriage to Richard-an-Iarainn is evident from the many references to them made by English administrators and military men who crossed their path. At their meeting in 1576, Sir Henry Sidney recorded that Granuaile 'brought with her her husband for she was as well by sea as by land well more than Mrs Mate with him ....'[3] Richard-an-Iarainn is usually referred to by the English as 'the husband of Grany O'Maile'.[4] While a brave chieftain by the standards of the time and skilled in feats of arms, Richard's martial attributes seemed ever to lack any coherent insight into the prevailing political complexities. It was his wife who excelled in this regard. But the combination of his military strength and her considerable political acumen, together with her sea power, made them a formidable couple. Granuaile brought a dowry to the marriage comprising cattle and horses, for which, as she later attested, she received from Richard-an-Iarainn 'sureties for the restitution of the same'[5] in case of divorce or death.

Their only son, Theobald, was born in 1567. He became known in history by his sobriquet, Tibbott-ne-Long (*Tibóid-ne-Long*), Toby of the Ships. He is said to have been born on board his mother's ship and de Burgo's *Hibernia Dominicana* acknowledges this theory as the source of his nickname:

...bellatorem strenuum et invictum, qui (sc Richardus) ex Grania (aliis Grisella) O'Maly, Dynastae O'Flaherti Vidua, genuit Equitem Theobaldum ny Lung id est, de Navibus quia

Mari in Navium Classe natum [... the mighty and invincible warrior that is Richard had by the widow Grania [alias Grisella] O'Maly of the O'Flaherty family, the knight Theobald ny Lung, that is of the ships, because he was born in a fleet of ships at sea.][6]

It was also traditionally held that the day after Tibbott's birth, Granuaile's ship was attacked by Algerian pirates. As the battle raged, her captain came below where she lay with her new-born son and begged her to come up on deck as her presence might rally her men. With the words 'may you be seven times worse off this day twelve months, who cannot do without me for one day',[7] she wrapped a blanket around herself and joined her men. Uttering a ferocious oath she roared them into action, while at the same time emptied a musket at the Algerians, crying, 'Take this from un-consecrated hands.' The fact that attacks by North African pirates on outlying areas along the south and west coasts of Ireland were recorded frequently during this period lends credence to this traditional account of Tibbott-ne-Long's birth. Granuaile's reference to 'un-consecrated hands' refers to a custom in the Catholic church (extant until recent times) that deemed a woman after childbirth unfit to participate in church ceremonies until she underwent a 'churching' or cleansing ceremony.

In a poem commissioned from the sixteenth-century poet Mathgamháin Ó hUigínn, and preserved in the Royal Irish Academy, Granuaile's youngest son is referred to as:

> Tiobóid a Burc of the valiant feats
> Of the hawklike blue eye ...
> He is the warrior whose curving neck
> With ringleted golden-yellow hair
> Is secretly loved by girls in every region ...
> He is the ruddy-cheeked heir of Gráinne.[8]

Another sixteenth-century poet, the renowned Eochaidh Ó hEoghusa, referred to Tibbott as:

Tiobóid, Tower of Achill
Salmon of Clár Gara
Emulator of the African Lion ...[9]

As was customary, the child Tibbott was fostered by Edmund
MacTibbot, a sub-chieftain of his father who resided at Castleleaffy
in the barony of Burrishoole. Fosterage was an integral part of
Gaelic life and was considered an honour by the family chosen
to foster the son of the chieftain, particularly one as powerful as
Richard Bourke.

> The practice [of fosterage] was of considerable political
> importance, for the person fostered could count on the
> adherence of his foster family through his life ... Conversely,
> the fosterers would also reap the benefits of support and
> protection.[10]

In fosterage, as the son of a chieftain and a future contender in the
ruling Bourke hierarchy, Tibbott's training placed much emphasis
on the use of weapons such as the sword, javelin and dart, and
proficiency in horsemanship and military tactics. Tibbott was
literate in both Irish and English, as his correspondence with the
English authorities demonstrates. He possessed a keen and able
mind and, as an adult, showed a consummate understanding of
both Brehon and English law, which he used to his advantage. The
fact that, towards the end of the century, Tibbott took control of
his mother's fleet of galleys is also testimony to his maritime ability.

In 1571 Shane MacOliverus Bourke became the MacWilliam
and Granuaile's husband Richard was elected his *tánaiste*. During
MacWilliam's reign the English administration continued to
expand its control over Connaught. In 1574 Mayo was surveyed
and divided into ten baronies. For the first time, the principal
clans and chieftains of each barony were listed. The barony of
Burrishoole was listed as 'Burris, containing Owle Clan Philbin,
Owel Eighter (iochtarach) and Sliocht MacTybbot's lands,
Richard-an-Iarainn, chief.'[11] In 1575 the English lord deputy, Sir

Henry Sidney, paid a second visit to Connaught to induce the lords and chieftains of the province to surrender their Irish tenures, take back their lands by the queen's patent, rule by English law, and accept sheriffs in their territories. Sidney returned again in 1576 and summoned the principal chieftains of Mayo to meet him in Galway.

Thinking that his power and forces made him immune, MacWilliam refused to comply with Sidney's order. The lord deputy succeeded in luring MacWilliam's Clandonnell gallowglass from him and, thus weakened, MacWilliam had little option but to comply. Together with his sub-lords, including the O'Malley chieftain, MacWilliam made his way to Galway. Sidney wrote to the English Court about the meeting: 'I found MacWilliam very sensible, though wanting the English tongue, yet understanding the Latin, a lover of Quiet and Civility.' MacWilliam, Sidney further maintained, was anxious 'to hold his Lands of the Queen and suppress Irish Extortion and to expulse the Scots, who swarm in those quarters'.[12] Whether voluntary or compelled, MacWilliam agreed to rule by English law, to pay two hundred and fifty pounds per annum in rent to the crown and to furnish the English governor with a force of two hundred soldiers as his own expense for two months each year. In return, Sidney conferred on MacWilliam 'his country ... by way of Seneschalship ... The order of Knighthood I bestowed upon him ... and some other little trifles ...', as well as appointing an English sheriff within his territory. MacWilliam had left Mayo to meet with the queen's deputy as an independent Gaelic chieftain, and returned an indentured English knight. MacWilliam also obtained a promise from Sidney to be created an earl but, he 'had no certain estate in land',[13] the promise was not fulfilled.

MacWilliam's submission had political repercussions for his *tánaiste*, Richard-an-Iarainn who, alone of the Mayo chieftains, had not accompanied his overlord to Galway. It demonstrated that the English were now more powerful than the strongest Gaelic chieftain. It undermined the age-old custom of clientship, the pillar on which Gaelic power rested, and revealed its inherent weakness when faced with a stronger and unified force. It was Granuaile who, more than her husband, realised the implications of MacWilliam's submission and prepared to do something about it. By English law, MacWilliam's eldest male blood relation would now succeed him, rather than his *tánaiste*, by Gaelic law Richard-an-Iarainn. Granuaile had first-hand experience of this reversal when her first husband, Dónal-an-Chogaidh O'Flaherty, had been set aside as *tánaiste* by an English-backed usurper. Her subsequent dramatic appearance in Galway was her way of demonstrating to the English lord deputy that she and Richard would not be as easily pushed aside.

On his return to Galway in March 1577, to quell a rebellion by the sons of the Earl of Clanrickard, Lord Deputy Sidney, accompanied by his son, the famous poet, courtier and soldier, Sir Philip Sidney, met with the most unusual leader he had ever encountered:

> There came to mee also a most famous femynyne sea capten called Grany Imallye, and offred her service unto me, wheresoever I woulde command her, with three gallyes and two hundred fightinge men, either in Ireland or Scotland, she brought with her her husband, for she was as well by sea as by land well more than Mrs Mate with him. He was of the Nether Burkes and now as I here [1582] Mackwilliam Euter and called by nickname Richard in Iron. This was a notorious woman in all the coastes of Ireland ...[14]

Granuaile's plan had the desired effect. Sidney noted her sea and military power and agreed to accept her offer of assistance, given that her army almost outnumbered his own. Anxious to view from the sea-side the defensive walls of Galway city which, as he reported, he found much decayed, he prevailed upon Granuaile to take him out on the bay in one of her galleys. But business being business, Granuaile demanded and was paid for the service, a receipt for which Sidney meticulously recorded in his accounts.

The Lord Deputy's son, Sir Philip Sidney, had recently accompanied his friend the Earl of Essex, the newly appointed earl marshal, to Ireland. From Dublin he had journeyed to Galway to meet his father. Sir Philip Sidney was captivated by Granuaile and, as his father reported to the queen's secretary, Sir Francis Walsingham: 'This woman did Sir Philip Sydney see and speake withal, he can more at large enforme you of her.'[15] What common ground the middle-aged, feminine sea captain and the sophisticated young Elizabethan courtier found, will never be known. That Philip Sidney had recently become a patron of the explorer Martin Frobisher, who was then preparing for a voyage to find the fabled North West Passage, perhaps provided them with one topic of mutual interest. That Granuaile could have informed him that an even greater explorer, Christopher Columbus, had visited Galway in 1492 en route to the New World, might well have been a further conversational topic.

Granuaile's submission to the English lord deputy in Galway was no more than a judicious gesture to enhance her husband's future claim to the MacWilliamship by the simple but effective expedient of a demonstration of their combined power. There was to be no change, however, in her activities on her return to Mayo. A few weeks after her meeting with Sydney, she set off south in her galleys on a plundering mission to the rich lands of the Earl of Desmond in Munster. The operation did not work out quite as she had planned. She was captured and hauled before the Earl at his great castle at Askeaton in County Limerick.

Desmond was fighting for his political survival. The most powerful independent lord in Ireland, he was being pressurised by forces within his own family who wanted him to protect the status quo, and by external powers who wanted to make him the symbolic leader in Ireland of the growing Counter-Reformation movement with its Papal and Spanish backers. At the same time he was being baited by land-hungry Puritan elements in the English administration both in Ireland and in England, who saw in the Earl's inflexibility and his vast acres as the means to their personal fortunes, if Desmond could be pushed over the edge into rebellion. The indecisive earl was playing for time. Under suspicion by

Queen Elizabeth—who had been recently excommunicated by the pope—of being implicated in a European Catholic crusade against her, Desmond badly needed a diversion and Granuaile was the opportune token to appease the queen's suspicions.

Desmond first imprisoned Granuaile in Askeaton and then sent her to Limerick gaol. Confinement for Granuaile must have been a living death but Limerick gaol was only the start of her long confinement. In March 1578, when the English President of Munster, Lord Justice Drury, came knocking on the door of Askeaton castle, Desmond produced his notorious prisoner as proof of his loyal intent. Drury communicated news of Granuaile's capture to Sidney in Dublin, describing his unusual prisoner as

> Grany O'Mayle a woman that hath impudently passed the part of womanhood and been a great spoiler and chief commander and director of thieves and murderers at sea to spoil this province ...[16]

In a letter to Sir Francis Walsingham, Drury further communicated how the Earl of Desmond had 'sent on also unto me Granny Nye Male one of power and force',[17] as a demonstration of his loyalty. The queen's Privy Council was suitably impressed:

> We pray you also to signify unto the Earle of Desmond in howe good parte her Majestie and we take it to understand of his so good and dewytfull behaviour, in making soche demonstration of his loyaltie, as you wryte of not only in words but also ... sending unto you Grany O'Mayle and other notorious offenders of his countrie.[18]

Drury ordered that Granuaile be transferred from Limerick to Dublin Castle. On 7 November 1578, having endured confinement for almost a year and a half in Limerick, she was taken in chains across the country. Drury met her and her escort at Leighlin in county Carlow, as he informed the Privy Council:

> To that place was brought unto me Granie ny Maille, a woman

of the province of Connaught, governing a Country of the Oflaherties, famous for her stoutenes of courage and person, and for some sundry exploits done at sea. She was taken by the Earle of Desmond a year and a half agoe and hath remained partly with him and partly in Her Mat.is' gaole of Limerick, and was sent for now by me to come to Dublin ...[19]

That Granuaile's capture and imprisonment were of such interest to the English administration in Ireland and to the Privy Council in England is testimony to her status and notoriety. Imprisonment in the dungeons of Dublin Castle was reserved for the most notable and politically important prisoners, and convicted inmates detained there were seldom released. Granuaile's three companions imprisoned with her were subsequently executed. Lost to her people, her husband and children, Granuaile must have despaired of ever being free again.

Sir Nicholas Malby succeeded Fitton as governor of Connaught. Malby was one of the new breed of Puritan military men sent to implement a more vigorous campaign against the Gaelic chieftains and lords. For men like Malby, the independent posturing of the Gaelic and gaelicised leaders in Ireland, the unstable situation which their individual power struggles created, and their resolute adherence to the spirit, at least, of the old religion, were anathema to their puritan Tudor minds. They saw in Ireland's disordered state both an opportunity for England's enemies and a means towards personal advancement and reward for themselves. The methods they employed, particularly in Munster and Connaught, had as their twin spurs zeal and avarice.

Granuaile's release came early in 1579, and the reason for it can only be surmised. Perhaps the tentative peace that had descended on the country contributed. Perhaps the English authorities decided that Granuaile, imprisoned for almost two years, had paid her dues. A more likely reason may have been her ability to prevent her husband from forming an alliance with her former gaoler—the Earl of Desmond. One way or another by March 1579 she was reinstalled at Carraigahowley.

It was not long, however, before she became embroiled in

further strife. Knowing that her release from Dublin Castle put the safety of their shipping once again at risk, the merchants of Galway city hired a strong sea-borne force of soldiers, under the command of a Captain Martin, and lay siege to her in Carraigahowley castle.

> This expedition sailed from Galway on 8 March but so spirited was the defence made by this extraordinary woman that they were obliged to retreat on the 26 of the same month and very narrowly escaped being made prisoner.[20]

The victory undoubtedly augmented Granuaile's reputation as a significant leader in the all-male Gaelic hierarchy, as well as giving further indication to the English authorities that she was some-one not to be tampered with. The military victory also gave leverage to Richard, still biding his time to become the future MacWilliam by Gaelic right.

On 18 July 1579, however, the tentative peace of the previous months was shattered by a holy thunderclap. It reverberated off the high mountain peaks of Kerry and sent shock waves careering across the country to frighten the English council in Dublin and make Elizabeth's nightmare, that Spain would use Ireland as a backdoor to England, a reality. With a fleet of ships, an army of some six hundred Europeans, a banner blessed by the pope and the promise of indulgences in the next life, James FitzMaurice Fitzgerald, cousin of the Earl of Desmond, arrived to unite and raise all Ireland in 'holy war'[21] against the 'heretic queen of England'. He appealed to the Gaelic chieftains and to the Earl of Desmond for support. While the indecisive Earl pondered his position, FitzMaurice was shot in a local tribal squabble. Goaded by circumstances over which he had little control, Desmond was forced to adopt the unlikely mantle of crusader in place of his cousin. Sir Nicholas Malby assumed temporary authority in Munster and, 'fired by puritanical religious zeal',[22] burned and looted his way to the very walls of Askeaton Castle. In November 1579, Desmond was proclaimed a traitor by the English and the dogs of war were let loose over Munster, which was to be ravaged and plundered for the next four years.

The Earl of Desmond wrote personally to the MacWilliam and to Richard-an-Iarainn to raise Mayo in support of the crusade. MacWilliam refused but Richard-an-Iarainn jumped into the fray and, with his Clandonnell gallowglass and some septs of the O'Malleys and O'Flahertys, marched into Galway. Once again he plundered the territories of his old adversaries, O'Kelly and Lord Athenry, as a decoy for raids by Desmond's forces in Limerick and Kerry. The reason for Richard-an-Iarainn's support for the Desmond rebellion is open to speculation. His hope of becoming MacWilliam had been reversed by the present incumbent Shane MacOliverus's conversion to English law. Like most of his contemporaries, Richard's discontent spread, not from any sense of religious persecution by the English crown, but from the crown's endeavours to take away his powers by denying him the MacWilliamship. He saw in Desmond's rebellion a chance to secure what he considered his by right of native law. MacWilliam had thrown in his lot with the English and it was logical that Richard would support England's enemy, the Earl of Desmond. It was unlikely, however, that Granuaile would readily have backed her husband's support of her former gaoler who had sacrificed her to save his own neck. Wisely, as it turned out, for both her husband and herself, she remained aloof.

In February 1580 Malby returned to Connaught to confront Richard-an-Iarainn. With MacWilliam's help, he drove him from Galway into Mayo. As Malby advanced, Richard-an-Iarainn's gallowglass began to desert him. When Malby took the castle of Donamona and, as he reported, 'put the ward, both men, women and children to the sword', [23] resistance began to crumble. Richard-an-Iarainn fled with a few followers to Clew Bay. 'The 16th I removed to Ballyknock', Malby recorded, 'whither Granny ni Maille and certain of her kinsmen came to me.'[24] With the initiative well and truly lost by her husband, a voluntary submission, rather than a forced one later, made obvious sense to Granuaile. That she was well-established as a leader, independent of her husband, is evidenced from Malby's statement, and was accepted as such by him and other English administrators with whom she came into contact. Malby and his army moved right into the heart of Burrishoole and placed a garrison at the abbey, close to Carrickahowley castle. Richard fled with a few followers to an island in Clew Bay and opened negotiations with Malby from a distance. Eventually he agreed to come ashore and submit in person but was prevented by a violent storm which blew for six days. As the rebellion in Munster intensified, Malby was ordered by the new lord justice, William Pellam, to report there for duty. Pellam further reported to England that 'Sir Nicholas Malbie has put an end to the stirs in Connaught by Richard Ineran, husband of Grany O'Maillie.'[25]

Richard-an-Iarainn's formal submission (see Appendix 1.1) was forwarded to Malby in Munster. Signed by his mark, it was couched in suitably remorseful tones. 'He hath fallen from his dewtie towards God and Her Maite …'[26] Richard admitted. But, while he may have been defeated in the field, he bargained for the best deal he could, most likely under his wife's direction. To regain control of his followers, the basis of his power, was his first objective. To this effect he offered to 'call backe his followers with theyre goodes to inhabyte the countrye', at the same time intimating that without them the queen would lose the 'rents and dewties' that were forthcoming from his territory. So that his authority over his followers would not be diminished, especially in the light of the presence of Malby's garrison in his territory, he demanded the restoration of his right as a chieftain 'to take up suche dewties and demands from tyme to tyme as is dewe upon his followers …'[27] By then fully-stretched with the rebellion in Munster, Malby had little option but to agree. Richard-an-Iarainn was subsequently pardoned and returned to Burrishoole.

The MacWilliam of Mayo died in November 1580. The succession was immediately claimed by MacWilliam's brother, also named Richard, his heir by English law. This time Richard-an-Iarainn and Granuaile combined their forces to protect Richard's right to the title. They mustered an impressive army, numbering '1,200 gallowglass, 700 Scots, 300 kerne and 200 horesmen',[28] to enforce Richard's claim. Together with the support of all the Mayo chieftains, the traditional client lords of the MacWilliam, as well as the more dubious support of the Earl of Clanrickard's sons, such a show of strength spurred the English, already committed in Munster, to act swiftly to defuse the situation. Malby was ordered back to Mayo this time to negotiate with Richard and Granuaile. After much sword-shaking a deal was eventually struck.

Letters patent from Queen Elizabeth, together with articles of indenture (see Appendix 1.II) were signed by Richard-an-Iarainn and by the English lord deputy, Sir Grey de Wilton, on 14 April 1581. They are written in Latin and confer on:

> Richard Bourke, alias Richard Inyeren Bourke, alias MacWilliam Eoghter Bourke, … that he be chief of his clan and seneschal of the feudal tenants and followers of our people and nation and of his own clans and their lands and tenements…[29]

The indentures detailed the duties required of Richard by the English crown, whom they refer to as having 'assumed the title and name of MacWilliam Eighter Burke … without permission from her Majestie.'[30] Richard promised to rule by English law, to obey the queen's representative and to pay 'each year 50 cows or fat martas [bullocks] or in place thereof 250 marks legal money of England at the Michelmas term each year', as well as providing food and lodging for two hundred soldiers for up to forty-two days each year. Most importantly, regarding the importation of gallowglass, the agreement stipulated that Richard 'would no longer suffer any Scotts or other rebels or enemies of her Majestie … within the limits of his authority and government.'[31] This stipulation fell to Richard-an-Iarainn's advantage. With Malby's help, he afterwards drove the Scottish mercenaries, numbering over one thousand men, whom he had hired to pursue his claim to the MacWilliamship, over the Moy river and out of Mayo, thus saving himself the considerable expense of paying for their hire.

The letters patent and indentures (Richard-an-Iarainn's copy was preserved for centuries in Westport House) are significant in so far that they are a rare, if unique, example of royal approval of a proscribed Gaelic title. Gaelic-sounding clauses such as 'chief of his clan', 'that he may tax, exact and levy', and that 'he shall have … profits and commodities which he the said Richard has by right possession in the province of Connaught', testify to the native ethos of the office. English aspirations to extinguish Gaelic titles such as the MacWilliam, on this occasion were secondary to the political reality on the ground. Richard and his formidable wife had flexed their combined military muscle and the English administration had taken note and acquiesced. From an English point of view, by granting Richard the MacWilliamship, albeit with the English embellishment of a knighthood, with which he was conferred in September 1581, expediency proved the wiser course and a costly war was thereby avoided.

Richard-an-Iarainn was subsequently created MacWilliam by native Gaelic custom at the prehistoric rath of Rausakeera, the ancient inauguration site near Kilmaine, county Mayo, where for generations MacWilliam chieftains had been invested. By virtue of Gaelic law, he acquired the overlordship of the extensive territories pertaining to the title: Lough Mask Castle with 3,000 acres, Ballinrobe Castle with 1,000 acres and Kinlough near Shrule with 2,500 acres, together with the demesne lands scattered over the baronies of Kilmaine, Carra and Tirawley. In addition, he received all customary exactions and tributes due to the MacWilliam by his numerous client chieftains in Mayo.

Richard-an-Iarainn had achieved the ultimate office of power. His accession to the MacWilliamship of Mayo was due in no small part to the intuitiveness and ability of his formidable wife, who gave his more overt methods a double edge with her sea power and political acumen. But the process by which they eventually succeeded marked a defining moment in the history of the MacWilliamship title. What should have been theirs by right of automatic succession by Gaelic law and custom they had to negotiate for and was granted by an outside power intent on the overthrow of the title and of the ancient world the title represented. And in the succeeding years this struggle for supremacy between the English and Gaelic systems of government intensified.

Granuaile and her husband Richard in Iron had won the first battle in the struggle for political survival in Mayo. It was a struggle, however, that had only just begun.

CHAPTER 6
'NURSE TO ALL REBELLIONS'

On his accession to the MacWilliamship, Richard-an-Iarainn and Granuaile moved their household inland to Lough Mask Castle, a large fortress situated on the eastern shore of the lake, located in the barony of Carra. The power, prestige and wealth conferred on them by the title made them the most powerful couple in the region. While Richard's ennoblement by English law added to their prestige.

In October 1582 they attended a gathering of the Connaught nobility, including the earls of Clanrickard and Thomand, at a function at the English governor's residence in Galway city. As Malby informed the Court

> ...Lord Bermingham, M'William, Richard M'Oliverus, Walter Burke, Murrough Ne Doe O'Flaherty, O'Maddin, M'Morris, M'Davy and besides very many gentlewomen, theyre wyves... among which Grany O'Mally ys one and thinkethherself to be no small lady...[1]

What Granuaile did to deserve the governor's appendage 'no small lady' is open to speculation. Perhaps, as befitted her new role as 'Lady Bourke', she simple outshone his other female guests.

Her son Tibbott-ne-Long, then twelve years of age, was removed from the care of MacTibbott chieftain in Burrishoole and placed in fosterage with Myles MacEvilly, a sub-chieftain of Richard in the barony of Carra. The MacEvilly clan (*Mac an Mhilidh*, i.e. son of the knight) were descended from the Anglo-Norman de Staunton family. They had come to Mayo with the de Burgos in the twelfth century and became lords of the barony of Carra. Like their overlords, the de Burgos, they eventually adopted Irish names and customs. At the time of Tibbott's fosterage the chieftain, Myles MacEvilly, possessed Kinturk, Kilboynell (later Castle Bourke), Castlecarra and Manulla castles together with the adjoining lands.

A strong local tradition linking Granuaile with the MacEvilly clan and with Kinturk Castle in particular survived to present times. Stories relating to her attacks on the castle and her eviction of MacEvilly are numerous and have been handed down from one generation to the next. Kinturk Castle is referred locally to this day as 'Granuaile's castle'. It was also said that she exacted a yearly tribute of 'a bag of meal, a fat pig and an ox'[2] from each family in the district. Her bravery in battle and her contempt for cowardice are portrayed in another story connected with Kinturk Castle. During one of her assaults on the castle, she observed her son Tibbott-ne-Long lose courage in the heat of the battle and sneak behind her for safety. Granuaile upbraided her son, saying: 'An ag iaraidh dul i bholach ar mo thóin atá tú, an áit a dtháinig as?' (Are you trying to hide behind my backside, the place you came from?)[3] Stung into action by her words, Tibbott-ne-Long resumed his place by her side.

While folklore may tend to embellish events and people, in the absence of historical records it is often the sole vehicle whereby the memory of an event or a person is preserved. In the case of Granuaile's connection with Kinturk Castle, a place far removed from her traditional stomping ground around Clew Bay, folklore merely supplemented what historical record had, it seemed, failed to preserve. However, among the original manuscripts preserved in Westport House, the factual evidence of Granuaile's connection with the MacEvilly clan and with Kinturk Castle reinforced what folklore had preserved.

In a deed dated 20 May 1582 (see Appendix 1.III) and signed (his mark) by 'Myles Mc Breyone alias MacEville, chiefe of his name', MacEvilly granted Richard-an-Iarainn in trust

> ... to the use and behoffe of my foster sonn Thibbott Bourk ... the castle and Bawne and ten quarters of land to me belonginge of and in Kintourk ... The castle Bawne and towne and eight quarters of land of Castlecarry and the four quarters of land of

Ballykally. The castle towne and barbican and foure quarters of lands of Moynulla … together with all the messuages buildings orchards gardynes moores meddowes feedinge pastures woodes and underwoode watter courses fishinges emollements and other hereditaments …[4]

This extensive property the MacEvilly chieftain conferred on Granuaile's son 'for and in consideration of a certaine some of money… and also for divers other good causes and considerations … be the consent of my sones and cousins.'[5]

While fosterage commanded extreme degrees of affinity, friendship and indebtedness between Gaelic clans, it seems extraordinary that a chieftain would willingly, even in consideration of a 'some of money', grant clan property to a foster son, albeit the son of his overlord. The fear of being dispossessed by outsiders, such as the wave of English adventurers who were making their way into Mayo, the need for MacWilliam's protection, or relief from financial pressure, may have been contributory factors. While Tibbott-ne-Long did not obtain access to the MacEvilly properties until the close of the century, the 1582 deed served as a device by which he eventually became the owner of most of the MacEvilly clan property in the barony of Carra. This included Kinturk Castle which was to become his principal residence. The deed was also to become the basis for the subsequent legends preserved in the area relating to Granuaile's association with Kinturk Castle and the MacEvilly family.

As the MacWilliam, Richard-an-Iarainn had attained his life's ambition. His agreement with the English, and the continued presence of a garrison of Malby's soldiers in his territory, did not deter him or Granuaile from enjoying the traditional benefits and status the MacWilliamship bestowed, or from settling old scores. In May 1582, using Malby's troops, under the pretext of collecting rents due to the crown, Richard-an-Iarainn, in time-honoured tradition, invaded the territory of his rival for the MacWilliamship, Richard MacOliverus. A battle ensued and up to twenty of Richard MacOliverus's followers, including his son, were slain. Richard-an-Iarainn's incursion was more to do with extracting the traditional tributes owing to the MacWilliamship by Gaelic right than collecting crown rent. Suspicious of his motives, but powerless to stop him, Malby ordered Richard 'to give either of his sons, Walter or Edmund'[6] as a pledge for his future conduct, an order Richard neglected to comply with.

In January 1583 Richard-an-Iarainn and Granuaile refused to pay the crown the rent agreed as part of the articles of indenture made with the crown for the MacWilliamship. Malby's rent collector, Theobald Dillon, wrote to the queen's secretary, Sir Francis Walsingham, about his encounter with both of them, when he attempted to extract the monies due:

> I went ther hence towardes the plas wher M'William was, who met me and his wyfe Grayn Ny Mayle with all their force, and did swer they wolde hav my lyfe for comyng soo furr into ther countrie and specialie his wyfe wold fyght with me befor she was half a myle nier me ...[7]

Dillon's observation confirmed the active role played by Granuaile in her husband's office, as well noting her fiery disposition. Their combined military strength of over two hundred men made the Englishman think hard, however, about extracting the rent they owed by force:

> I being but a C [100] and fyftie [50] foot men and fyftie [50] horse-men ... they were afar greater in number ...[8]

Gaelic-born leaders like Granuaile and her husband considered Englishmen, such as Dillon, no more than servants. To endure the insolence of such brash, avaricious, low-born officials was anathema to their pride and provoked their anger, as much as did their efforts to undermine their status and power. As part of the machinery set in motion to undermine, overthrow and replace a culture and a political system that to them appeared reprehensible, such minor administrators represented the bullying face of English colonialism. To justify their actions against the Gaelic chieftains inferiority and fault had to be shown in the people and customs of the country that had come to conquer.

Refusing to deal with such low-born servitors as Dillon, Granuaile and her husband would deign to do business only with the governor.

> M'William and Shee came to Sir Nicholas to agree with hym for 600 marks of areradges [arrears] due upon ther countrie which they thought never to pay.[9]

Richard-an-Iarainn did not live long to enjoy his hard-won honours as the MacWilliam and he died on 20 April 1583. Recording his death the Four Masters referred to him as

> A plundering, warlike, unquiet and rebellious man, who had often forced the gap of danger upon his enemies and upon whom it was frequently forced…[10]

His was the last recorded appointment to the MacWilliamship by right of the Gaelic custom of tanistry, albeit with the acquiescence of the crown. On his death his former rival by English law, Richard MacOliverus, succeed to the title but his appointment was hotly contested by the more senior sept of Burrishoole who took to the field to assert their claim by right of Gaelic law. They were opposed by Malby who arrived in Mayo and with a large army spoiled the two Owels and 'burned and totally destroyed Cathair-na-Mart.'[11] Eventually local opposition to the English-appointed MacWilliam abated, for a time.

Richard-an-Iarainn proved to be a worthy consort for Granuaile. While often forced to play a supporting role to her, they were a well-matched couple who together, as well as individually, made an impact on political events. Richard-an-

Iarainn was content and even encouraged his wife's unusual role, and his standing in the male-dominated society of Gaelic Ireland does not appear to have been diminished by her unorthodox ways. In an age that was more male-oriented than most, Richard-an-Iarainn emerges as a man sufficiently liberated from the shackles of misplaced male pride to have acknowledged, encouraged and capitalised on his wife's ability and success.

In 1583 the death of her husband, Granuaile, by then in her mid-fifties according to her own testimony,

> ... gathered together all her own followers and with 1000 head of cows and mares departed and became a dweller in Carrikahowley in Boroswole.[12]

Granuaile quickly established claim to one-third of her second husband's property. She later testified that, Gaelic law did not provide for the restitution of the dowry of a widow of a second husband, so she simply took the law into her own hands and seized one of her husband's castles in lieu. Her independence during her marriage to Richard is further reiterated in her statement that she 'gathered together all her *own* followers'. The extent of her wealth at this time was substantial. As well as her fleet of galleys, one thousand head of cattle and mares was no mean fortune in the sixteenth century.

Her youngest son, Tibbott-ne-Long, then almost sixteen, left the fosterage of MacEvilly and entered into his inheritance in Burrishoole, as co-inheritor with his half-brothers, Edmund and Walter of his father's personal estate.

The English governor of Connaught, Sir Nicholas Malby, died the following year. During the period of his governorship major changes had occurred throughout the province of Connacht. English authority had gradually but steadily extended its influence with a system of rent-paying to the English crown and the imposition of the contentious issue of 'cess', whereby Gaelic chieftains were forced to maintain a specified number of English soldiers in their territories, had become widespread. Court sessions by right of English law were being held and English legal practice was being enforced, especially in the trial and punishment of malefactors and Malby had laid the foundations for its future extension. Well might the Irish annalists write of him that 'he placed all Connaught under bondage.'[13] In Munster after three years of incessant warfare, the Desmond rebellion had finally petered out with the slaying of the Earl of Desmond as he took refuge in a cave in the woods of Glenageenty, near Tralee, in November 1583. For a short time an exhausted peace descended on the country.

John Browne, the newly-appointed sheriff of county Mayo and, as he wrote, 'the first Englishe man that in the memory of man hath settled hymselfe to dwelle in the countie of Mayo',[14] reported:

> … that Connaught standeth on good terms and the people live and keep their goods in more safety and travel with less fear and in less danger than in any other part of Ireland.[15]

But it was an uneasy peace. As the English administration continued to undermine the power and privileges of the native chieftains, repercussions were inevitable as the chieftains fought back to protect their rights and privileges. The situation came to a head in 1584 on the appointment of Sir John Perrot as Lord Deputy of Ireland and Sir Richard Bingham as governor of Connacht. Diametrically opposed, on both a personal and political basis, the methods they employed in their dealings with the Connaught chieftains were equally divergent. A policy of conciliation by Perrot contrasted with a policy of the sword by Bingham, which was destined to bring him into direct confrontation with almost every Gaelic leader in Connaught and especially with Granuaile.

Richard Bingham came to Ireland with sound military credentials. Born in Dorset, from his youth he had been trained in military service. He served in Scotland, fought at the famous Battle of Lepanto against the Turks, as well as in France and in the Netherlands. He was in the army of Grey de Wilton at Smerwick harbour when the ragged Italian and Spanish force, which had been sent to aid the revolt of James FitzMaurice FitzGerald, was unconditionally slain. He was fifty-six when he was appointed governor of Connaught. Described as 'a man eminent both for spirit and martial knowledge, but of very small stature',[16] his narrow visage, accentuated by a pointed, neatly-trimmed beard and dispassionate eyes, proclaimed a narrow and inflexible personality and a zealousness for duty. 'The Irish were never tamed with words but with swords'[17] was his opinion, and one which he diligently sought to put into practice during his tenure as governor of Connaught.

Bingham's at times brutal oppression must, however, be examined within the context of pertaining social and military conditions and attitudes. Popular opinion has painted him the villain, the 'Flail of Connaught', executioner of innocent women and children. The methods he employed in subduing Connaught are usually attributed to his individual brand of cruelty instead of, as they were, the accepted rules of sixteenth-century warfare but reinforced by his own racist attitude towards the Irish in general. Bingham's singular failing was his inability to adapt his political policies to the realities of Gaelic Connaught. It could be said that his thoroughness and inflexibility as an administrator, coupled with a narrow perception of duty, made it impossible for him to convert the Gaelic chieftains to English ways without resorting to excessive force. At the same time, his relative honesty as an official of the crown, and his diligence to duty, assured him the ill-will and envy of many of his fellow English administrators.

In Munster the English crown had reaped a high price for the rebellion of Gaelic leaders such as the Earl of Desmond. The ruthless and systematic destruction of the countryside by both sides in the war had resulted in what the poet Edmund Spenser described as 'a most populous and plentiful country suddenly void of man or beast.'[18] It was a poor return on the crown's substantial expenditure in overcoming the Desmond rebellion. Rather than repeat the experience of Munster, Elizabeth I was not averse to inducing rather than coercing the chieftains of Connaught to abandon their independent status and clientship power over their sub-chieftains, and conform to English law and customs. Weary of the desultory conflict over succession and privilege, and conscious too that time had caught up with the outmoded structures and customs by which they ruled their lordships, many chieftains were willing to conform and seek title to their position and lands by English law.

In 1585 Perrot introduced a formula known as the Composition of Connaught, which provided for, not only the continuance of the 'surrender and regrant' policy of Henry VIII, but for the extension of English control over other issues hitherto governed by Gaelic law and custom. The Composition sought to abolish the customary exactions and tributes paid to chieftains by their client lords, as well as ending the English custom of 'cess'. In their place a fixed rent of ten English shillings or one Irish mark on each quarter of tillage and pastureland was to be payable to the English crown by every chieftain, and a similar rent payable to the chieftain by his client lords. A specified amount of land was allowed rent-free to each chieftain. To eliminate the system of clientship, every chieftain was made responsible for his own sept only. Primogeniture was to replace the native customs of election and tanistry.

For the Bourkes of Mayo, the Composition effectively ended the power of the MacWilliamship. While MacWilliams continued to be chosen up to the close of the century by various dissatisfied factions, the title never again commanded the same power, prestige, privilege and wealth. To the holder of the office by English law, it brought security of tenure and provided for the inheritance of the title by his eldest male heir. To those denied access to the title by right of Gaelic law, it provided the focal point for future rebellion against the Crown. In the expectation that Tibbott-ne-Long would one day succeed his father to the title, Granuaile must have viewed the Composition of Connaught as a reversal of her son's fortune. Whether willingly, through duress or fear, or as a mere temporary convenience, the Composition was duly signed by the principal chieftains of Mayo, including Edmund Bourke of Castlebar, *tánaiste* to the MacWilliam by Gaelic law.

While Perrot temporised with the Connaught chieftains on the legalities of change, Sir Richard Bingham's methods of reducing their powers by more confrontational methods stirred up anger and opposition among them. Bingham singled out Granuaile for special treatment. As a deterrent to her continued threat by sea and by land, he captured Tibbott-ne-Long and sent him as a hostage to the house of his brother, George Bingham, the sheriff of county Sligo. Tibbott was kept under restraint for more than a year with the sheriff and his family at Ballymote castle, which Bingham had confiscated from the chieftain Donough O'Connor Sligo. It was the expressed English policy of the period that the sons of the Gaelic aristocracy, thus held in captivity, should be educated and indoctrinated in English ways in the hope that they might conform. It would take longer to transform Tibbott-ne-Long from Gaelic chieftain to anglicised lord, but the process had been set in motion. During his captivity, Tibbott learned to speak and write English, a fact commented on by Queen Elizabeth in 1593, and evidenced in his numerous letters and dispatches preserved among the Elizabethan State Papers.

In 1584 Tibbott-ne-Long married Maeve O'Connor Sligo— 'Meadhbh of the yellow-gold hair, daughter of Cathal',[19] as a sixteenth-century poet described her. She was the sister of Tibbott's future ally, Donough O'Connor Sligo. The O'Connor Sligo family was one of the three branches of the royal O'Connor family, once kings of Connaught and High Kings of Ireland. By the sixteenth century they ruled an area corresponding to the present-day county Sligo. Their lordship was strategically situated between Ulster and Connaught. To the north lay the extensive territory of the O'Donnell chieftains of Tirconail, who claimed a traditional overlordship of Sligo. Through alliances with O'Donnell's enemies, the O'Connor Sligo chieftains constantly sought deliverance from their more powerful neighbour. Their most recent alliance was in 1568 when Maeve's uncle Donal made an indenture with Queen Elizabeth, which he interpreted as a reaffirmation of his overlordship of all Sligo, but which the crown later claimed was confined merely to the barony of Carbury. Sir Richard Bingham duly effected the crown's claim by seizing the castle of Ballymote and installing his brother there.

Whether Tibbott's marriage to Maeve occurred before or during his captivity in Ballymote castle is uncertain. If, as is more likely, it occurred prior to Bingham's arrival in Sligo, it would seem that his detention by Bingham's brother was intended to deter Granuaile and the Bourkes of sept Ulick from aiding O'Connor Sligo against Bingham as they had, in the past, aided O'Connor against his traditional enemy, O'Donnell. For Granuaile, the captivity of her son, following on the death of her husband, must have been a severe blow. It was the first of many she was to endure at the hands of Richard Bingham and his relations in Connaught.

While Sir John Perrot was the architect of the Composition of Connaught, its implementation was left to Bingham. In the summer of 1585 he held the first sessions in county Mayo. The Bourkes of sept Ulick refused to attend and fortified themselves in Hag's Castle on Lough Mask, which Bingham subsequently besieged and demolished. The incident seemed of little significance until later in the year when the MacWilliam of Mayo died and his *tánaiste*, Edmund Bourke of Castlebar, claimed the title by right of Gaelic law. Bingham, however, bestowed the bulk of the lands and property pertaining to the title on MacWilliam's eldest son, according to English law. The Bourke septs rose in a second rebellion against the Governor. This time they were joined by their traditional allies, the O'Malleys, Clan Gibbons, the Joyces, Clan Philbin and, covertly, by Richard Bourke, known as 'The Devil's Hook' (*Deamhán* and *Chorráin*), chieftain of the Corraun peninsula who was married to Granuaile's daughter, Margaret

O'Flaherty. They were also joined by Sir Murrough-ne-Doe O'Flaherty, the senior chieftain of Iar-Chonnacht. Among the names of the rebels sent by Bingham to Sir Francis Walsingham is that of Tibbott-ne-Long who, by August 1586, had been released from captivity in Sligo.

Granuaile's eldest son, Owen O'Flaherty, was married to the daughter of Edmund Bourke of Castlebar. There was no evidence to suggest that Owen was involved in the rebellion of his father-in-law, other than Bingham's later contention that he 'was an open rebel.'[20] When the governor's brother, Captain John Bingham, entered the barony of Ballinahinch in July 1586 in search of booty and cattle, in time-honoured tradition Owen and his followers hid with their herds and belongings on Omey Island. Granuaile and Sir Richard Bingham both give varying accounts of the events leading to Owen's death. According to Granuaile's testimony, John Bingham discovered where Owen was hiding with his cattle herds and

> ... came to the mainland right against the said island calling for victuals, whereupon the said Owen came forth with a number of boats and ferried all the soldiers into the island where they were entertained with the best cheer they had ... The said Owen was apprehended and tied with a rope ... The next night ... being fast bound ... the said Owen was cruelly murdered having twelve deadly wounds ...[21]

In a deposition later, when charged with complicity in the killing of Granuaile's son, Bingham claimed that he had been 'an open rebel being prisoner with the marchall's deputy made his escape and in pursuit was slain because he would not stay and yield himselfe ...'[22], a claim that hardly justified the number and severity of the wounds inflicted on Owen O'Flaherty.

Devastated by the murder of her eldest son, Granuaile became an active leader in the revolt against Bingham. With her ships she sailed north to Scotland for reinforcements. On learning that O'Donnell had Scottish mercenaries for hire, to save time she negotiated a deal with the O'Donnell chieftain, a fact noted by Sir

IRELAND circa 1530
Showing principal lordships

Inishowen
O DOGHERTY

The Rout
MAC QUILLIN

MAC DONNELLS

O CAHAN

Tyrconnell
O DONNELL

Tyrone
O NEILL

O NEILL of
Clandeboy

SAVAGE

Lecale

Fermanagh
MAGUIRE

Iveagh
MAGENNIS

O HANLON

Sligo
O CONNOR O ROURKE

Oriel
MAC MAHON

Tyrawley
O DOWD

BARRET

O CONNOR
MAC DONOGH   Brefny

O REILLY

Lower MAC WILLIAM

O HARA
MAC JORDAN
MAC COSTELLO
MAC DERMOT
THE TWO
O CONNORS

MAC MORRIS

Annaly
O FARRELL

DALTON

O MALLEY

MAC DAVID
BURKE
BERMINGHAM

O MELAGHLIN
MAGEOGHAGAN

Iarconnacht
O FLAHERTY

UPPER MAC WILLIAM
Clanrickard

O KELLY

O MADDEN

O MOLLOY

EARL OF
KILDARE

Galway

Ormond
O KENNEDYS

Ely
O CARROLL

Offaly
O CONNOR

O TOOLE

Arra
MAC UI BRIAIN

MAC GILLA
PATRICK

Leix
O MORE

O BYRNE

Thomond
O BRIEN

O MULRIAN

Kilkenny

MAC MURROUGH

Limerick

Clanwilliam
BURKES

BUTLERS

Fermoy
ROCHE

FITZGERALD
of the Decies

POWER

EARL OF DESMOND

Duhallow
MAC DONOGH

BARRY MOR

Desmond
MAC CARTHY MÓR   Muskerry

O SULLIVAN
MOR

O SULLIVAN BEARE

Carbery
MAC CARTHY REAGH

0   80 Km
0   50 Mls

Principal sixteenth-century Gaelic lordships. (*Private collection*)

O'Malley coat of arms.
(*Private collection*)

Galley—Jobson map of Ulster
1590.

Impression of Granuaile's galley.
(*Illustrated by Monica Kennedy*)

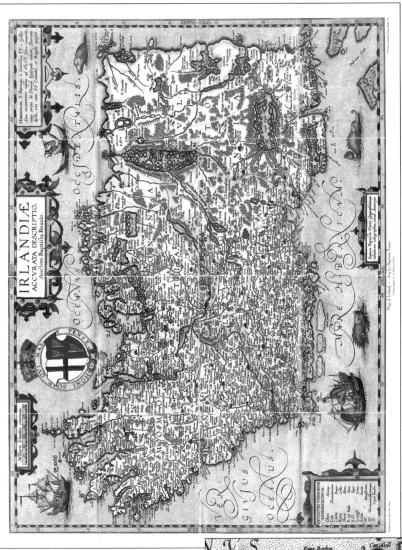

Boazio map of Ireland, 1599 (with name 'Grany O Male'). (*Private collection*)

Gaelic chieftain and kerne. (*Derrick, 1581*)

Galway city, 1610.

Chieftain and entourage, summer feasting. (*Derrick*, 1581)

Clare Island Castle. (*Dúchas, The Heritage Service*)

Kildawnet Castle, Achill Island. (*Dúchas, The Heritage Service*)

Warfare—sixteenth-century Ireland. (*Derrick, 1581*)

Sir Henry Sidney, English Lord Deputy, leaving Dublin *Castle*. (*Derrick*, 1581)

English military tactics
in sixteenth-century
Ireland. (*Derrick, 1581*)

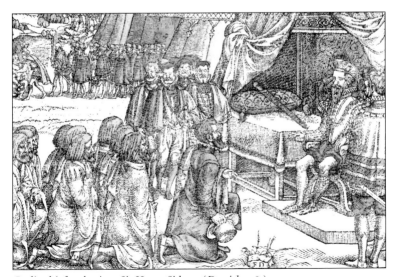

Gaelic chiefs submit to Sir Henry Sidney. (*Derrick, 1581*)

Howth Castle, County Dublin. (*Private collection*)

Carraigahowley (Rockfleet) Castle. (*Dúchas, The Heritage Service*)

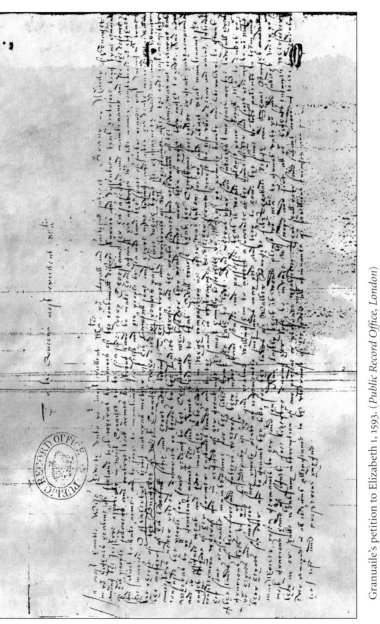

Granuaile's petition to Elizabeth I, 1593. (*Public Record Office, London*)

Meeting of Granuaile and Queen Elizabeth I. (*National Library of Ireland*)

Maude Bourke (b. 1642), great-great-granddaughter of Granuaile. (*Westport House*)

Sir Richard Bingham,
Governor of Connaught.
(*Private collection*)

Westport House. (*Private collection*)

Sir William Cecil
(Lord Burghley)

Thomas (Black Tom),
10th Earl of Ormond.
(*Private collection*)

Traditional resting place of Granuaile, Clare Island Abbey. (*Dúchas, The Heritage Service*)

Stone plaque, Clare Island Abbey. (*Dúchas, The Heritage Service*)

Bronze sculpture,
Granuaile,
Westport House.

Seamus Cashman, the late Lord Sligo, Anne Chambers, Lady Sligo, the late
Dr T. K. Whitaker. Launch of the original edition, Westport House, 1979.

John Perrot when he condemned O'Donnell to the queen as one 'ready to send aid to any that were evil disposed in your kingdom, as of late he did to Grany ne Male to see if they would make any stirr in Connaught.'[23] Alarmed at the extent of Granuaile's power and influence, and with an eye to her extensive cattle and horse herds, Bingham sent his brother, John Bingham, the murderer of her son, with an army into her territory. In a deposition to Queen Elizabeth's Secretary of State, Lord Burghley, Granuaile gave an account of Bingham's actions.

> She was apprehended and tied with a rope, both she and her followers at that instant were spoiled of their said cattle and of all they ever had besides the same, and brought to Sir Richard who caused a new pair of gallows to be made for her where she thought to end her days. [24]

With Granuaile under lock and key, Bingham next targeted her relations. The Bourke hostages in his custody were executed by martial law. They included Moyler and Tibbot Reagh Bourke, her late husband's nephews, who according to Bingham were 'the worst Bourks then living.' [25] Other Bourke hostages in the keeping of the sheriff, John Browne, were also summarily executed, including another nephew, Ulick, son of William, nicknamed the 'Blind Abbot'. All were accused with her of plotting 'to draw in Scotts', the evidence for which being based mainly on hearsay and on dubious letters which Bingham claimed to have been written by them while in prison. The importation of Scottish mercenaries was deemed a treasonable offence and Granuaile's life hung by a thread. Her reputation as a 'drawer in of Scots' was well established and Bingham now wrote of her to the English court as being the 'nurse to all rebellions in the province for forty years'.[26] She was surprisingly set at liberty, as she later related, 'upon the hostage and pledge' of her son-in-law, the Devil's Hook, who was not in open rebellion. Once he had secured Granuaile's freedom, however, the Devil's Hook immediately joined his relations.

On her release from custody Granuaile lost little time. With her fleet of galleys she headed for Scotland to ferry in additional gallowglass. When later required to justify her actions she maintained that when the guarantor of her freedom, the Devil's Hook, went into rebellion '*fear* compelled her to fly by sea into Ulster',[27] an unlikely excuse, but politic and necessary under the circumstances in which she made it in 1593. En route to Ulster she encountered a severe storm at sea which severely damaged her galleys, and she was forced to make landfall in Ulster where she remained for three months while her ships were being repaired. During that time she met with both O'Neill and O'Donnell. The two Ulster chieftains, Hugh Dubh O'Donnell and the English-educated Hugh, Earl of Tyrone, *tánaiste* to the overall O'Neill chieftaincy, traditionally bitter enemies, had laid aside their differences. Alarmed that what was being visited on Connaught by the English could soon extend to Ulster, they prepared to unite against a common enemy. Hugh O'Neill had married O'Donnell's daughter. O'Donnell himself was married to the formidable Finola, the *Ineen Dubh*, daughter of James MacDonald, Lord of the Isles, and cultivated close links with the royal court of Scotland. Their son, Red Hugh, then a youth, was destined, a few short months after Granuaile's visit to his father, to become a prisoner of the English in Dublin Castle.

What matters Granuaile discussed with O'Neill and O'Donnell during her stay in Ulster in 1587 have not been documented. As in the rest of Ireland, rumours of a Spanish invasion of England were rife there. Merchants and seamen carried stories of the mustering of ships, troops and arms in Spanish ports for an unprecedented attack on England. The Spanish king, Philip II, was determined to embark on a crusade against Elizabeth and 'to visit the censure of God upon a middle-aged female'.[28] The religious aspirations of the king's Armada would have cut little ice with the Gaelic chieftains, but the political fall-out from such a venture for them and for Ireland was a different matter. The Ulster chieftains heard from Granuaile a first-hand account of Bingham's rule in Connaught and his attempts to overthrow the power of the Gaelic chieftains there.

In Mayo Bingham continued *his* vendetta against the Mayo Bourkes and captured and executed many of the leaders who offered resistance. He executed by martial law the main contender for the MacWilliamship, the aged Edmund Bourke of Castlebar, so decrepit that he had to be carried to its scaffold. In late September he defeated a huge force of Scots mercenaries who, with Granuaile's galleys out of commission, had made their way by land into Mayo. On the banks of the Moy, Bingham routed them with great slaughter; over 1,400 were killed or drowned. The rebellion subsequently collapsed and the Bourkes sued for peace. In May 1587, urged by the newly appointed lord deputy, Sir John Perrot, Bingham's severest critic, the queen ordered Bingham for military service to Flanders.

With Bingham sidelined, seizing her chance, Granuaile set out for Dublin to meet Perrot. Aware of the antagonism that existed between Bingham and the lord deputy, she was determined to take advantage of the situation for herself and her family. Perrot received her in Dublin castle and listened to her complaints against Bingham. According to her testimony, she duly received 'her Majesty's pardon by Sir John Perrot'.[29] The pardon, preserved in the Elizabethan Fiants, also granted pardons for past 'offences' to Granuaile's sons, Murrough O'Flaherty and Tibbott-ne-Long and to 'Margaret O'Flahertie daughter of Grany'. The slate against Granuaile and her family was thereby wiped clean. Granuaile's shrewdness had paid dividends, in the short term at least. On her return from Dublin, she claimed to be living 'in Connaught a farmer's life ... and did give over her former trade of maintenance by sea and land,'[30] but in reality, with Bingham out of the picture, she acquired additional galleys and resumed her seafaring enterprises with renewed vigour.

CHAPTER 7
'A NOTABLE TRAITORESS'

On the evening of 29 July 1588 the long-threatened Spanish Armada was sighted off the Lizard. From beacon to beacon the news was relayed across England. The king of Spain's meticulously planned crusade against his 'heretic' sister-in-law had become a reality. The 'invincible' Armada of 134 ships and over 30,000 men, commanded by the flower of Spanish aristocracy, moved slowly and menacingly in a crescent formation along England's southern coast. After a series of naval skirmishes with the faster and more skilfully captained English fleet, the Armada ships became scattered. English fire ships wreaked havoc among the great carracks, galleons and galleases before the elements took a hand. As the wind shifted, the Spanish ships were swept up the Channel towards the North Sea, pursued by the English fleet. On 21 August, having failed to make landfall in England, the Armada set course to return to Spain, only to be buffeted by fierce storms and heavy seas. Some of the ships were driven towards the north and west coasts of Ireland, where rocky headlands, underwater reefs and sandy shallows took a heavy toll. Some twenty-six Armada ships were eventually wrecked along the Irish coastline

Fearing that the Spanish survivors might land on the west coast of Ireland and make common cause with the Gaelic chieftains there, Sir Richard Bingham was hurriedly returned as Governor of Connaught. The governor's adversary, Sir John Perrot, was recalled and replaced as lord deputy by Sir William FitzWilliam. As the Armada ships were driven onto the Irish coast, messengers and spies brought exaggerated tidings of great numbers of Spanish soldiers holed up in castles and towers of the Gaelic chieftains along the west coast. Inadequately armed to repel such an invasion, the English administration in Dublin panicked. FitzWilliam proclaimed it a crime punishable by death to harbour or aid the Spanish castaways. The Armada ships were rumoured to contain untold treasure, the salvage of which was an added attraction to English and Irish alike. Consequently the Spanish survivors who managed to land on Irish soil, in the main, received a less than hospitable reception.

It was estimated that five ships were wrecked on Mayo's jagged coastline. English reports suggested that many of the survivors were summarily killed by treasure-seeking clansmen. Given the remoteness and inaccessibility of the region, the inaccuracies—both deliberate and inadvertent—of English accounts, and the distinct lack of information from an Irish perspective, it is virtually impossible to assess the true story behind many of the Armada wrecks.

The single most controversial incident occurred on Clare Island, where around 22 September 1588 a huge ship, the square-rigged, cumbersome, converted merchantman *El Gran Grin*, of some 1,160 tons, carrying 329 men and 28 guns when she sailed for England, was driven helplessly before the wind towards Clew Bay. With little or no space to manoeuvre, she drifted onto Clare Island towards the cliffs on the southwest shore and was presumed to have been wrecked. English accounts record that her commander, Don Pedro de Mendoza, and some one hundred crew, scrambled ashore to safety but were killed on the orders of the island chieftain Dubhdara Rua O'Malley. The remainder of the crew were said to have drowned.

The facts regarding the wreck and supposed massacre on Clare Island are scanty. That *El Gran Grin* was driven towards the island is most likely true. That she was wrecked there and that her commander and crew were killed by the islanders is less certain. There is no deep-rooted tradition on the island of such a massacre having taking place. The O'Malleys, in particular, were well used to piloting and trading with the Spanish for generations. Only the English accounts testify to the massacre, and these must be viewed in the context in which they were written and the motivation and racist attitude of their authors.

On the other hand, the presence of some one hundred foreigners on Clare Island would undoubtedly have put the islanders under extreme pressure. Plunder and wrecking were part and parcel of seafaring people everywhere, and the O'Malleys were no exception. The foreigners outnumbered the islanders and, despite their plight, posed an imminent threat. To find food and shelter for so many would have put an immense strain on the island's slender resources. There is mention in the English State Papers that O'Malley had imprisoned the Spanish castaways initially, but that they had broken out and may well have attempted to fight their way off the island, commandeering boats on which the livelihoods of the islanders depended. Three of the officers accredited to *El Gran Grin,* however, were later identified as prisoners of Bingham in Galway. Whether O'Malley handed them over to the English or whether they were captured by the English bands who were scouring the coastline for survivors is uncertain. At this time the O'Malleys were one of the clans least likely to have co-operated freely with the English administration, particularly with Sir Richard Bingham. One way or another, whether the Spanish castaways were massacred by the O'Malleys, as the English reports claim, or were secretly taken off the island by them, to get passage back to Spain on other Armada ships, the truth rests beneath the fathoms with the many other secrets of the Armada wrecks.

A further complication to the theory of the Clare Island wreck is that it may have been mistaken for a ship that went aground at Fynglass (present-day Toorglass) on the Corraun peninsula, a few miles west of Granuaile's castle of Carraigahowley. Some accounts maintain that this was the 834-ton *San Nicholas Prodaneli,* while others claim that it was in fact *El Gran Grin,* which had been driven past Clare Island onto the mainland at Toorglass. The lands on which she was wrecked were claimed by the Earl of Ormond, 'Black' Tom Butler, as part of the original Anglo-Norman Butler estate in Burrishoole. Black Tom was not slow to send messengers to Mayo with orders to make an inventory and lay claim to the ship's treasures, most of which by then had been picked clean by the local O'Malley and Bourke clansmen.

Among the reports concerning both wrecks in Clew Bay there is no mention of Granuaile. Whether she was absent on some business of her own or was too closely watched by Bingham's officers to intervene, is open to speculation. The lure of treasure and plunder was a way of life and there is no reason to assume that Spanish cargo would have been immune from her attention. Her attitude to the Spanish survivors was another matter. Her family's connections with Spain were long-established and her understanding of the Armada's ambitions may have been clearer to someone who had recently been in contact with O'Neill, one of the few Gaelic chieftains who assisted the Spanish castaways. But, in any event, with Bingham's bands of soldiers in close proximity, any help or protection she may have given to the survivors, had to be done with the utmost secrecy.

Derided by FitzWilliam for being ineffective in his pursuit of the Spanish survivors, Bingham intensified his efforts along the Connaught coastline. He ordered his deputy marshal, Robert Fowle, to seek out, dislodge and kill any of the unfortunate survivors. With her 'rebellious' record, as well as her maritime capability, by then well-established, Granuaile's activities by sea were now especially monitored. That she assisted the Spanish survivors who came her way is likely, especially since Bingham later accused her son-in-law, the Devil's Hook from nearby Corraun, and his son, as well as the Bourkes of Erris and Sir Murrough-ne-Doe O'Flaherty in Iar-Chonnacht, of sheltering the Spanish who, Bingham claimed, 'had an intention to remayne in the county of Mayo and that the inhabitants of the same were agreed to join with them …'[1] Providing assistance to the Spanish survivors carried great personal risk. The English Council in Dublin proclaimed any chieftain found harbouring the Spanish to be, in effect, in rebellion and his lands thereby subject to confiscation.

It was a combination of Bingham's harsh actions and the bad blood that existed between John Browne, the newly appointed sheriff of Mayo, and the Bourkes of Corraun and Erris that, in

1589, sparked off the third Bourke rebellion. A controversial commission was issued to John Browne by Bingham, empowering him to enter the territory of the Burrishoole and Erris Bourkes with orders

> ... to prosecute and followe all and every of the said traytors ... yt shall be lawful for you and yr, said companies to praie, burne and spolie ... (giving them notice of the daunger thereof beforehand ...)[2]

The commission bore only Bingham's signature, instead of the two commissioners' signatures legally required, proof to the Bourkes that the enterprise was purely at Bingham's personal instigation and of his continuing animosity towards them.

On 7 February 1589 the sheriff arrived at Granuaile's castle of Carraigahowley with an army of some 250 men. Granuaile's grandson, Richard Bourke, the son of her daughter, Margaret, objected to the sheriff and attempted to prevent the English forces from proceeding any further. In the official correspondence relating to the incident, there is no mention of Granuaile, but in view of her previous attitude to English intruders on her property, it is certain that she would have found English presence at her castle as disagreeable as she had on previous occasions. Disregarding Richard Bourke's objection, Browne persisted and followed the main body of his army towards Corraun where he was attacked and killed, together with his escort of some twenty-five soldiers.

The Browne incident signalled the start of the most widespread rebellion against the administration of Sir Richard Bingham in Connaught. The Bourkes of Burrishoole, Corraun, Erris and Tirawley were joined by the O'Malleys, Clandonnells and Clangibbons. Sir Murrough-ne-Doe O'Flaherty (despite the fact that his son was a hostage with Bingham and was subsequently executed) crossed Lough Corrib with an army of five hundred men and joined the Bourkes. Granuaile struck by sea and, as Bingham reported, 'byrned and spoyled the isles of Aran'[3] which had recently been granted to an Englishman, Sir Thomas

LeStrange. Her son, Tibbott-ne-Long, and his half-brother, Edmund, were named by Bingham as being among the rebel leaders. Mayo was in turmoil. The Bourkes raided Kilmaine and Clanmorris, taking substantial booty, before moving into Galway where they plundered right up to the walls of Galway city.

Alarmed by the strength and extent of the rebellion, Lord Deputy FitzWilliam ordered Bingham to desist from any further action against the Bourkes and a tentative truce was arranged. Negotiations between the Bourke leaders and the English took place at Newcastle, the Bourkes having refused to enter Galway city. The contentious issue of the MacWilliamship title reared its head once again. The Bourkes demanded that Richard-an-Iarainn's brother, William Bourke, the Blind Abbot, *tánaiste* by Gaelic custom, should be restored to the title, and that Richard Bingham be removed as governor of Connaught. Many in the English administration, including FitzWilliam himself, were in agreement with the second of the Bourke demands, which simply mirrored the conspiracy then afoot among Bingham's own colleagues in the Irish service to effect his removal from office.

The queen wrote of her disquiet at the extent of the rebellion in Connaught and ordered FitzWilliam to adopt a conciliatory attitude to the Bourkes. The lord deputy set out for Connaught, while ordering Bingham to remain at Athlone Castle. The appeasement policy proposed by the queen was beyond Bingham's comprehension, as he angrily confided to a colleague at the English court:

Truly I have not heard of the like between a prince and her subjects and much less with a race of such beggerly wretches as these ... This dalliance with these rebels makes them most insolent and without the sword ... it is impossible to govern the Irish people ... They believe this is their time and have hope of foreign aid.[4]

On 12 June FitzWilliam met representatives of the Bourkes in St Nicholas' Church in Galway, where they presented him with a book of complaints against Bingham and his relations in the Connaught service. Granuaile was undoubtedly present at the meeting because much of which Bingham stood accused of concerned herself and her family. A similar book was also presented to the Lord Deputy by the chieftains of Sligo against George Bingham, the governor's brother.

Many charges were laid against Bingham, including breaches of the Composition, quartering of English soldiers on the people, and encroachments by officials in his administration on the lands and livings of the chieftains. Specific charges of murder, cruelty and torture were also cited, including the murder of Granuaile's eldest son, Owen O'Flaherty and her Bourke nephews; the hanging of the elderly chieftain Edmund Bourke of Castlebar, her eldest son's father-in-law; and the execution of the young Bourke hostages, including Ulick, son of the Blind Abbot, the MacWilliam *tánaiste*. The Bourkes made a token submission to the lord deputy, appropriately contrite in tone, and promised to 'forthwith deliver to the lord deputy such Spaniards, Portugalls and other foreigners of the Spanish fleet as are now amongst them.'[5]

The submission was no more than a ploy to buy time. The Bourkes were careful not to hand over the customary hostages as pledges to the agreement. On the other hand, they had prevailed on the lord deputy to curb English incursions on their lands and, more significantly, to remove Bingham from the governorship of Connaught. The Bourkes knew that they held the advantage, with Mayo, part of Roscommon, Iar-Chonnacht, Sligo and Galway under their control.

To supplement their forces on the ground Granuaile went to Scotland to hire mercenaries. Their arrival back in Mayo in early September was reported to Bingham, who advised Burghley and the Privy Council of '7 gallies to be arryved in Erris with Scottes ... having for their guyde and conductor one of Grany O'Malleys sons'.[6] However, Bingham's claim was rebutted by no less a personage than the lord deputy who told Burghley, 'that she [Granuaile] shold be gon over into Scotland to drawe over Scotts into these parts ... nothing could be untrulie written or reported ...'[7] and he added, 'this man Bingham is shameless'. Now fully in control of Mayo, in October the Bourkes assembled at Rousakeera, near Kilmaine and inaugurated the Blind Abbot as the MacWilliam. They then recaptured Lough Mask Castle, part of the traditional seigniory of the MacWilliamship, and plundered the countryside from the Neale to Shrule.

As the rebellion continued, Elizabeth's patience and purse became exhausted. She ordered FitzWilliam to determine once and for all whether or not Bingham was guilty of the charges brought against him by the Bourkes. After a trial in Dublin Bingham was acquitted, and in spring 1590 he was reinstated as governor with orders to bring the rebellion to an end. He immediately set about doing so the only way he knew—by the sword. Aided by the earls of Clanrickard and Thomond, with an army of over one thousand, Bingham marched into Mayo and took Castlebar. From there he set out through the mountain pass of Barnagee into Tirawley. Marching through the mountain fastness and boglands, he was shadowed by the Blind Abbot and Edmund Bourke with a small force of horsemen. The Bourkes launched a sudden attack, and in the ensuing skirmish the Blind Abbot's foot was cut off from the ankle. The Bourkes withdrew and ferried their injured leader to a small island in Lough Conn. The Blind Abbot's injury ended his reign as the MacWilliam, his disability making him unfit to hold the office.

Bingham pressed home the advantage and marched through Tirawley and into Erris, relentlessly killing and plundering as he went. The people fled before him and hid themselves and their belongings in the mountain recesses. Bingham's army looted whatever was left behind and swept the land clean of livestock. By the time he left Erris, Bingham had amassed a herd of over two thousand cattle. Arriving in Burrishoole, he found most of the inhabitants had fled before him into the islands in Clew Bay. Lack of boats prevented him from pursuing them, but he took retribution in another way as he reported: 'I took 100 cows and I slew all the churls, women and children'.[8] The rebellion began to crumble. The Clandonnells, the standing army of the Bourkes, were first to submit, and they were followed by the leaders of the Bourkes and their allies, with the exception of the sept of Ulick, led by Granuaile's stepson, Edmund, and her son, Tibbott-ne-Long, who in June 1591 ambushed John Bingham near Cloonagashal.

Granuaile aided her son and stepson by sea and her territory around Carraigahowley bore the brunt of Bingham's retribution. The sea was now her sole refuge. With her galleys she swooped once more on the Aran Islands where, as Bingham later testified, she 'committed some spoile ... to the value of 20 mark.'[9]

When news reached her that her second son, Murrough-ne-Maor O'Flaherty, had submitted and had allied with her arch enemy, Bingham, her fury knew no bounds. Like most of the chieftains, Murrough-ne-Maor was more concerned with his personal vendetta against his neighbour, Sir Murrough-ne-Doe O'Flaherty and his son, Teig, who had recently plundered his lands. Operating a divide-and-rule policy, Bingham offered to assist Murrough-ne-Maor against them, in return for his allegiance. But Grace was having none of it. Her attack on her son was later communicated by Bingham to Lord Burghley in an attempt to discredit her further at the Elizabethan court:

> His [Murrough's] aforesaid mother Grany (being out of charety with her sonne for serving her Matie) manned out her Navy of Galleys and landed in Ballinehencie where he dwelleth, burned his towen and spoiled his people of their cattayle and goods and murdered 3 or 4 of his men which offered to make resistance ...[10]

Bingham cites the incident to Burghley, hoping 'to gyve your Honour Knowledge of her naughty disposicion towards the state.'[11] Little is heard of Murrough-ne-Maor in the war against Bingham after his mother's chastisement. That Granuaile would take arms against her own son is testimony to her grim determination and single-mindedness in pursuit of her aims, allowing neither maternal instinct nor emotional ties to get in the way. Little wonder that the incident was to become the talk of the English court and of particular fascination to Queen Elizabeth.

In June 1591 a force of seven hundred Scottish mercenaries hired by the Mayo chieftains arrived in Erris. Finding neither an outlet nor payment for their hire, they ravaged north Mayo in lieu. In the mêlée that followed, some of Granuaile's Bourke and O'Malley relations were killed, including two of the Blind Abbot's sons. Granuaile hurried northwards to help, but by the time she arrived in Erris the Scots had fled by sea back to Scotland. Undeterred Granuaile gave chase in her galleys, as Bingham reported to the English Privy Council, hoping sardonically as he stated, 'that all or the moste part will take their journy towardes heaven and the province ridd of manie badd and ill disposed persons.'[12] Bingham's hope regarding Granuaile was not fulfilled. She survived the journey and continued to be a thorn in his side. Her actions demonstrate the lengths to which she was prepared to go to avenge a wrong committed against her extended family, and how she, in turn, was now regarded by them as their matriarch, their defender and avenger—a privilege and a duty formerly deemed the preserve of a chieftain.

With the removal of the Blind Abbot from the leadership of the Mayo Bourkes, and the death during 1591 of most of the senior leaders, Granuaile's stepson, Edmund, and her son, Tibbot-ne-Long, emerged as the principal men in the Bourke hierarchy. Together with Granuaile, they were the two remaining chieftains who by spring 1592 had not submitted to Bingham. In the struggle between the English and Gaelic worlds in Mayo, no likely victor had as yet emerged. Under Bingham's harsh rule, English control had undoubtedly advanced. Yet, as the various Bourke rebellions demonstrated, when confronted by a Gaelic alliance English power was still, in effect, quite fragile. However, despite their victories over the English, the Bourkes and their allies suffered from the prevailing Gaelic malaise. Gaelic leaders in Mayo, including Granuaile and her sons, like those elsewhere in the country, merely fought their own corner. Their wars were local and, as it had been for their ancestors, their spur was that of survival in the political as much as in the physical sense. They were products of their time and of a society which still nurtured the outmoded Celtic tradition of individual and fragmented tribalism, which seemed incapable of producing a single centralised authority. Gaelic Ireland had fallen behind the rest of Europe.

> Such a life had been an anachronism in the medieval system and there was no place for it in Renaissance Europe … the fundamental divergence between the Celtic conception of a ruler and the new conception of the state.[13]

This concept of a common cause and the need for unity among the Gaelic clans was slowly being fostered by two chieftains in Ulster.

In the spring of 1592 Tibbott-ne-Long was approached by bishops Hely and O'Boyle to raise a rebellion in Mayo in tandem with Red Hugh O'Donnell, the young chieftain of Tirconail, lately escaped from captivity in Dublin Castle. Spanish aid was promised and the prospect of re-establishing the MacWilliamship was held out as an additional incentive. Tibbott-ne-Long reacted cautiously. The concept of waging battle at the behest and in the cause of an outsider, particularly an O'Donnell of Tirconail, was an alien concept. Moreover, since the last rebellion, Bingham had Mayo firmly under control and had established a garrison at Castlebar thus cutting off the western Bourkes from their traditional allies in the north of the county. However, on the appeal of the Clandonnells to rescue one of their leaders imprisoned by Bingham at Cloonagashal castle, Tibbott-ne-Long initiated a rising in Mayo and attacked the castle as Bingham was holding sessions there. The attack was beaten back by the garrison. Tibbott-ne-Long held out for as long as he could until he heard that O'Donnell himself had submitted and that the promised Spanish aid had failed to materialise.

Tibbott-ne-Long's action brought the full wrath of Bingham once more down on Burrishoole, with disastrous consequences for Granuaile, who was still operating from nearby Carraigahowley castle. Since Bingham's devastation of her territory, the sea had become her sole source of survival as she tried desperately to regroup and replenish what Bingham had taken from her. In retaliation for her son's attack on Cloonagashal, Bingham once more entered her territory and stripped it bare of cattle and produce. For the first time he also penetrated Granuaile's sea domain, as he informed the Privy Council:

> At Burrishoole we met our shipping and so continued there two nights altogether. The shipping has done great service for the same had cleared all their islands.[14]

With English warships in Clew Bay, the unique shelter of mountain, inlet and island, which had maintained Granuaile's seapower for so long was, for the first time, revealed. The network of harbours, channels and fortresses that had provided a safe haven for her activities and given her the freedom of movement her trade by sea required, was now exposed. There was nowhere to hide and nowhere her ships could run to before the wind, safe from pursuit. Bingham's invasion of her sea domain and his subsequent impounding of most of her fleet was a reversal of fortune and one from which she was never fully to recover.

It was not in her nature, however, to submit without a fight and initially she resisted Bingham's efforts to deprive her of her sea power. Shortly afterwards she is recorded as having seized a galley from 'an Englishman of Sir Richard Bingham's, who was there killed',[15] in lieu of her galleys impounded by Bingham.

With Bingham in the ascendant further resistance was, for the moment, futile. In September 1592 it was recorded that Tibbott-ne-Long, on behalf of the neighbouring clans, met with Bingham at Aghagower near Westport and agreed to terms: 'Tibbott Burke Mac Richard-an-Iarainn came into us and agreed into all things for the Burkes, O'Malleys and Clangibbons to be received into her Majesty's mercy and protection laying in his foster-father Edmund MacTibbot and one Tibbot MacGibbon to remain as pledges ...'[16].

The terms were severe. Bingham set out to reduce the influence of chieftains like Tibbott-ne-Long by stripping them of the foundation on which their power was based—their client chieftains. Henceforth, a chieftain could only represent his own sept in his dealings with the English administration. Tibbott-ne-Long was required to pay a proportion of the cost of the war expended by Bingham in quelling the rebellion, and to make restitution for the spoils committed. He was also fined a certain number of cattle. Well might Bingham subsequently write in his report to court that Tibbott-ne-Long and his step-brother Edmund were 'men of no possessions or to have of any goods so much as half a dozen cows apiece.'[17]

An uneasy peace descended on Mayo, devastated by the long series of wars and disorder which had reduced it to a virtual wilderness. Politically the inadequacies of the age-old Gaelic system had been cruelly exposed and as cruelly dismantled by the relentless pressure of Richard Bingham. More than most, Granuaile had been a victim of Bingham's oppression. Now in her sixties, an astonishing age in the sixteenth century, especially given her perilous career, she witnessed her Gaelic world crumble before Bingham's onslaught.

Reduced once more to the status of dependent widowhood, her eldest son and many family members murdered, her ships, cattle and horse herds confiscated, her territory destroyed and, most of all, her freedom of movement by sea restricted—all had as their source Sir Richard Bingham. For another of similar age, sex and circumstances, it would have been understandable to have surrendered to such seemingly insurmountable difficulties, to lay down the sword and bow to the inevitable. But for someone who had fought for survival for over forty years, who had fearlessly sailed the wild western coastline, who had endured imprisonment and deprivation, who had led with sword in hand by land and sea, who had skilfully outmanoeuvred every major figure in the English administration in Ireland for the space of thirty years, who, as a later poet wrote of her, had

 … dared the tempest in its midnight wrath
 And through opposing billows cleft her fearless path,[18]

it was simply not in her character, even at this late stage of her life, to capitulate without a fight.

  And in the spring of 1593, in her stark fortress of Carraigahowley, despite the setbacks, far from being a spent force, Granuaile was already plotting her next audacious move.

CHAPTER 8
THE MEETING OF
THE TWO QUEENS

There were many factors which compelled Granuaile to put her case directly to Queen Elizabeth I and equally there were many more that well might have deterred her from so doing. The reasons for her decision are evident in her correspondence to the queen and to the English Privy Council, especially to Lord Burghley. Perhaps this single episode in Granuaile's chequered life contributed most to her exclusion from Irish historical record. Later generations of historians, intent on eulogising Irish heroes, could find no place for one who, it appeared, had 'bent the knee' to 'perfidious Albion'. On the other hand, folklore, legend and poetry conversely sought to highlight the episode by putting a patriotic gloss on the meeting, fashioning it into an encounter between two queens of equal standing, with the Irish queen getting the upperhand of her rival. Somewhere in between lies the reality.

Political conditions obtaining in Ireland when Granuaile opened correspondence with the Queen of England were, to say the least, convoluted. The native system of government in Connaught had fallen foul of the power and Machiavellian tactics of a determined neighbour, as had happened a decade earlier in the Munster of Granuaile's old adversary, the Earl of Desmond. The Gaelic world was caught in a time warp. Its inflexibility and inability to adapt and to become part of the new Europe, which had long since divested itself of the vestiges of medievalism, had become the trap within which it must surely perish, taking with it those who continued to champion its cause. Gaelic resistance was piecemeal, undisciplined and lacked a coherent and unifying policy. Most importantly it lacked a centralising authority or figurehead which in England was embodied in the person of Elizabeth Tudor. The Gaelic code, with its emphasis on the individual rather than on the commonweal, seemed incapable of producing such a leader. Gaelic chieftains were still more apt to fight one another than to consolidate against the English.

Mayo's resistance to the encroachment of English power, in which Granuaile had played her part, now lay in ruins. The leadership hierarchy in Mayo, through death and execution, was decimated. The land lay waste. English garrisons were established in the forfeited castles of the chieftains and monitored every movement. Granuaile had suffered more than most: death of kith and kin, imprisonment, impoverishment, confiscation and finally the seizure of her ships. At sixty-three years of age, the future looked bleak.

Granuaile was a product of the Gaelic world of her birth and rearing. Her quarrel was not with England or its queen, but with individual representatives of England working in the Irish service when they threatened her, her family and their property. She had experienced at first-hand the promises and pacts made and broken, the ambiguity and deception and finally the ruthless subjugation as the incomprehension and incompatibility that lay between the Gaelic and English worlds exploded into bloody confrontation. When the representatives of the English world, like Sidney and Perrot, appeared to deal with her in a way that did not unduly dilute her power and freedom, she, like most of her fellow chieftains, was prepared to deal, even to make token submissions. The earlier breed of Elizabethan officials like Sidney were content, for the most part, to be facilitators of such nominal submissions in order to preserve the peace and to avoid, on their queen's orders, expensive warfare. But international politics and changing religious and social attitudes in England and in Europe gave a more urgent and ruthless edge to Ireland's conquest.

It was also the age of exploration and discovery; new lands to conquer; fortunes to be made. For many Englishmen Ireland offered a less distant location to fulfil such ambitions than the far-off Americas. After the death of the Earl of Desmond and the collapse of the Desmond rebellion in 1583, the once repugnant Irish service became more attractive, especially when Desmond's 500,000 acres, innumerable castles, woodlands, fisheries and limitless rights and tributes in Munster came to be parcelled out among the avaricious victors. The spoils attracted a new breed of English adventurer: younger sons of landed gentry, lawyers and entrepreneurs, who saw in Ireland's disordered political state, her rich pasturelands and virgin forests, the way to personal fortunes. But such exploitation had to be justified. The natives over whom these English adventurers come to plunder had to be presented as 'savages', as a race unfit to govern themselves, unworthy owners of such prime lands and properties, a race inferior in every way. If they could be provoked to rebel, like Desmond, then by English law their lands and properties were automatically forfeited to be picked up at a nominal cost. The bigoted strain of the new, puritanical, religious fervour that was sweeping England and, to her unease and personal dislike, which had infiltrated Elizabeth's administration, added another dimension to fuel the incompatibility and hatred between native and newcomer. For the first time religion had been introduced as a divisive issue in Ireland. Sir Richard Bingham, his family and many in his administration in Connaught epitomised these traits and Granuaile and her family had borne the brunt of their anatagonism, prejudice and cruelty.

It is against this background that she first opened correspondence with the Queen of England in June 1593. Her motivation was primarily one of survival and to get Bingham off her back. There was no one in the Irish administration to whom she could turn. Sir Henry Sidney had died in 1586; Sir John Perrot had been removed from office. Bingham's star that was now in the ascendant. He had eliminated any Spanish threat in Connacht, crushed the Bourke rebellion and his success had, for the present, silenced his critics in the Irish council. It is obvious that Granuaile understood how the English administration operated and was sufficiently *au fait* with the political process to know that a direct approach to the queen was both feasible and was her only recourse. She was also sufficiently confident in her ability to navigate her way through the labyrinthine channels of Tudor officialdom.

How her first petition to the queen, written while she was still in Ireland, was delivered to the Court is unclear. One of her later petitions was endorsed by the powerful Earl of Ormond, Black Tom, then a court favourite of Elizabeth and related to her through her mother Ann Boleyn. Ormond had revived a claim to part of the barony of Burrishoole, which had subsequently brought him into direct contact with Granuaile at Carraigahowley Castle.

With characteristic cunning, diplomacy and a sophisticated ability to negotiate, knowing that Bingham had already fed the queen damning evidence of her disloyalty, Granuaile was quick to put on record her version of events (see Appendix 1.IV). In the opening lines of her petition she outlined to the queen how

> ... the continual discord stirres and dissention that hertofore long tyme remained among the Irishrye especialey in West Conaght by the sea side everie cheeftaine for his safeguard and maintenance and for the defence of his people, followers and countrye took armes by strong hand to make head against his neyburs which in like manner constrayned your highness fond subject to take armes and by force to maintaine her selfe and her people by sea and land the space of fortye yeares past.[1]

Then in almost chatty vein she tells of her two marriages, her sons and her present situation as a widow. She claims that the Gaelic system, as it operated in Connaught, never yielded 'thirds' to the widows of chieftains who, because of the disordered state of their territories and their constant warring, on their deaths had little to leave in any event. She also took the English-imposed Composition of Connaught to task for failing to make provision for the widows of chieftains. Playing the sympathy card, in the knowledge that Elizabeth was of similar age, she asked the queen:

In tender consideracion whereof and in regard of her great age ... to grant her some reasonable maintenance for the little tyme she hath to lyve.[2]

She offered in return 'a surrender at her hands' the lands of her two sons and also the lands of her two surviving Bourke nephews. Then to her main objective, to return to the sea and circumvent Bingham's embargo, she asked the queen to

... grant unto your said subject under your most gracious hand of signet free libertye during her lyve to envade with sword and fire all your highness enemyes wheresoever they are or shall be ...

and the crunch clause: 'without any interruption of any person or persons whatsoever'.

It was an ingenious stroke to return to her old ways but this time with the queen's personal approval, thereby making herself untouchable by Bingham.

While her petition made its way by sea to London an incident occurred which lent it greater urgency. Ulster was secretly preparing for war, urged on by the fear of English expansionism and a renewed hope of Spanish assistance. The English-educated Earl of Tyrone, Hugh O'Neill, now chieftain of the great O'Neill clan, amidst much subterfuge and outward protestations of loyalty to the queen, had secretly confederated with the young Tirconail chieftain, Red Hugh O'Donnell. Tyrone had personally witnessed at first hand the destruction that had been wrought in Munster where, a decade earlier, as an ally of the Crown, he had ridden with the English hordes as they lay waste to the lands of the Earl of Desmond. He had seen the earl hunted like a wild animal across his own lordship, running from one wretched bolthole to the next before his ignoble death in a bleak cave in the winter of 1583. He had seen the Desmond estates parcelled out among the English victors. Closer to home, Bingham's subjugation of Connaught had made the alarm bells ring even louder. Now the English were knocking on the doors of Ulster. Breifny had already been burned and looted by Bingham's bands. The whole of Monaghan had been proclaimed, its chieftain MacMahon executed. Next in line to face the English onslaught stood Maguire's country of Fermanagh. From the sidelines Tyrone waited and watched the build-up of Gaelic resentment against English excesses, fanned by the counter-reformation exhortations by a new wave of Irish clerics from the Papal and Spanish courts, spark into the flames of all-out rebellion.

Reduced in power and wealth by Bingham, any road to reverse the humiliation and deprivation he had suffered was welcomed by Granuaile's son, Tibbott-ne-Long. In May 1593, Maguire finally broke into rebellion and burned Ballymote, then under the control of Sir George Bingham. In the ensuing conflict one of Maguire's men was captured and, under torture, implicated Tibbott-ne-Long in a wider Tyrone-inspired conspiracy against the English. Tibbott was promptly captured by Sir Richard Bingham, consigned to prison in Athlone castle and charged with treason, as Bingham subsequently reported (see Appendix 1.vi):

Tibbot Burke had even then written a lettre in Irishe to Brian oge O'Rourke to raise sturres in the Breny [Breffni] and to hold out but two monthes and he would undertak that the banished rebell the Devills Hoke and the rest should retourne to Mayo againe and with his help mak warres there ...[3]

In the heightened political situation the air was thick with claim and counterclaim, subterfuge and intrigue. Whether Tibbott was implicated or whether he had been framed by Bingham was irrelevant. Treason was a capital offence, punishable by death, and Bingham's preference for martial law was by now well-established.

Her son's imprisonment by her avowed enemy galvanised Granuaile into action, to undertake the most hazardous voyage of her career. Haste was imperative if she was to save the life of her son. From experience she had every reason to believe that Bingham would not be slow to resort to summary execution, as she explained to Queen Elizabeth:

> The poor youth of the countrey are so extreamly used as they
> are most comonly executed before they be justly tryed or ther
> cause only hearde ...[4]

Coupled with the imprisonment of her son, Granuaile's half-brother, Dónal-na-Píopa O'Malley, who resided at the clan fortress of Cathair-na-mart, was also arrested by Bingham and charged with the murder of some English soldiers. Very little was heard of Donal during the late rebellions and, as his nickname suggests, he perhaps was given more to either playing the pipes or drinking wine, than making war.

Folklore and tradition maintain that Granuaile captained one of her own ships for her voyage to England and there is certainly no reason to doubt her capability in that regard. Folklore and tradition also state that she was accompanied by a troop of her hardy kerne and that, barefoot, dressed in her Irish costume, the beautiful Irish 'queen' cut an impressive, figure in the court of Queen Elizabeth. On their introduction, it was said that Elizabeth held out her hand, but she was forced to raise her hand to the Irish 'queen' Granuaile being the taller of the two. When it was perceived during the course of their meeting that Granuaile required a handkerchief Elizabeth offered her a lace-edged one of fine cambric. Upon using it, Granuaile threw it into the nearby fire, bringing the surprised retort from Elizabeth that it was meant to be put in her pocket. Equally surprised, Granuaile told the queen that in Ireland they had a higher standard of cleanliness. When Elizabeth offered to confer her with the title of countess, Granuaile is said to have declined the offer on the basis that a title could not be conferred on one of equal status. When Elizabeth bemoaned the cares of royalty, looking around her sumptuous surroundings, Granuaile witheringly told her 'that the poor women of Mayo had greater cares and greater industry to their credit'[5].

It is not surprising that the meeting of two of the century's most remarkable women would give rise to such fanciful tales, particularly in Ireland where, over the intervening centuries, the oral tradition of storytelling embellished the event. The factual evidence relating to the meeting rests mainly on the correspondence of Granuaile, Lord Burghley, Sir Richard Bingham, Tibbott-ne-Long, the Earl of Ormond and Queen Elizabeth. That Granuaile was at the court from June until September 1593 is certain and in the course of that time she was granted an audience with Queen Elizabeth. The circumstances leading to the encounter, the reasons for it and the outcome, though fundamentally different from the folklore and fiction, are all the more fascinating.

Granuaile did not go alone on her journey to England. She was accompanied by at least three other people, who were expressly mentioned as being with her at Court. One was her first husband's cousin and former adversary, the elderly O'Flaherty chieftain Sir Murrough-ne-Doe, who was seeking redress against a relation, a protégé of Sir Richard Bingham, who had encroached on his property. Granuaile is also said by Bingham to 'have carried over into England'[6] the son of Ulick Bourke of Erris and her grand-nephew, the son of Tibbot Reagh Bourke who, it was recorded, 'attended uppon Grany O'Maille at her late beyinge at Court.'[7] This implies, as folklore has always maintained, Granuaile sailed her own ship to England and consequently would have been accompanied by a crew. Her advanced age, although she was not averse to use it as bargaining ploy with Elizabeth and Burghley, did not mitigate against her undertaking long voyages. As late as 1597 she is recorded as being in action at sea. Consequently in 1593 she was physically more than capable of captaining her ship to England. The south coast of Ireland was familiar territory to her and well within her sailing capabilities.

Her journey was, nonetheless, daunting. Few Gaelic chieftains with such a documented and established record of rebellion and piracy would have dared put foot on English soil, particularly in the prevailing political climate. Granuaile possessed great confidence in her powers of persuasion that her case would firstly be entertained, that she would gain the ear of the queen, where so many others had failed, and that she would not be hanged as a rebel. As her galley passed alongside Wapping Stairs on the river Thames, the rotting corpses hanging in iron cages suspended over the river's edge was evidence of the terrible fate meted out to pirates. Rumours abounded of another Spanish invasion and the seas around the southern coasts of Ireland and England were patrolled by English warships. The capture of an Irish ship, captained by a notorious pirate leader, would have been no mean prize for any privateer.

Nothing daunted, her ship sailed around the south coast of Ireland, past the Old Head of Kinsale and into St George's Channel, past Land's End and the Scilly Isles, through the straits of Dover and finally into the estuary of the Thames, to anchor at one of the many landing places below London Bridge. There her galley was dwarfed by the soaring mastheads of the great cargo ships in the port of London, then one of the busiest and wealthiest in the world. All along the bustling waterfront ships from Antwerp, Hamburg, Bordeaux, Genoa, Venice and the Levant discharged cargos of wines, spices, silk, carpets, metalware, pottery, glassware, pitch, and timber and were loaded with English produce: tin, corn, coal and the lucrative woven cloth. Barges, lighters and the traditional Thames 'wherries' ferried passengers and products up and down the teeming water highway. Upriver towards the palaces of Whitehall and Westminster the new mansions of wealthy merchants and influential aristocrats rose imposingly above the waterside.

Behind the façade of wealth and commerce lay the crowded, noisy streets of London, reverberating to the shrill cry of trader, shopkeeper and huckster and through which permeated the stench of open sewers and rotting refuse. Through the narrow streets and laneways, bounded on either side by wooden-framed houses, shops and taverns, a constant mass of people jostled and pushed their way: tradesmen, porters, pickpockets, beggars; drovers driving herds of sheep, cattle and pigs vied for space with sword-swinging aristocrats spoiling for a fight and richly attired ladies, perfumed handkerchiefs held at the ready to stifle the stench as they flitted from goldsmith to haberdasher. All was noise and movement, a far cry from the silent, empty spaces of the west of Ireland.

Granuaile's impressions of this vast metropolis must remain in the realm of fancy. Like every visitor to London during the reign of Elizabeth, she was doubtless impressed by the city's vibrancy and wealth as much as she was repelled by the stench, filth and overcrowding. As one who had spent her lifetime on the open, invigorating sea and in the underpopulated Irish countryside, city life must have been anathema. Granuaile's mission, however, was not to sightsee or trade with merchant or shopkeeper, but to barter with the Queen of England for the life of her son.

Elizabeth moved her court regularly from one palace to another. During the summer months, when disease flourished in London, she progressed between her country palaces of Richmond, Hampton Court and Greenwich. In the summer of 1593, an outbreak of the plague had sent the court scurrying out of the city to the more salubrious air of the countryside. Tradition has always held that it was at Greenwich Palace on the banks of the Thames that the 'Pirate Queen' finally met the Queen of England.

From the recorded evidence it is clear that from early July 1593 Granuaile was in England. Like the hundreds of petitioners who hung about the fringes of the court in the hope of capturing the ear of the queen, Granuaile had to conform to the required protocol and wait her turn. Great formality was attached to the court of Elizabeth and access to it was difficult and restricted. Other than Shane O'Neill in 1562, few Irish chieftains were recorded as having been granted an audience with the monarch. Granuaile was not the only Irish petitioner at court that summer. She herself mentions the presence of her son's brother-in-law, Sir Donogh O'Connor Sligo, who had also come to seek redress against Bingham and his family.

There too was Eleanor Butler FitzGerald, the tragic widow of the 'rebel' Earl of Desmond, Granuaile's gaoler in 1577. Stripped of the vast wealth, lands and property of her husband which, since his death in 1583, had been snapped up by such court 'favourites' as Sir Walter Raleigh, the poet Edmund Spenser, Warham St Leger and Sir Christopher Hatton, the Countess of Desmond was forced to beg her bread on the streets of Dublin, while her son, the rightful heir, was a prisoner, shut away and forgotten in the grim dungeons of the Tower of London. Then at court to plead her case, her plight was a sobering example of the cruel outcome of rebellion.

The year 1593 was a time of great political unease in England. The prospect of another Spanish invasion loomed large, as English privateers such as Raleigh, Howard, Frobisher and Grenville continued to attack the King of Spain's treasure ships returning from the New World. Across the English Channel, King Philip was attempting to gain a foothold on the western coast of France and Elizabeth strove to keep him out at all costs. The queen's support of the Protestant French king, Henry of Navarre, against the French Catholic League, which in turn was supported by Philip, received a setback in July. Deciding that his alliance with England could no longer guarantee him power or protection, Henry of Navarre agreed to turn Catholic, declaring that *Paris vaut une messe* (Paris was worth a mass). The prospect of an alliance between France and Spain provoked great unease in the English court, leaving England alone with only the Netherlands to stem the Catholic tide. The court circles throbbed with rumour and counter-rumour as diplomatic delegations, ambassadors, emissaries and spies came and departed. Grace O'Malley's petition for the life of her son seemed insignificant by comparison.

Undaunted by the obstacles, Granuaile opened her campaign firstly through the influence of Black Tom, the Earl of Ormond, cousin and favourite of the queen, who gave her an introduction to the Lord Treasurer, William Cecil, Lord Burghley. Then the most powerful man in the queen's service and referred to by Elizabeth as 'her spirit', William Cecil had served his temperamental and autocratic mistress loyally and long. In his seventy-third year, gout and old age had slowed Burghley physically but mentally he was ever as vigilant in his queen's interest. Subterfuge, diplomacy, patronage, even murder he employed during his long tenure, to ensure the mission for which life had ordained him—to serve his queen and fulfil the criteria she had demanded of him when she first came to the throne:

> ... that you will not be corrupted with any manner of gift; and you will be faithful to the State and, without respect of my private will, you will give me the counsel that you think best.[8]

Throughout his career, William Cecil had negotiated, outwitted and outmanoeuvred the best minds in Europe as he steered his sovereign through the difficult years of her reign.

It was to this international statesman that Granuaile turned in her need, a man she later referred to as her 'best frende since her cominge hyther.'[9] Burghley was not ignorant about Granuaile; in fact he knew more about her than she perhaps realised. From Sir Henry Sidney to Bingham, over the space of twenty years, in the dispatches of those employed in the Irish service, he had read the reports about this female leader from Connaught. He had written her name and attempted to untangle her complex family connections in his own hand on various state documents which detailed her nefarious activities. But before he advanced her petition to the queen, Burghley was determined to know more.

To this effect, he forwarded Granuaile a list of 'eighteen articles of interrogatory to be answered by Grany ne Maly'[10] (see Appendix 1.v). The questions and Granuaile's answers are preserved in the Elizabethan State Papers and contain written observations in the margin in Burghley's hand. They not only provide an informative résumé of Granuaile's life, her family and relations, her observations and opinions on the social and political practices obtaining in her native Connaught, but are also a testimony to her remarkable political acumen.

To negate Bingham's damning evidence, in her answers

Granuaile sets out her version of events since the death of Richard-an-Iarainn, to her arrest by Bingham and her narrow escape from hanging at his hands. She speaks of the tragic death of her eldest son, Owen O'Flaherty, and hints at Bingham's implication in his murder. She explains that her flight into Ulster to O'Neill who, as she is aware, is by then under suspicion by the English of being in collusion with Spain, was she maintains through fear of Bingham. She tells of the pardon she received from the queen by her deputy Sir John Perrot in Dublin and how Bingham set the pardon aside in his actions against her and her family. Her replies are always guarded and she concentrates on aspects of her life least objectionable to the English. She adroitly neglects to mention her participation in the Bourke rebellions, her plundering exploits by land and sea and her importation of Scottish mercenaries. Her replies show a cunning and subtlety of mind that is more than a match for Burghley.

While Granuaile awaited a response, Burghley received a letter from Bingham, bristling with indignation

> … There be 2 notable traitors gon over Sir Morrow ne doe and Grainy O'Maly both rebelle from their childhoode and continually in accion … for notwithstanding that they have many pardons there ys matter ynough of late found out against them to hang them by justice …[11]

Knowing that the two Irish petitioners would have little positive to say on his behalf at court, Bingham sought to pre-empt their accusations:

> … if they be drawn to make generall exclamations against me, I do not doubt but your honour will most honorably and indifferently consyder of it …[12]

Bingham's damning indictment did not, however, adversely affect Granuaile's chances to obtain a royal audience. Her replies to Burghley's questions seem to have been at once satisfactory and intriguing enough for the queen to agree to see her. That Granuaile undoubtedly had some influence at court is commented on by Bingham, disgruntled at 'having bin advertised from thence that some in Court hath comended her for doing her Matie [Majesty] good service ...'13

Trouble was brewing in the province of Ulster. Stories of the Earl of Tyrone's intrigues with the Spanish king and of a secret confederacy being formed among the Gaelic chieftains in the province made English fears that Ireland would join Spain in a grand alliance against her now appear more likely. To pardon rather than punish past offenders and rebels, to maintain influential leaders like Granuaile in some semblance of loyalty, from Burghley's perspective, despite Bingham's objections, he deemed the wiser course to follow.

In July, Granuaile received her summons to appear before the Queen. Elizabeth was at the apex of her power, the beloved Gloriana of her people, the 'Goddesse Heavenly Bright' of Edmund Spenser's *Faerie Queene*, Good Queen Bess, the saviour of England from the tyrannical ambitions of Spain. For thirty-five years she had steered England through turbulent political waters, by a strategy of delay, procrastination, secrecy, compromise and prudence, and had more than proved her worth as well as her right to rule. While she may have had 'the body of a weak and feeble woman', she had shown that she possessed, as she told her troops at Tilbury in 1588 when the Armada was bearing down on England's shores, 'the heart and stomach of a king, and a king of England too.'14 By sheer graft, personality and an inherited Tudor belief in her God-given right to rule, this bastard daughter of Henry VIII and Anne Boleyn, without a clear title to the throne, had won the respect and adoration of her subjects.

She could be coarse and bawdy, she spat and picked her teeth, was given to swearing, had a temper to match her red hair and boxed the ears of her ministers, who constantly despaired of her making up her mind. A brilliant scholar and linguist, she had a cruel wit and a razor-sharp tongue. She bullied and cajoled her quarrelsome courtiers like children and demanded and received their devotion and symbolic love in return. In her sixtieth year, age had not spared even the deified figure of Elizabeth Tudor. Her eyes peered shortsightedly out of her sharp-featured face, her red hair had given way to a wig, her face was a mask of rice powder and rouge, her nose 'grew hooked as a harridan's'[15] and her teeth were decayed and blackened. What age had ravaged, Elizabeth Tudor sought to conceal by the sheer opulence and radiance of her wardrobe and she strutted her court like an exotic bird:

> The Queen's dresses were not distinguished by refinement of taste: it was rather at a magnificent display that she aimed and her predilection was for gowns richly embroidered and sewn with jewels, so that they were as encrusted with ornament as the buildings of the early English Renaissance.[16]

This was the vain, autocratic, supreme ruler with whom Granuaile sought to do business. The similarities between them were marked. They were the same age. Both were women who had usurped what was perceived to be a man's role and by sheer determination and obstinacy, had prevailed. Both were used to ruling men, to having their orders obeyed, as the poet wrote of Granuaile:

> She seemed well used to power, as one that hath
> Dominion over men of savage mood …[17]

Both displayed a certain magnetism, a charisma that kept their followers in thrall and loyal until the end of their lives. Both sought to protect their 'country' from whatever enemy who might try to take it from them. For Elizabeth, the enemy was Spain; for Granuaile, the enemy was Elizabeth's own military men in Connaught.

Age and the harsh environment in which she operated had undoubtedly left its imprint on Granuaile. Unlike Elizabeth, the furrows and wrinkles of age, salt spray and wind lay exposed on her face for all to see. It is unlikely that she could have survived her long battle with the elements over the space of forty years without some outward scar or blemish. Granuaile's dress, while doubtless the best in her wardrobe, was hardly a match or a threat to the opulence of the queen's.

More blatant differences were apparent. Each woman represented a culture totally incompatible and incomprehensible to the other and which were set on a collision course from which there could be only one winner. Despite Elizabeth's assertion of 'having the heart and stomach of a king' she had never personally led her army into battle and, despite her claim to be 'mistress of the seas', she had never sailed further down river than Greenwich. Elizabeth ruled from the protection and comfort of her palaces surrounded by a retinue of loyal and able advisers. Granuaile led alone by land and sea. She had taken two husbands and according to tradition at least one lover. She was the mother to four children. Elizabeth could hold onto power only at the expense of her personal happiness and fulfilment. Marriage was incompatible with her crown, as she told Robert Dudley, the most persistent of her many suitors: 'God's death, my Lord, I will have but one mistress and no master.' 18 Only in solitary virginity could Elizabeth hope to rule her bickering courtiers by appearing as a lover to all of them and a wife to none, while England became her substitute child. By comparison, in this regard, Granuaile seemed to have had it all.

On a summer's day in late July, within the lavish surroundings of Greenwich palace, the two elderly women finally came face to face. Their conversation was believed to have been conducted in Latin, the language often used by the English in their dealings with Irish chieftains and in which the queen was one of the most proficient of her age. However, both from her correspondence and from the observations of many Englishmen in the Irish service who had come into contact with her over the decades, it was obvious that Granuaile understood and spoke English. As befitted the occasion, she would undoubtedly have dressed with as much care as she had in 1581, at Sir Nicholas Malby's celebrations in Galway, when she had been singled out among the other guests as being 'no small lady'. She could not, and perhaps wisely choose not to, compete with Elizabeth in the fashion stakes. Far better to achieve what she came to seek by invoking the queen's compassion rather than her resentment. It was a successful ploy and one that paid dividends, because Elizabeth later ordered Bingham 'to have pity for the poor aged woman,'[19] who had come before her, blithely ignoring the fact that they were the same age.

The correspondence emanating from the meeting is the only extant evidence remaining to what transpired between the two women. In a later letter to Lord Burghley, Granuaile writes of 'the clemencie and favour,'[20] displayed by the queen towards her at their meeting. It is the queen's letter regarding the meeting, however, which is the more revealing and is testimony to how well Granuaile negotiated her case (see Appendix 1.VIII). The only unlawful act attributed to Granuaile by the queeen during the course of the meeting, was her dramatic chastisement of her son Murrough-ne-Maor O'Flaherty, by which the queen seemed to have been amazed. She glances over her other 'unloyal' activities by merely noting that she 'hath in times lived out of order.'[21] With a mixture of admiration and compassion she listened as Granuaile outlined the harsh actions of Sir Richard Bingham against herself and her family and her plea for the life of her son and her half-brother. She listened too as Granuaile, with some audacity, sought protection from her own governor and for her reinstatement to her trade of 'maintenance by land and sea'[22] which she couched in such a way that, as the queen noted, she would 'fight in our quarrel with all the world',[23] and to which she agreed, so that, as she wrote, it might 'yield to her some maintenance for her living the rest of her old years.'[24]

With the queen's promise to have her requests investigated, Granuaile gratefully took her leave to await the outcome. The queen subsequently ordered her Privy Council to seek an explanation from Sir Richard Bingham regarding his treatment of Granuaile and her family and to investigate how her situation could best be relieved. Indignant and self-righteous, Bingham replied 'in defence of my own innocency...'

> ... to shew me instance of any one that ever I used violence
> against, havinge alwayes (I thancke the Lord) had that
> consideracion of christian dutye as I never sought any man's
> bloode otherwise then by course of her Maties. comon lawes
> to take away.[25]

Outraged that the queen and her Council should contemplate
reinstating Granuaile and Sir Murrough-ne-Doe, both of whom
he had gone to such lengths to destroy, he contended, perhaps not
without some semblance of truth, that

> ... for so long as Grany Ne Malye and he were of power to make
> any sturres the state was nevr trobled with theyr complaints but
> now that they are pulled dowen and forced in speight of their
> hartes to submit themselves to her Ma.ts lawes they pretend
> many wronges and are not ashamed to aske recompence.[26]

In relation to Granuaile, Bingham was undeterred and determined:

> ... how great soevr any may make her wch knoweth her not I
> will nevr aske but a boat of xxx tonnes to beate her ... and wth
> gods assistance dryve her and all her fleet into the sea.[27]

Burghley digested the intemperate tones of Bingham's letter
before making final recommendations to the queen.

Biding her time in London while awaiting the outcome of the
queen's deliberation, Granuaile began to fear that Bingham might
execute Tibbott-ne-Long in the meantime. In early September,
she wrote once more to Burghley (see Appendix 1.VII) reminding
him that 'hir Matie ... hath promised hir hir letters to Sir Richard
Bingham', and begging him to ensure that her 'sonne maye take
no harme in body or goods untyll her Maties pleasure be further
known.'[28]

Towards the end of September Granuaile finally achieved

her goal. The queen wrote her recommendations to Bingham (see Appendix 1.VIII). She ordered the release of Tibbott-ne-Long and Dónal-ne-Píopa from prison. Regarding Granuaile's personal plight, which Elizabeth described as 'having not by the customs of the Irish any title to any livelihood or position or portion of her two husbands' lands, now being a widow,'[29] she ordered that provision be made for her out of her sons' estates, the amount to be deducted, at her personal command, from their crown taxes. She urged Bingham to ensure that they were allowed the ownership of their lands and property and 'that you also shall with your favour in all their good causes protect them to live in peace to enjoy their livelihoods'. She further noted that Granuaile had 'departeth with great thankfulness and with many more earnest promises that she will, as long as she lives, continue a dutiful subject, yea and will employ all her power to offend and prosecute any offender against Us'[30]—a promise that, knowing the opportunities it presented to Granuaile on her return to Connaght, Bingham determined to disregard.

CHAPTER 9
END OF AN ERA

Granuaile's visit to the court of Queen Elizabeth undoubtedly raised her profile and prestige at home and became the subject of discussion and the source of stories and folktales for generations there long after her death. That she likewise made an impression on those who met her at court, including the queen, is obvious from the success of her mission there.

Her bona fide and status as a political leader was further consolidated by the inclusion of her name in the famous Boazio map of Ireland. Drawn by the acclaimed Italian cartographer, Bapista Boazio, the beautifully engraved and decorated map entitled Irlandiae Accurata Descriptio was first published in 1599 in Sudbury. (Another edition was published in 1609 in Antwerp) It is likely that the map was being prepared during the time of Granuaile's appearance at court. Her name written as 'Grany O Male' figures prominently on the map among the otherwise all male principal chieftains and lords of Ireland of the period, perhaps the only female to be so recognised anywhere. What Irish annalists and historians choose to conceal others were more willing to acknowledge that Granuaile was as valid a chieftain as any of her male peers.

The practical results of her mission to the Elizabethan court, however, took longer to manifest themselves than perhaps either she or the queen intended. From the tone and content of his dispatches to court it is obvious that Sir Richard Bingham was not in favour or in agreement with the outcome. He would have to live with the results of what he considered as the queen and Burghley's inappropriate largesse to someone he regarded a traitor and rebel. There is distinct note of pique in his correspondence that Granuaile should go behind his back and even more so that her case should have been entertained at Court. Initially he refused to act on the provisions of the queen's instructions which Granuaile had personally delivered to him on her return to Ireland. But Granuaile was not prepared to let her hard-won concessions be negated by Bingham's hostility and threatened him 'that she would else repaire againe into England'[1] if he did not comply. Rather than risk the queen's censure Bingham eventually agreed, as he reluctantly acknowledged, 'to enlarge Grany O'Mally, her son Tibbott and her brother Donal na Pippe,..[albeit] upon such slender surytes [sureties].'[2]

Granuaile, as Bingham realised, had pulled a fast one on his queen who, in acceding to her requests, had neglected to obtain the usual sureties or pledges in lieu of favours granted. Pardons and favours usually cost, but Granuaile had extracted them from Elizabeth gratis. Elizabeth and Burghley had underestimated the capabilities of the 'aged woman' who had come before them, whose advanced years belied her endurance as well as her capability to plot and to negotiate as ably as themselves scheme. With first-hand experience of her ability, Bingham, knew her as a determined and cunning foe. For all that he had expended to stop her, the queen had, in effect, granted her *carte blanche* to return to sea with her galleys and resume her old trade of 'maintenance', this time under the guise of fighting the queen's 'quarrel with all the world'. There was little Bingham could do but obey the queen's instructions and await an opportunity to clip the wings of this 'notorious woman'.

Tibbott-ne-Long was released from prison in Athlone in late September 1593. Such was the deprivation he endured while in Bingham's custody that, as he wrote, 'he could not stand upon his legges through that durance and misery he suffered there.'[3] Granuaile's half-brother, Dónal-ne-Píopa, was also released. With her family free from Bingham's clutches, Granuaile prepared to take full advantage of the queen's letter regarding her own situation. She started to rebuild her fleet and with three large galleys, which English records describe as being capable of carrying three hundred men apiece, commenced a new chapter in her trade of 'maintenance by land and sea'. The countryside around still bore the scars of warfare, and the sea was once again her only salvation. With mounting alarm Bingham noted her movements and determined on a course of action to stop her without openly disobeying the orders of his queen.

As Granuaile prepared to return to her trade by sea with her newly-acquired galleys, Bingham struck. To monitor her activities he quartered a troop of his soldiers on her ships with orders to accompany her on all her voyages. He next pressed her crew and galleys into service against some of her family's kinsmen who he claimed were in rebellion. As she later complained in court she and her son were forced 'to repair to the seas wher in certain illandes eighteen chiefest of the Bourkes being proclaimed traytours were killed.'4 These were the remnants of the army of her grandson, Richard Bourke, the son of the Devil's Hook who, while acting as a decoy for the activities of Hugh O'Neill and Maguire in Ulster, had plundered north Mayo from where he had been routed by a detachment of Bingham's troops. On his return to his own territory, Richard was attacked by the Bourkes of Erris and was forced to take refuge on the lonely island of Inishkea, where the massacre subsequently took place. Richard and four of his companions, however, managed to escape.

To be a party to the slaughter of their relations must have been a bitter pill for Granuaile and her son to swallow. It is highly unlikely, however, that they did so voluntarily, as Granuaile's son-in-law, the Devil's Hook, and his son Richard Bourke, continued to be Granuaile's, and later Tibbott-ne-Long's, most steadfast allies. In April 1595 Tibbott initiated a military campaign against the Bourkes of Erris and killed a number of their leaders. Under the guise of 'service to the crown', it was, in reality, a revenge attack for the murder of his kinsmen in 1593.

To curb Granuaile's activities on land, Bingham quartered another detachment of his soldiers on her property in Burrishoole where, as she complained to court (see Appendix 1.ix), they did

> … place and cesse themselves taking up meat and drinke after their own serving and six pens per diem for every souldier and four pens per diem for his mann, where they do remain all these seven moneths …5

The result on her depleted resources was, as Granuaile vividly described to Burghley, the total impoverishment of herself and her family.

Unable to bear the financial strain, together with her sons, cousins and followers in tow, Granuaile was forced 'to withdrawe themselves into the province of Mounster, where they do remaine in great distresse.'[6] We can envisage this exodus from Mayo—the band of refugees, whose hope of salvation lay in the courage and the contacts of their indomitable matriarch. Their faith in her limitless energy, political acumen and sheer nerve propelled them to abandon their lands to undertake the hazardous journey south. They sailed from Clew Bay southwards, rounded the south coast and anchored in the river Suir where, in April 1595, Granuaile once more sought the help of the influential Earl of Ormond, at his newly built Elizabethan manor at Carrick-on-Suir. She prevailed on him, as he informed Burghley,

> for my letter to you on her behalf as I could not refrain to write these fewe lines unto your Lordship by her. Though I was verie lothe considering your Ls. weightie causes to trouble you with her private suite, the declaration whereof I refer to herself …[7]

Granuaile desperately needed to be free from Bingham's scrutiny by sea which was rendering her both powerless and penniless. In order to regain unfettered control of her fleet she offered the queen:

> … to serve with a hundred men at her owne charges at seas upon the coaste of Ireland in her Majesties warres uponn all occasions from Easter to Michelmas …[8]

This was a remarkable offer from a woman, who, despite her advanced years, was still prepared and able for such a physically demanding and dangerous role. The idea of this woman, very old by the standards of the day, an active leader of an army of 100 men and a fleet of ships, offering to engage in warfare is, from a mere physical perspective, quite remarkable. The strategy behind Granuaile's offer to the queen is testament to a mind that is sharp and calculating, unaffected by the passing years. While her offer was not immediately availed of by the Crown, it acted later as a means by which her two sons, Tibbott-ne-Long and Murrough-ne-Maor O'Flaherty, were made captains of their own armies, paid for out of the queen's purse, but which they used mainly to advance their own cause.

From the Earl of Ormond's covering letter, and from a further petition dated 5 May 1595 (see Appendix 1.x) from Granuaile to Burghley, in which she refers to 'at my last beinge here'[9] (at the English court), it is clear that some time between 17 April, and 5 May, 1595, Granuaile returned to England to plead her case, this time to Lord Burghley. Granuaile informs him that because of 'Sir Richard Binghams hard dealinge'[10] of her, and contrary to the earlier provision made for her by the queen, she had been prevented by the queen's governer Sir Richard Bingham to 'posses and injoie the third parte of the lands and comodities of MacWilliam and Oflahertie as lawful wife unto each of them ...'[11] She also requested of Burghley to order Bingham to leave her and her family in peace so, as she wrote

I may lyve secure of my life which hath been attempted sundrie tymes be the said Sr Richard Bingham his brethren and others by his direcsion ...[12]

She also asked for the Lord Treasurer's 'favourable letters in me owne and me sonnes behalf to the Lo. Deputie and to Sr Richard Bingham' and craved 'his lordship's pardon for my contynuall boldness'.

Her 'boldness' was rewarded when, in August 1595, a commission was granted by the queen and the Privy Council to investigate the lands in Mayo claimed by her sons, Tibbott-ne-Long and Murrough O'Flaherty, her grandson Dónal O'Flaherty, son of Owen, Owen, Dermot and Dónal O'Malley of 'Owel O'Maillie', and Miles MacEvilly, Tibbott-ne-Long's foster-father, 'with the intention of the Queen accepting their surrenders of the premises and re-granting them by letters patent ...'[13]

Burghley's interest in her welfare and his intervention with the queen on her behalf is testimony to the impact of Granuaile as well as her insistence to have her case heard by those in power in England, rather than suffer the indignity of dealing with antagonistic administrators, like Bingham, in Ireland. But favours had to be reciprocated, and from the time of this, her final visit to the English court, a marked shift began to emerge in the allegiance of her family.

By mid-1595 Hugh O'Neill shed all semblance of loyalty to the English crown by sending his brother, Art, to capture the English-garrisoned fort on the Blackwater, which Tyrone had previously helped the English to establish. A formidable confederacy, spear-headed by O'Neill and his ally, Red Hugh O'Donnell, was being shaped from out of the traditional whirlpool of Gaelic disunity. In their dispatches to the Spanish court, O'Neill and O'Donnell now represented their cause as an 'all-Irish' one. They offered the 'crown of Ireland' to Philip, 'if he would deliver them from their English oppressors.'[14] But personal vendettas and individual power struggles threatened the confederacy from the start. Nowhere else was this to become more apparent than in Mayo, where O'Donnell's aggression against her family was to alienate Granuaile and her sons and thereby lose the Ulster confederacy valuable allies.

Traditionally the O'Donnell chiefs of Tirconail claimed over-lordship of north Mayo—a claim that had always been forcibly resisted by the ruling septs of the Bourkes. To secure the passage from Tirconail into Connaught, in 1595 Red Hugh O'Donnell sought to reactivate that claim. In June he captured Sligo Castle, regarded as the key to the passage into Connaught, thus giving him unhindered access into Mayo. In a demonstration of power to the yet unaligned chieftains of Mayo, O'Donnell looted and plundered the county. The Mayo chieftains were caught between two opposing forces, that of Bingham and O'Donnell, and felt the brunt of both, as one observer recorded:

Through the fear the people have of Sir Richard Bingham, their necessity drives them to depend on O'Donnell, whom they hate for his pride and ambition and are weary of the burdens he daily lays upon them.[15]

Bingham's days as governor were, however, numbered. A new conspiracy was afoot among his fellow administrators in Ireland to remove him from office. Fearing that the charges were stacked against him, Bingham abandoned his post and fled to England in September, and was promptly imprisoned. Sir Conyers Clifford was appointed governor of Connaught in his place.

While doubtless celebrating the removal from office of her most determined enemy, a new threat to Granuaile and her family emerged. O'Donnell sought to capitalise on his initial success in Mayo by attempting to exact unlawful tributes and payments from the Mayo chieftains. In December 1595 he further announced his intention to revive the MacWilliam title which had been declared illegal by the English administration and summoned the Bourkes throughout the county to the traditional inaugural site at Rousakeera. O'Donnel arrived at the site accompanied by an impressive array of his client chieftains and by a large army. Disregarding the Bourke's selected candidate he imposed his own choice, MacWilliam, Theobald, the son Walter Ciotach of Tirawley, the least eligible of the candidates but chieftain of a territory that was essential to O'Donnell's strategic plans. The selection was received with uproar from the various Bourkes and the meeting broke up in anger and disorder. Such rashness and lack of judgement on O'Donnell's part not merely drove a wedge between him and the Mayo Bourkes but also served to alienate them from the Ulster confederacy.

> Hitherto the old customs were the alternative to the queen's government. Now, the choice was between the queen's government and the old customs subject to the very heavy burden of O'Donnell's domination.[16]

With Bingham out of the picture, Granuaile took to the sea again. The lands of her son, out of which the queen had granted her maintenance, were repeatedly ravaged by O'Donnell and his puppet MacWilliam. To sustain herself and her dependants she raided and plundered. Her ships were reported operating off the coast of Thomond, where the Earl of Thomond was forced to do battle with some of her followers who came ashore in search of plunder. In 1597 the Dean of Limerick, writing to the English council in Dublin, reported that 'Grany ny Maly and Mac Neil of Barra invaded one anothers possessions though farre distant …'[17] The fact that she was prepared and physically able to sail in such a dangerous retaliatory mission as far away as the Island of Barra, off the coast of Scotland, is testimony to her incredible courage and endurance. The sea took a heavy toll on life and health. Few seamen in the sixteenth century lived to such an advanced age. Fewer still could continue to operate in such a demanding and dangerous environment as she did to the end of her life.

As her family fought to protect their positions and properties in Mayo, as much as from O'Donnell as from the English, like Granuaile, survival continued to be their motivation. By now her son Tibbott-ne-Long had emerged as the most influential leader of the Mayo Bourkes.

In February 1597, the new English governor, Sir Conyers Clifford arrived in Connaught. His style of government differed greatly from Bingham and he sought the allegiance of the local chieftains by conciliation rather than by coercion. He was acquainted with Tibbott-ne-Long's brother-in-law, Donough O'Connor Sligo, whom he had known at the English court. On his arrival in Connaught, Clifford immediately rewarded that friendship by recapturing Sligo Castle from O'Donnell and reinstating O'Connor Sligo. O'Connor Sligo then 'established friendship and concord between his brother-in-law, Theobald-ne-Long … and Sir Conyers Clifford.'[18] Tibbott-ne-Long, together with Richard Bourke, the Devil's Hook's son, O'Malley, MacJordan and other Mayo clans subsequently met with the governor and agreed to terms. By the terms of the agreement they were pardoned of all past 'offences', made secure in their lands and provided with cattle in lieu of those confiscated by Bingham. In return, they agreed to pay the arrears of the Composition rent, support the governor and give pledges for their continuing loyalty. Tibbott-ne-Long, with the help of the

English governor, subsequently marched into Tirawley and as the *Annals of the Four Masters* recorded, 'expelled and banished MacWilliam ... to O'Donnell ... The Country generally on this occasion adhered to Tibóid-ne-Long and the Governor.'[19]

Now emerging as the most powerful leader in Mayo Tibbott-ne-Long realised his worth and put a price on his loyalty. Alienated from the Ulster Confederacy by O'Donnell, on 25 April 1597 he presented the English governor with a list of fourteen demands which Clifford agreed to forward to the Privy Council for consideration. To secure his allegiance the Council granted Tibbott the extensive lands of the MacWilliamship, as well as the lands of leaders within his own sept who had been killed in rebellions against Bingham. He was made captain of a private army which, although paid for by the government, was at his sole command and discretion. He secured pardons for his half-brother, Murrough-ne-Maor, and for his ally Richard Bourke, for whom he also secured a pension, as well as pensions for his mother's half-brother, Dónal-ne-Píopa and other relations.

Tibbott-ne-Long's decision to agree to terms with the English in 1597 emanated from an overwhelming sense of insecurity, as the Gaelic world of his ancestors was brought crashing down around his head, its laws and customs, whereby he hoped to attain power, overturned by O'Donnell, as much as by the English. While his uneasy alliance with the English was to experience many relapses, over the following years leading up to the Battle of Kinsale in 1601, his agreement with the English government served as a basis by which he eventually emerged as the most powerful and influential leader and the largest land-owner in Mayo. His rise marked the end of inheritance and succession by Gaelic Brehon law and its replacement by English civil law.

From surviving records it appears that Granuaile and her extended family backed and profited from her son's arrangement with the English authorities. In August 1597 Clifford indicated to the lord deputy that he had 'given him [Tibbott-ne-Long], his mother and brother amongst them in money and other necessaries, £200'[20] for their services by sea.

On 14 August 1598, when the English were overwhelmed by the forces of O'Neill and O'Donnell at the Battle of the Yellow Ford, many of the Connaught chieftains who had stood aloof or who had aligned with the English governor, changed sides. Now virtually unopposed, O'Donnell raided at will throughout Mayo, Galway and Thomond. In the autumn he sent MacWilliam and O'Doherty to plunder Tibbott's territory around Burrishoole and also Granuaile's castle of Carrickahowley.

Now almost seventy years old, in her declining years, Granuaile eventually left her struggle with the sea and with the world in the capable hands of her sons. While their activities and the part they played in the concluding years of the century are well documented, there are few additional references to Granuaile. One of the final recorded notices about her appears in the State Papers in July 1601, in a dispatch by the captain of an English warship. It is, fittingly, an account of his encounter with one of her galleys, which the captain claimed was on a mission of plunder:

> All the sails I have seen since I came upon the coast was a galley I met withal betwixt Teelin and Killibegs, where I made her run on shore among the rocks, notwithstanding she rowed with thirty oars and had on board ready to defend her 100 good shot, which entertained skirmish with my boat and had put her to the worst. But coming up with my ship to her rescue, I quickly with my great shot made an end to the fray. This galley comes out of Connaught and belongs to Grace O'Malley ... this with one other galley was set out and manned with a people called the Flaherties who was proposed to do some spoils upon the countries of MacSwyne Fanad and MacSwyne ne Doe about Lough Swilly and Sheephaven ...[21]

That Granuaile was still alive appears likely and it seems that under her direction her trade of 'maintenance by land and sea' still flourished.

Thus the extraordinary life of Granuaile ends as it begins—shrouded in uncertainty. It appears that her death occurred at Carraigahowley castle about the year 1603. She probably survived to hear of the defeat of O'Neill and O'Donnell at the battle of Kinsale, the final and conclusive milestone in the long and bloody struggle between the Gaelic world of her birth and the new world of her sons' adoption. Perhaps she also lived to hear of the death in March 1603 of Queen Elizabeth, her adversary and benefactor. Tradition maintains that she is buried in the ruins of the Cistercian abbey on Clare Island, an appropriate resting place for a Sea Queen.

While denied a place in the annals and history of Ireland, Granuaile's memory remained alive in the folk memory of the area where she once lived. The English also had good reason to remember her long after her death. Writing in 1623, an English lord deputy, seeking to justify the seizure of fishing rights on the borders of Mayo and Galway, reminded the Privy Council that the inhabitants of Mayo

> … have been always more apt to rebellion than any in that kingdom in soe much that the very women have borne armes there, whereof Grany ne Maly was famous and is yett renowned by them …[22]

In the west of Ireland many of the stone fortresses associated with her name stand solidly still in remembrance of their audacious chatelaine. Her main abode, Carraigahowley castle, stark and brooding, the sea waves lapping its stone walls, is today a mecca for the many Granuaile enthusiasts, from all points of the compass, who venture up the dark, spiral stairway to view her forlorn but still evocative chambers. Across the bay on Clare Island the ruins of 'Grania's castle' evoke images of the Pirate Queen.

More recently her story has fired the imagination in a wide range of creative disciplines, and her life has been depicted in fiction, music, dance, drama, and documentary. She has become the inspiration for women's self-awareness groups, for yacht races and diving clubs even uisce beatha (whiskey) named in her honour, while she is the subject of thousands of enquiries on the world-wide-web. Her life and contribution to the eventful era in which she lived is now part of school's curricula both in Ireland and around the world. The modern-day O'Malley clan, its members scattered throughout the world, come together each year to commemorate and celebrate their remarkable antecedent. The passenger ferry *The Pirate Queen* brings visitors to Clare Island to view her castle and final resting place, while the Irish Lights vessel *The Granuaile* keeps a watching brief on the coasts once traversed by this intrepid seafarer.

But it is the swirls and flourishes of the handwritten parchment manuscripts of the sixteenth-century English State Papers, the letters, dispatches and memorabilia of the Tudor conquest of Ireland, which have preserved for posterity the tantalising character and career of Granuaile and of the impact she made on a traumatic period of history. These relics, now brittle and faded with age, challenge our predisposed sense of convention, our assumptions regarding what is possible, and rip apart the shallow boundaries that society tends to impose on women—boundaries which Granuaile, by 'overstepping the part of womanhood', dared to breach. Above all they provided an insight onto one of the world's most remarkable female leaders.

CHAPTER 10
THE DESCENDANTS OF GRANUAILE

Granuaile left her struggles in the capable hands of her two sons, Murrough-ne-Maor O'Flaherty and Tibbott-ne-Long Bourke. Both were to prove as able as their indomitable mother in the art of survival. Pragmatic and ambitious, each possessed the traits of compromise and cunning that, as the sixteenth century drew to its inevitable close, were the essential weapons necessary to survive. Of similar outlook and character, the two brothers tended to operate in tandem and, as well as being blood-related, they became close political allies. Although older, Murrough-ne-Maor seemed content to be directed by his younger and more influential half-brother and lived to reap the rewards. Their lives are a unique commentary on a period of fundamental transition and change. Theirs is the story of the minor chieftains who at the close of the sixteenth century occupied the middle ground between the fixed battlelines of two incompatible protagonists. Trapped by events outside their control, many became pawns in a momentous game of strategy. Others, like the sons of Granuaile, 'plotted their own moves and in a game within a game, became intrepid knights charting their own survival.'[1]

Initially it was their sea power and seafaring expertise, inherited from their mother, combined with their status as influential leaders, that made them much sought after by the opposing sides in the final conflict. By 1597 both were allied, ostensibly, with the English against O'Donnell. In the final years leading up to the battle of Kinsale, as the balance of power constantly shifted between the Ulster confederacy and the English crown, they flirted with both sides, to the utter consternation of the English. 'I know not of one day's service that Tibbott ne Longe hath performed,'[2] the Machiavellian president of Munster, Sir George Carew, complained to the Privy Council while an English spy in a dispatch to the Earl of Essex in 1599 confirmed that

Tibbott ne Longe was within with O'Donnell and O'Donnell did send out of him as pledges ... the best of his country. Tyrone himself say they are agreed, but they will not have any know of it.[3]

When his erstwhile ally, Governor Clifford, was attacked and killed in the Battle of the Curlew mountains in 1599, it was the issue of the MacWilliamship and O'Donnell's continued support of his protégé that kept Tibbott-ne-Long from changing sides and throwing in his lot with the Ulster confederates. The lands pertaining to the title, rather than the title itself, which through O'Donnell's intervention had lost its status and prestige, was the magnet. The English Privy Council had conferred Tibbott with part of the MacWilliamship lands and property, including Belcarra Castle where he resided with his family, and he was determined not to lose them. In 1600 when Sir Henry Docwra landed behind O'Donnell's lines in Lough Foyle and set up his rival, Niall Garv O'Donnell as chieftain in his place, the confederate leader could no longer support his protégé MacWilliam in Mayo. Seizing his chance Tibbott-ne-Long subsequently convened a meeting of all the Bourke septs at Rousakeera and conferred the MacWilliamship on his long-time ally, Granuaile's grandson, Richard Bourke, the son of the Devil's Hook.

To confer the MacWilliamship on a subordinate rather than assume the title himself was a shrewd move on Tibbott's part. He already possessed most of the lands and privileges pertaining to the title. If he was to maintain credence with the English, he could not be seen to assume a proscribed office. Moreover, by conferring the title on a lesser chieftain, he demonstrated that he had become, in effect, greater than the once all-powerful MacWilliam. The struggle for the ancient title of his ancestors in itself symbolised the final struggle being waged by the Gaelic world that had bred and sustained it through the centuries. Tibbott-ne-Long had moved on and declined the opportunity to be the last holder of a doomed office or the champion of the doomed world that it represented.

On 23 September 1601, Spanish troops under the command of Don Juan del Aquila, arrived to support the Ulster chieftains against the English. They landed, however, at Kinsale in the southernmost part of the country. The entire length of Ireland lay between them and their allies, O'Neill and O'Donnell in Ulster. In late October the Spaniards were besieged by an army, ostensibly English but in reality composed of as many Irish, commanded by Lord Mountjoy.

In Ulster Red Hugh O'Donnell mustered his army and in an incredible feat of endurance and military ability, outmarched and outmanoeuvred the English forces sent to bar his way to Kinsale. At the end of November his more cautious ally, Hugh O'Neill, also made the long journey south. With a combined army of 6,000, the two leaders besieged the besiegers.

At the beginning of December, leading an army of 300, Tibbott-ne-Long marched out of Mayo and also headed south. As he approached Kinsale, neither Mountjoy nor O'Neill knew with certainty on which side he intended to fight. At Kinsale, after months of vacillation, Tibbott-ne-Long finally showed his hand and fought alongside the victorious Mountjoy.

After Kinsale a new war for ownership of the land of Ireland commenced. Despite the defeat at Kinsale, at the beginning of the seventeenth century, most of the land of Ireland was still in Gaelic hands. With the collapse of the Gaelic system and the subsequent flight of O'Neill and O'Donnell in 1607, vast areas of Ulster lay open to exploitation by a new wave of English and Scottish planters, adventurers and entrepreneurs, armed with vague and suspect titles to the properties of the Gaelic chieftains. In this new war, waged with maps, quill and parchment, inquisitions and legal rhetoric, Tibbott-ne-Long's instinct for survival endured its greatest test. For the space of three decades he successfully competed within the framework of an alien legal system and increased his patrimony substantially, despite the Crown's suspicions and against the concerted efforts of the many English adventurers and speculators who sought to deny him. By mortgage, purchase, claim and counter-claim, by right of both Gaelic and English law, he amassed the largest estate in Mayo, mostly at the expense of his legally less astute relations, in particular the O'Malleys, various septs of the Bourkes and his foster family, the MacEvillys of Carra, whose castle of Kinturk eventually became his principal residence. After Kinsale he abandoned his seafaring activities to consolidate his position on land. The remains of his mother's fleet continued to be operated by her O'Malley relations into the middle of the new century but without the effectiveness or flamboyance of the 'Pirate Queen'.

Tibbott-ne-Long was knighted by the new king of England, James I, on 4 January 1603 in recognition of his 'loyal and valorous' service. He was styled Sir Tibbott (ne Longe) Bourke. The letters patent relating to his enoblement were preserved in Westport House. They are written in Latin on six pages of fine parchment and decorated with the de Burgo arms, Tibbott-ne-Long's personal arms and a portrait of King James I. In 1627 he was created Viscount Mayo by Charles I. Despite his royal honours, however, Tibbott's loyalty to the English crown continued to be suspect. Until his death at Kinturk castle in 1629, he continued to scheme and intrigue with exiled elements of the Gaelic resistance, against whom he had fought at Kinsale, and endured imprisonment and investigation by the English authorities in the process. Being the survivor he most certainly was, he managed to retain both his head and his newly-acquired lands and titles and, paradoxically, the esteem and loyalty of his Gaelic followers and neighbours. He is buried in Ballintubber Abbey, county Mayo. His death notice was registered at Athlone Castle:

The right Honorable sr Theobald Burke Kt viscount Burke of Mayo, deceased the 18 June 1629. He had to wife Maude, dr of Charles O'Connor Sligoe, by whome he had issue, the right Ho. Miles, Viscount Burke, David, Theobald, Richard, Mary, Onore and Margaret ...[4]

His half-brother and ally, Murrough-ne-Maor O'Flaherty, died at Bunowen Castle in Connemara in April 1626. According to his wishes he was buried in the Abbey of St Francis in Galway. Murrough-ne-Maor O'Flaherty predeceased his half-brother by three years. He died at Bunowen castle in April 1626 and was buried, according to his instructions, in the Abbey of St Francis in Galway, the city from where his O'Flaherty ancestors had once been debarred. In his will, (see appendices) by which he appointed Tibbott-ne-Long his executor, he provided for each of his eight sons and two daughters out of his large estate which stretched from Bunowen, north to Renvyle and south to Kilkieran. One of the stipulations of his will was the provision for 'my fifth son Patricke who is become a scholler, £20 when he is ready and determined to goe beyond the seas to studie, together with £10, everie year during his continuance beyond the seas.'[5] His eldest son, known as Murrough-na-Mart (of the Beeves), succeeded him and was knighted by the Lord Deputy, Sir Thomas Wentworth, in 1637. He was subsequently dispossessed of his estates by the Cromwellian confiscations in 1653 and his descendants were gradually reduced to the status of impoverished farmers on their former ancestral lands.

The descendants of Granuaile through the marriage of her daughter, Margaret O'Flaherty, to Richard Bourke, the Devil's Hook of Corraun, are unknown, as are her descendants through her eldest son, Owen O'Flaherty.

Tibbott-ne-Long's eldest son, Miles, succeeded him as Viscount of Mayo. Named after his foster father, Miles MacEvilly, whose lands and castles of Kinturk, Kilboynell (afterwards Castlebourke) and Manulla were by that time subsumed into the Viscount Mayo estate, like his father, Miles endured the continuing distrust of the English establishment. For a time he was confined at the Gatehouse at Westminster accused of plotting with elements of the Gaelic resistance movement overseas. In 1640 he played a nefarious role in the massacre of Protestant settlers at Shrule, on the borders of Mayo and Galway. His son, Theobald, the third viscount, who made a valiant attempt to avert the slaughter, was subsequently tried, found guilty and executed by the Cromwellians, more with an eye to his confiscated estates than to his alleged involvement in the crime. Theobald, the fourth viscount, was regranted part of his estates on the restoration of Charles II. By the time of the last acknowledged viscount, John Bourke, who died in 1767, the original Mayo estate, so deftly amassed by Tibbott-ne-Long, was reduced through confiscation and mortgage to Castlebourke and a few hundred acres of land.

On the death of the eighth Viscount Mayo, without a male heir, the title officially lay dormant. There is much evidence to suggest, however, that David Bourke, from Asgalan in the barony of Murrisk, a direct descendant of Richard, the fourth son of Tibbott-ne-Long, was the rightful claimant. His claim was supported by the depositions of the sister of the eighth viscount, the dowager countess of the seventh viscount and many of the retainers and friends of the family. To the doctor who attended him on his deathbed in 1790, David Bourke claimed to be the ninth Viscount Mayo. Richard Bourke, his uncle from Ballyhaunis, county Mayo, claimed as tenth viscount but had not the means to pursue his case through the courts. On his death, his son and heir, Michael Bourke of Lavalaroe, county Mayo, submitted additional sworn affidavits that he was 'the fourth cousin in the male line of collateral descent to the late John, lord Viscount Bourke of Mayo,'[6] but owing to his meagre means, his claim was not successful and he died sometime after 1814. The Viscount Mayo title was subsequently subsumed into the Earldom of Mayo, a more recent creation.

The descendants of Granuaile are mainly traceable through her Bourke line, and her bloodline is to be found among many pedigrees of both aristocrat and commoner in Ireland and Britain. Some of her descendants, like Granuaile herself, made an impact on their age. Her great-great-great grandaughters, Maria and Elizabeth Gunning, known as the 'gorgeous Gunnings' from Castlecoote, county Roscommon, in the eighteenth century took English society by storm with their beauty. One married the Earl of Coventry and secondly the Duke of Hamilton; the other married the Duke of Argyle.

In 1669 Granuaile's great-great-grandaughter, Maude Bourke, daughter of Theobald the third Viscount Mayo, married John

Browne of Westport. Their mansion, Westport House, was built near the old O'Malley fortress of Cathair-na-Mart, where Dónal-ne-Píopa, Granuaile's half-brother, once resided. In modern times Westport House was the first stately home in Ireland to open its doors to the public, and has since become one of Ireland's premier tourist attractions. The descendants of Maude Bourke and John Browne Granuaile's 14th great granddaughter continue to live on Westport House estate. In 2003 a life-size bronze sculpture of Granuaile was unveiled in the grounds.

Claiming a similar descent from Granuaile was the late award-winning film producer John Brabourne, married to the daughter of the late Lord Louis Mountbatten. With tragic perversity, their son, Nicholas, a fourteenth great-grandson in descent from Granuaile, was killed, together with his grandfather, grandmother and a young friend, when their fishing boat was blown apart by a terrorist bomb off Mulloughmore harbour in Sligo in 1979, in waters once traversed by his remarkable 16th century ancestor.

The descendants through Granuaile's O'Malley relatives, particularly her half-brother, Dónal-ne-Píopa, are less certain. Confiscation, deprivation and famine scattered the clan O'Malley throughout the world. Tracing individual O'Malley family branches back as far as the sixteenth century and unravelling their connections to Granuaile has been made more difficult by the passage of time and the lack of authentic records.

But O'Malleys everywhere can take pride in the fact that they originate from the same seafaring clan from the lordship of Umhall on the west coast of Ireland, and that they share a common heritage with the most famous member of the clan to bear the name O'Máille—Granuaile.

APPENDICES

1.   Manuscript Decipherments (I–XI)
2.   Poems and Songs
3.   Family Trees

APPENDIX 1.I

The Humble Peticone of Richard Bourke to His Wo.Ship Sir Nicholas Malby, Knight. Governor in Thomond, 22 April 1580

He most humbly beseechith the same in respect he hath fallen from his dewtie towards God and her Matie. And he and all his according theyrin to defect been attempted and plagged by your worship and her Mati's force under your chardge. And driven to flye into remote places with theyre goods and cattle whereby these his lands lye and are become waste. That it will pleas yr worship of yr great goodness as you have received him into grace without distress so likewise it will please you to graunt commission to deponent not only to call backe his followers with theyre goodes to inhabyte the country whereby her Matie may be assured of her rents and dewties and the deponent and followers theres without any assurances of theyre pay: but also that the said deponent may have commission to restore your peticonars to suche demaunds and challenge as he hath against any person or persons in that the county of Mayo. And that moreover yor peticonar may have yor wor.s commission to take upp suche dewties and demaunds from tyme to tyme as is dewe upon his followers of the baronies of Carrowe [Carra] Oweles and Irryes [Erris] as all by sea as land. The same to continue during suche tyme as he shall remayne dewtyful towards her Matie. And that no deponent may have to deale with him or his saving only suche a one as your wor. shall make choyse of. And according his most bounden he shall pray.

Richard + Bourke

Source: SPI 63/170 no. 62 (Public Record Office, London)
Deciphered from the original by the author

APPENDIX 1.II

Letter Patent Queen Elizabeth I, 14 April 1581

Elizabeth by the Grace of God, Queen of England, France and Ireland, defender of the Faith etc to all who receive this letter, greetings.

Know you that of our special grace, certain knowledge and free will, together with the advice and consent of our beloved and faithful counsellor Arthur Grey of Wylton, knight of our order of the Garter and our deputy general in our Kingdom of Ireland, and with the advice and consent of our Council in that kingdom we grant give authorize and confer upon our beloved subject Richard Bourke, alias Richard Inyeren Bourke, alias Mac William Eoghter Bourke that he be chief of his clan and seneschal of the feudal tenants and followers of our people and nation and of his own clans and their lands and tenements in our province of Connaght and of the border castles with their manors, lands, tents and hereditaments with their revenues and privileges which he now lawfully possesses in the said province. And that for the protection of the said castles, lands, tents and hereditaments and of the rest entrusted to him as well as for the protection of our subjects therein dwelling against enemies or rebels, invaders or plunderers, or violators or disturbers of our peace he may call to arms our subjects therein dwelling and lead them in pursuit as often as and whenever it shall be necessary for our service and the defence of these same our subjects and his own people and that he protect and advance our peace and good government and a similar life among our good subjects within the boundaries of his jurisdiction and that he be minister of our justice and laws within the same boundaries for as long as he occupies the office of our seneschal. Finally that he may tax, exact and levy within the limits of the said office (except for free church lands and waste land) his reasonable expenses whenever he shall be ordered to appear at Dublin, Athlone or Galway—by the chief of our ministers in the government of our said kingdom or by our lord president or governor or our councillors for the province of Connacht—for any cause relating to the said office of seneschal or in the interests of our subjects within the said boundaries or for any other reason for our service.

The said office, authority and the manors, castles, lands, tents, hereditaments and the rest above-mentioned shall belong as is fitting to the said Richard Bourke, alias Richard Inyeren during his natural life. Provided always that the said Richard shall meanwhile be well-affected to us, our heirs and successors and shall observe, do, pay, render and fulfil all and every condition, provision, agreement, article and clause specified and contained in the indenture annexed to this our letter patent and which are to be observed and fulfilled by the same Richard.

In witness whereof we have had this letter patent of ours drawn up. Our aforementioned deputy being witness thereto this 14 April in the 23rd year of our reign.

Source: Westport House Manuscripts
Translated from Latin

APPENDIX 1.III

Milly Mac Evilly His Deed of Kinturk, 1582

To all christiane people to whom this writtinge shall come to be heard read or seene, Meyle Mc Breoyne alias McEville chiefe of his name in the countie of Mayo gent. Sendeth greeting in our Lord God everlastinge. Knowe ye that I Meyle Mc Breoyne alias Mc Eville shall for and in consideration of a certaine some of money, bestowe, then seallinge and delivery hereof receved at and by the hand of Sr Richard Bourk alias Richard Ineryn otherwise McWilliam Bourk cheefe of his name of Ballyloughmask in the countie of Mayo, Knight, as also for divers other good causes and considerations me thereunto speceally movinge be the consent of my sones and cousins have given granted bargained sold enfeoffed and confirmed like as by these pr.nts. I doe give grant bargaine sell enfeoffe and confirme unto the said Sr Richard Bourk alias McWilliam Knight and his heires to the use and behooffe of my foster sonn Thibbitt Bourk one of the sons of the said Sr Richard Bourk and the heirs of his body lawfully begotten or to be begotten of the said Tybbott. The castle and Bawne and ten quarters of land to me belonginge of and in Kintourke viz. the half town of Kintourke Eighter and Kintourke Uaghter the four quarters of Ballyclay and the four quarters of Ballybonhane with thappurtenances. The castle Bawne and towne and eight quarters of land of Castlecarry and the four quarters of land of Ballykally with thappurtenances. The castle towne and barbican and foure quarters of land of beinge in the barony of Carry within the countey of Mayo aforesaid, together with all the messauges buildings orchards gardynes moores meddowes feedinge pastures woods and underwoodes wayes watter courses fishings emollements and other hereditaments whatsoever beinge or reputed to be part parcel member or apendant of or therefore granted. To have and to hold the premises before expressed granted and specified with thappurtances to the said Sr Richard Bourk Knight alias McWilliam and to the said Thibbott Bourk and to the heires of the body lawfully begotten or to be begotten of the said Thibbott Bourk his heires lawfully begotten and for want of such heires and assignes all and singular therefore granted promised with thappurtances to the said Sr Richard Bourk alias McWilliam Bourk Knight and his heires forever. To hold of the cheefe Lords of the fee by the services thereunto and accustomed and I the said Mylie Mc Breyone alias Mc Eville cheefe for my selfe my heires and assignes all and singular therefore granted promised with thappurtenances to the said Sr Richard Bourk alias Mc William Knight and to the said Thibbott Bourk and to his heires of his body lawfully begotten or to begotten in manner aforesaid against all manner of attacks shall save warrant acquit and defend forever by these pr.nsts. And further knowe yee that I the said Meyli mc Breyone alias Mc Eville cheefe has consented ordained and appointed my wellbeloved Gilleduf Mc Jonnock Mc Gibbon of the said countie of Mayo gent. my true and lawfull attorney fore me in my name in all and singular the pr.nts or unto any part thereof in the name of the whole to delyver the quiet and peaceable possession by levery and seisin to the said Sr Richard Bourk or to any other to—wordinge to the—of this deed. In witness wherof I have sett hiarunto my hand and seale the tynth day of May in the yeare of our Lord God aforesaide five hundred and eighty and two.

Beinge pr.sent at the signinge seallinge and deliverancy thereof and also at the deliverancy and seisin and possession by the within named Gilleduff Mc Jonnocke Mc Gibbon balliff and attorney to the within named Sr Richard Bourk Knight of the castle and Towne of Kinturk for and in the name of the whole and in the name of all and singullary the heritamente viz. the pr.ent within menconed according the purpot of this deed.

Source: Westport House Documents
Deciphered from the original by the author

APPENDIX 1.IV

Granuaile's Petition to Queen Elizabeth I, July 1593

To the Queen's Most Excellent Majesty

In most humble Wise showeth unto your most excellent Majestie your loyall and faithful subject Grany ny Mally of Conaght in your highness realm of Ireland:- that wheras by meanes of the continnual discord stirres and dissention that hertofore long tyme remained among the Irishrye especially in West Conaght by the sea side everie cheeftaine for his safeguard and maintenance and for the defence of his people, followers and countrye took armes by strong hand to make head against his neyburs which in like manner constrayned your highness fond subject to take armes and by force to maintaine her selfe and her people by sea and land the space of fortye yeares past. During which tyme she married Offlahertye being natural mother of his lawfull sone and heire nowe living and after his death married Mac William the cheefe of the Bourkes of West Conaght who died x yeares past, since which tyme she remained widowe and is likewise the mother of his lawfull sone and heyre nowe living. The countries and territories of which chieftains after the rude custome of their ancestors never yielded doweries or thirds to the ladies thereof, and the rents services and reservation of the same was not certayne but confused the people for yelding to the cheeftains whatever they would crave more than of right they aught to have. And now whereas by your gracious meanes the said province is reduced to that civil course that the cheeftaines freeholders or gents. hath compounded and is assigned what and how much he is to have; in which composition no order was taken for your fond subject what maintenance she aught to have of her former husbands lands and by the same is

151

restrayned to use her former course to her utter decay and ruine: In tender consideracion whereof and in regard of her great age she most humbly besechethe your Majestie if your princely bounty and liberaltye to grant her some reasonable maintenance for the little tyme she hath to lyve. And whereas your said subjects two sones are the lawfull heyres of the lands of there foresaid fathers whereof they nowe stand seized and possessed, that it would please your Royall Majestie to direct your gracious letters to your L. Deputy of your said realme willing him to accept a surrender at her hands of her said sones yelding to Your Majestie your heyrs and successors such yearly rents as conventiently such lands may yeld and they to hold the same by letters patents to them and ther heyres for ever and to grant the like for the lands of Walter Burgh Fitz Theobald Reogh and Shane Burke Mac William Mac Moiler cosen germaine to her said son. And lastly that it would please your Majestie to grant unto your said subject under your most gracious hand of signet free libertye during her lyve to envade with sword and fire all your highness enemyes whersoever they are or shall be without any interruption of any person or persons whatsoever. Thus shall your said subject according to her bounden duty ever remayne in all obedient alleagance to resist all remnants of rebellious enemies and pray continually for your Majesties long life and prosperous reygne.

Source: SPI 63/170 no. 204 (Public Record Office, London)
Deciphered from the original by the author

APPENDIX 1.V

The Eighteen 'Articles of Interrogatory', July 1593

TO BE ANSWERED BY GRANY NI MALY

1. Who was her father and mother?
2. Who was her first husband?
3. What sons she had by him? What be their names and where they live?
4. What countries they have to maintain them withal?
5. To whom they be married?
6. What kin was O'Flaherty her first husband to Sir Mourrough M'Ne Dough O'Flaherty that is here now at the court?
7. To answer the like question for her 2 husband and for his sons and their livings.
8. If she were to be allowed her dower, or thirds of her husband's living, of what value the same might be of?
9. Where upon the Composition of Connaught there hath been any provisions for the wives?
10. Whether it be not against the Customs of Ireland for the wives to have more after the deaths of their husbands than they brought with them?
11. How she hath had maintenance and living since her last husband's death?
12. Of what kindred is Walter Bourgh fitz Tibalds and Shane Bourke mc Moyler to her son?
13. What captains and countries lie next to her husband's possessions?
14. Who doth possess the house of Moriske upon the seaside in Owle O'Maly?

15. What lands doth McGibbon possess in that country?
16. Who doth possess the country named Carramore and Mayn Connell?
17. Who doth possess the island of Achill and Kill castle?
18. What kin was her last husband to Walter and Ulick Bourke?

ANSWERS OF GRANY NY MALLY TO THE ARTICLES

To the first

Her father was called Doodarro O Mailly sometime chieftain of the country called Opper Owle O Mailly now called the barony of Murasky her mother was called Margaret ny Mailly daughter to Conogher Omailly of the same country and family. The whole country of Owle O Mailly aforesaid have these islands vis. Inish Bofyne Cleria Inish Twirke Inish arke Caher Inishdalluff Davellen and other small islands of little value which and the rest of the mainland are divided into the towns to the number of twenty and to every town four quarter or ploughs of land is assigned; out of every such quarter of land is yearly paid to her Majesty ten shillings called the composition rent. There is also in Connaught a country called Owle Eighter, otherwise the Lower or Nether Owle, containing fifty towns at four quarters the town, yearly paying the same rent, whereof the Sept of the Mailles in general hath twenty towns, the Bourkes of Mac William country other twenty towns and the Earl of Ormond ten towns.

To the second

Her first husband was called Donell Ichoggy Offlaherty and during his life cheiftain of the Barony of Ballynehenssy, containing twenty-four towns at four quarters of land to every town paying yearly the composition rent aforesaid. After his death Teige Offlaherty the eldest son of Sir Morough now at court entered into Ballynehenssy afore said there did build a strong castle and the same with the demain lands thereof kept many years. Which Teige in the last rebellion of his father was slain.

To the third

She had two sons by her said first husband the eldest called Owen Offlahertie married Katherine Bourke daughter of Edmond Bourke of Castle Barry by her he had a son named Donell Offlahertie, now living which Owen all his lifetime remained a true subject to Her Majesty under the government of Sir Nicholas Malby while he lived and under Sir Richard Bingham until July 1586 at which time the Bourkes of the MacWilliams country and the sept of the Shoose [Joyce] began to rebel. The said Owen, according to Sir Richards special direction, did withdraw himself his followers and tenants, with all their goods and cattle into a strong island for their more and better assurance. Then having been sent against the said rebels five hundred soldiers under the leading of Captain John Bingham appointed by his brother Sir Richard Bingham as the lieutenant in those parts. When they missed both the rebels and their cattle they came to the mainland right against the said island calling for victualls; whereupon the said Owen came forth with a number of boats and ferried all the soldiers into the island where they were entertained with the best cheer they had. That night the said Owen was apprehended and tied with a rope with eighteen of his chief followers; in the morning the soldiers drew out of the island four thousand cows, five hundred stud mares and horses and a thousand sheep leaving the remainder of the poor men all naked within the island [they] came with the cattle and prisoners to Ballynehenssy afor said where John Bingham afor said stayed for their coming; that evening he caused the said eighteen persons without trial or good cause to be hanged among whom was hanged a gentleman of land and living called Thebault O Twohill being of the age of four score and ten years. The next night following a false alarm was raised in the camp in the dead of the night the said Owen was cruelly murdered having twelve deadly wounds and in that miserable sort he ended his years and unfortunate days—Captain William Mostyn now at court and Captain Merriman and Captain Mordant were of that company. Her second son called Moroghe Offlahertie now living is married to Honora Bourke daughter to

Richard Bourke of Derivillaghny in the Magheri Reagh within the county of Galway.

To the fourth
Moroghe her second son aforesaid and Donell son to her first son the aforesaid Owen murdered do possess and enjoy the fourth part of Barony of Ballynehenssy aforesaid unto them descended from their ancestors which is all the maintenance they have.

To the fifth
This is answered more at large to the third article.

To the sixth
Her first husband by the mother's side of Sir Moroghe now at court was his cousin germain and also cousins both being descended of one stock and root of nine degrees of consanguinity asunder.

To the seventh
Her second husband was called Sir Richard Bourke Knight alias McWilliam chief of the Bourkes of Nether or Low Connaught by him she had a son called Theobald Bourke now living he is married to Mewffe O'Connor sister to O'Connor Sligo now at court, his inheritance is about 40 quarters of land situated in the three baronies of Carry [Carra], Nether Owel and Galling [Gallen].

To the eighth
The countries of Connaught among the Irishry never yielded any thirds to any woman surviving the chieftain whose rent was uncertain for the most part extorted but now made certain by the composition and all Irish exactions merely abolished.

To the ninth
The Composition provided nothing to relieve the wife of any chieftain after his death wherein no mention is made of any such.

To the tenth

Among the Irishry the custom is that wives shall have but her first dowry without any increase or allowance for the same time out of mind it hath been so used and before any woman do deliver up her marriage portion to her husband she receives sureties for the restitution of the same in manner and form as she hath delivered it in regard that husbands through their great expenses especially chieftains at the time of their deaths have no goods to leave behind them but are commonly indebted; at other times they are divorced upon proof of precontracts; and the husband now and then without any lawful or due proceeding do put his wife from him and so bringeth in another; so as the wife is to have sureties for her dowry for fear of the worse.

To the eleventh

After the death of her last husband she gathered together all her own followers and with 1,000 head of cows and mares departed and became a dweller in Carrikhowlly in Borisowle parcel of the Earl of Ormond's lands in Connaught and in the year 1586 after the murdering of her son Owen the rebellion being then in Connaught Sir Richard Bingham granted her his letters of tuition against all men and wiled her to come and dwell under him, in her journey as she travelled she was encountered by the five bands of soldiers under the leading of John Bingham and thereupon she was apprehended and tied in a rope, both she and her followers at that instant were spoiled of their said cattle and of all that ever they had besides the same and brought to Sir Richard who caused a new pair of gallows to be made for her last funeral where she thought to end her days, she was let at liberty upon the hostage and pledge of one Richard Bourke otherwise called the Devil's Hook when he did rebel fear compelled her to fly by sea into Ulster and there with O'Neill and O'Donnell staid three months; her galleys by a tempest being broken. She returned to Connaught and in Dublin received her Majesty's pardon by Sir John Perrot six years past and so made free. Ever since she dwelleth in Connaught a farmers life very poor bearing cess and paying Her Majesty's composition rent, utterly did she give over her former trade of maintenance by sea and land.

To the twelfth
Walter Bourke FitzThebalt and Shane Bourke FitzMeiller are cousins germain removed of one side vis. Walter son to Thebault, son to Meiller son to the said Walter Faddy. Thebault Bourke mentioned in the seventh article and borne by Grany Ny Mailly is son to Sir Richard Bourke her last husband, which Sir Richard was brother to the said Walter Faddy.

To the thirteenth
The country of her first husband is situated between Owle O'Mailley on the north west part, Mac William's country to the north east towards the country of Sligo, Sir Moroghe Offlaherties country on the east side towards Galway and the great bay of Galway on the south.

To the fourteenth
The castle town and lands of Morrisky is possessed by Owen M'Thomas O'Mailley now chieftain by the name of O'Mailley.

To the fifteenth
The Mac Gibbons have no lands by inheritance in any part of the country; farmers they are at will both to the Bourkes and to the O'Maillies.

To the sixteenth
She doth not know or understand Caremore or Moinconnell.

To the seventeenth
The island of Ackill is occupied by some of the Mailleys as tenants to the Earl of Ormond, as for Kill Castle, she knoweth no town of that name.

To the eighteenth
Her last husband had two brothers Walter and Ulligge [Ulick]

Bourke both died before she married Sir Richard Bourke, her said husband, their father was called David Bourke.

A set of 18 questions by Lord Burghley, the Lord Treasurer of England, dated July 1593 with appropriate answers by Granuaile.

Source: SPI 63/170/63 (Public Record Office, London)
Deciphered from the original by the author

APPENDIX 1.VI

Sir Richard Bingham to the Lord Treasurer, July 1593

It may please yo.r most honourable good L: yo.r hono.rs lrs [letters] of the xi and the xiii of Julye I have recevyed the first fower dayes agoe and the laste but yesterdaye and in all humbleness do answere to the particularyes hereof as the trewth is in this sort following viz. I was bolde to advertise yo.r hono.r of Sr. Morough Oflahertie & Grany ne Malye because I knew their going into England was drawen on of purpose to complayne againste myself albeit sithence (as it should seeme) they have better considered with themselves. And although I am at a point (I thancke God) w.th them and all the rest so they say no more than the trouth yet being so well acquainted w.th the practise of this Countrye and shamles disposicion of the worst sorte of their people I thought it convenient both for yo.r hono.rs better informacion of theis two persons and defence of my owne innocency to write my humble letters to yo.r hono.r in sorte as I did w.th humble desire of yo.r L. good and most honourable acceptance ... for so long as Granye Ne Malye and he were of power to make any sturres the state was nev.r trobled w.th theyr complaints but now that they are pulled dowen and forced in speight of their hartes to submit themselves to her Ma.ts lawes they pretend many wronges and [are] not ashamed to aske recompence.

Yo.r hono.rs second letter toucheth Grany Ne Malye and her sute to her Ma.tie that her two sonnes alledged by her to be in holde should be spaired from execucion etc and in the former letter mencion was made of a brother of hers called Donell O piper Right honourable she hath a sonn called Moraghe Ne Mayre Oflahertie a chiefe man in the barony of Ballinahensie within Eir

Conaught w.ch she had by a former husbande called Donall O
Flaherty and her other sonne by the said husband was slayne in
rebellion vii yeres agoe this Morough is held for the best subject
in all that parte of Eirconaught although till of late yeres he was
a barbarous and wilde person. In the last Accion against the
Burks this tyme twelve monthes he came by boat w.th such other
shippinge as I had prepaired against the Burks having two small
Gallies after the countrey manner manned w.th his owne people
and behaved himself very well in that service. In requital whereof
his aforesaid Mother Grany (being out of charity w.th her sonne
for serving her Ma.tie) manned out her Navy of galleys and
landed in Ballinehenchie where he dwellethe burned his Towen
and spoiled his people of their Cattayle and goods and murdered
3 or 4 of his men w.ch offered to make resistance this was the last
noteable Act w.ch she did in particular I could set dowen many
more [M.r Fraunces Shaen can report this and much more] but
that I hope this shalbe sufficient to gyve yo.r hono.r Knowledge
of her naughty disposicion towards the state having bin advertised
from thence that some in Court hath commended her for doing
her Ma.tie good service but in hope of her amendment hereafter
I forbeare to write any more of her Accions now assuringe myself
if she contynew nev.r so ill mynded she shall not be liable to do
much for how great soev.r any may make her w.ch knoweth her
not I will nev.r aske but a boat of xxx tonnes to beate her and all
the boates and Galeyes belonging to the county of Mayo and [w.th
gods assistance] dryve her and all their fleet into the sea.
Then the sayd Grany had a sonne by S.r Richard Burke alias
McWilliam named Tibbot Burke who is now in holde here in
Athlone and a daughter who is wife to the nothable Tratoure the
Devills hooke and the cause of Tibbotts apprehension was this. In
may last when Magwire burnt Ballimote my brother S.r George
toke one Albenagh a man of Magwires who he detayneth yet in
prison and this Albenagh amongst other thinges confessed how
that Tibbot Burke had even then written a lettre in Irishe to Brian
oge O'Rourke to raise sturres in the Breny [Breffni] and to hold
out but two monthes and he would undertak that the banished

rebell the Devills hoke and the rest should retourne to Mayo againe and with his help mak warres there w.ch letter the sayd prisoner affirmith he hard red to Magwire in a place between him and Brien oge O Rourke and this is all the matter I knowe against Tibbot Burke sithence the generall accion for w.ch he hath his pardon yet cause sufficient for me to lay holde on him knowing by long experience the bad affeccion of theis low Burks speciallie the sept of Ulick whereof he and his [step] brother Edmund are now the chief this Tibbot both speakith and writith English being brought up a while in my brother S.r George howse and is marryed to Donogh Oconnors Sister and in respect of his Cyvill behaviour above the rest he hath had of late the whole doing of thinges in that parte of Mayo myself willing ynough to favoure him the best I might and if her Ma.tie please to pardon him some such assurance may be taken of him by way of bonds as he is liable to give and so inlarge him. But her other sonn was nev.r meddled w.th all or otherwise reputed by her will sithence his last submission and considering the present tyme and how all the sept of the Omayles and the worst sept of the Burks called the Sept of Ulick were wholie at Tibbotts comaundent I could do no less then restrayne him of libertye not hastening him to any tryall unless further matter had appeared then yet is knowen to me and nevr.theles I holde him hereby touched in the highest degree. And her brother Donell Opiper was apprehended 6 or 7 monthes agoe for conspiring new matters of treason viz the murdering of some souldie.rs w.ch were there placed in ward in that Countrey but if her Ma.tie like the same he may be pardoned upon the like security for his good behavoure hencefourth. The said Tibbot hath the chiefe doing in the half of the barony of Owles OMalye and the like in the whole Barrony of Borowshowle the one barony conteyning xx Towens allowinge iiij.or quarters of land to every Towen and the other barony xxxij Towens wherof the Erle of Ormonde hath x Towens free and so both the Barronyes contagne 168 qrs of land charg able w.th the Compisicion w.ch maketh 84 li per annum the Countrie of Eir Conaught w.ch is the Oflahertyes countrye was charged w.th 150 li per annum the whole and god willing at this next colleccion I will make out a perfect booke of the Composicion rent by the severall barronyes throughout the province and for each Countye w.ch notes of the chiefe men in the sayd Barronyes and will send the same to yo.r hono.r for yo.r L. satisfaction in that behalf.

Now right honourable how her Ma.tie might consider Grany OMaly w.th somewhat out of her former livings I knowe not unless it be by allowing her the thirds of both the livings w.ch her sayd husbands lefte their sonnes and I have nev.r harde her complayne of either of them or do I think they will see her want themselves having it. What course yo.r hono.r shall please I shall holde towards her and the rest I am in all duty most willing to performe the same having many tymes tried to reclame them by lenity and faire meanes and when they conforme themselves and begin once to live quietly as becomith Subjects I never restrayne them of any lawfull and convenient favoure being most desirous of peace and some quiet dayes …

Source: SPI 63/171 no. 62 (Public Record Office, London)
Deciphered from the original by the author

APPENDIX 1.VII

Petition of Granuaile to The Right Honourable Lo. Burghley, Lord High Treasurer of England, September 1593

The humble petition of Granny ny Maylly

In most humble manner beseecheth your Honourable lord, your poor suppliant Granny ny Maylly where the Queens most excellent Matie. hir gracious clemencie and pardon hath promised hir hir letters to Sir Richard Bingham for the delivery of her sonne who hath lately since her cominge from thence confined to prison by the sd Sir Richard. And for as much my very good Ld. as the poor youth of the countrey are so extreamely used as they are most commonly executed before they be justly tried or ther cause hearde whereof she humblie beseecheth your hon. Ld. And since her cominge there that yt may please your Ld to graunt her your letters to the said Sir Richard willinge hym so that your suppliants sonne maye take no harme in body or goods untyll her Maties pleasure be further known. And shee shall praye your lordships good health.

Source: SPI 63/171 no. 44 (Public Record Office, London)
Deciphered by the author

APPENDIX 1.VIII

Queen Elizabeth I to Sir Richard Bingham, September 1593

Where our Treasurer of England by his letters in July last, did inform you of the being here of three several persons of that Our province of Connaught under your charge, that is Sir Morogh O'Flaherty, knight, Grany ne Maly and Roobuck French, requiring to understand your opinion of every of them concerning their suits; we perceive by your late letters of answer what your opinion is of them and their cause. But where Grany ne Maly hath made humble suit to us for our favour towards her sons Morogh O'Flaherty and Tibbott Burk, and to her brother Donnell O'Piper, that they might be at liberty, we perceive by your letters that her eldest son Morogh O'Flaherty is no trouble but is a principal man of his country, and as a dutiful subject hath served us when his mother, being then accompanied with a number of disorderly persons did with her 'galleys' spoil him: and therefore by you favoured and so we wish you to continue. But the second son Tibbott Burk, one that hath been brought up civilly with your brother and can speak English, is by you justly detained because he hath been accused to have written a letter to Bryan O'Rork, the late traitor's son, though it cannot be fully proved but is by him utterly denied: and for her brother Donald, he hath been imprisoned 7 months past being charged to have been in company of certain that killed some soldiers in a ward. But for these two you think they may be both dismissed upon bonds for their good behaviour, wherewith we are content, so as the old woman may understand we yield thereto in regard of her humble suit; so that she is hereof informed and departeth with great thankfulness and with many most earnest promises that she will, as long as she lives, continue a dutiful subject, yea, and will employ all her power to offend and prosecute any offender against Us. And further, for the pity to be had of this aged woman, having not by the customs of the Irish any title to any livelihood or position or portion of her two husbands' lands, now being a widow, and yet her sons enjoying their father's lands, we require you to deal with her sons in our name to yield to her some maintenance for her living the rest of her old years which you may with persuasion assure them that we shall therein allow of them and you also shall with your favour in all their good causes protect them to live in peace to enjoy their livelihoods. And this we do write in her favour as she now sheweth herself dutiful, although she hath in former times lived out of order, as being charged by Our Treasurer with the evil usage to her son that served us dutifully. She hath confessed the same with assured promises by oath to continue most dutiful, with offer, after her aforesaid manner, that she will fight in our quarrel with all the world.

From the Queen
Drafted by Lord Burghley
Source: Cecil Papers no.169/128, Hatfield House

APPENDIX 1.IX

Granuaile's Petition to The Right Honourable The Lord
Treasurer of England, April 1595

May it please your honourable good Lordshipp Grany Ny Mailly
of Conaght in her Majesties Realm of Ireland widowe. Whereas
accordinge her earnest promes made in September 1593 shee
beinge then at Court to continue a dutiful subject to the Quenes
most excellent Majestie, sethens which tyme shee procured all
her sons, Cusens and followers of the Mailles with a number of
gallies (whereof some were made and built after her last return)
fournished with menn and victwelles at their own chardges,
accompanied with Capten Strittes and his band of souldiers to
repaire to the sease, wher in certaine illandes eighteen of the
chiefest of the Bourkes here under named, being proclaimed
traitors and a great number of souldiers, came to that parte of
the country where your suppliant, her sons, cusens and followers,
dwelled, and ther did place and cesse themselves taking up meat
and drinke after their own serving and sixe pens per diem for
every souldier, and four pens per diem for his mann, where
they do remain in all these seaven monthes, without any cause
of service in that part of the counytey to be dun. But if privat
respect impoverished the poore enhabitantes: wasted the countrey
disabled them to serve her Majestie, diminished her heighnesses
rentes and inforced your suppliant and the rest (being not hable
to sustain the burthen of that cesse and to pay the said rent) to
abandon and leave the countrey and to withdrawe themselves into
the province of Mounster, wher they do remaine in great distresse;
which cesse is contrarie to the couvenauntes on her Majesties
behalf in discharge whereof your suppliant and the rest with all the

inhabitants of Conaght have yielded to pay unto her heighness that yearlie rent by the name of the compossission rent. In regard of all which and that your suppliant, her sonne, cusens and followers will serve with a hondreth menn at their owne chardges at sease upon the coaste of Ireland in her Majesties warres upon all occasions every yeere from eister till mighelmas, and ever hafter to continue dutifull unto her Majestie, as true and faythfull subjectes ought to do; most humbly do beseech your Honorable lordship, to be a meane to the Quenes most excellent Majestie to accept a surrender of your suppliants sonnes and cusens, of all their maners, castles, illandes, townes, lands and hereditamentes in Conaght aforesaid to be immediately holden from her Majestie her heirs and successors, in maner and form, as in the schedall herunto anexed is sett down, and to that effect to grant her gratous letters to the Lord Deputie of Ireland upon the acceptance of the said surrenders to pass the same over to your suppliants sons and cusens, under the great seale of that Realm and to call befor him the said William Fieldy and finding the surmise true to take present order as your supliantes sons cusens and followers may be suffered to inhabit and dwell upon their ancient patrimony and inheritance paing the said rentes and other duties comprised in the indentures past and confirmed in her Majesties behalf and all the lordes and Chieftains, gentlemen and friholders of Conaght aforesaid. And your suppliant her sons and the rest will not onely put their lives at all tymes in daunger to the advancement of her heighness service but also pray for your honourable lordship's successe longe to lyve in all happiness.

Endorsed by Lord Burghley: Letter to Ormond to mye by Grany Maly
Source: SPI 63/179. no. 36 (Public Record Office, London)
Deciphered from the original by the author

APPENDIX 1.X

Petition of Grany ny Mally to the Lord Treasurer, 5 May 1595

To the right honourable and my very good lord high treasurer of England.

Right Honorable and my very good Lo. maye it hath pleased her Matie. At my last beinge here by her highness letters to Sr Richard Bingham to demand hime to take present order that I might posses and injoie the third parte of the lands and comodities of MacWilliam and O'Flahertie as lawful wife unto each of them so it is right honourable that I cane not have nor can injoie the same by meenes of Sir Richard Binghams hard dealinge. I therefore most humblie beseeche your honours to be a meynes to her Matie to addres mye her highness letters to the Lo. Deputie to put me in the possession of the third parte of the said mac William and O'Flahertie my late husbands and lyvinge and that likewise I may lyve secure of my life which hath been attempted sundrie tymes be the said Sr Richard Bingham his brethren and others by his direcsion, humbly I beg your Treas.'s favourable letters in me owne and me sonnes behalf to the Lo. Deputie and to Sr Richard Bingham so cravinge pardon for my contynuall boldness … the living God to blesse and preserve yor Lord.

Source: SPI 63/179 (Public Record Office, London)
Deciphered from the original by the author

APPENDIX 1.XI

Surviving part of a deposition made in the Court of Chancery in 1626 in a dispute over ownership of lands in the Barony of Murrisk between Sir Theobald Bourke (son and heir of Grace O'Malley) and the O'Malleys

Rejoinder of Sir Theobald (Tibbot-ne-Long) Bourke

... when the premises descended to Conor Oge O'Malley as son and heir to the said Conor, who was accordingly seised and died so seised leaving issue only a son and a daughter: vizt Dowdarra mc Connor O'Mally and Margarett, after which the said Dowdarra Mc Connor O'Mally entered and was seised and died so seised without heirs of his body lawfully begotten, after which the said premises descended and came to the said Margarett ny Connor og O'Mally as sister and heir, who accordingly entered and was seised and died so seised when the premises came to Grany ny Mally, the defendant's mother, as dau. and sole heir to the said Margarett, who accordingly entered and was seised and being so seised by good conveyance conveyed the premises to the defendant who according entered and is seised thereof, except of the part thereof as before in the answer excepted. He denies that the moiety of the lands in the bill descended and came to Hugh O'Mally as son and heir to Conor, son and heir to Melaghlin O'Mally as in the bill is surmised, for defendant avers and hopes to prove that the said Hugh supposed to be son and heir of Dowdarra Mc Connor was a bastard begotten and born out of wedlock upon the body of one ... reputed a common whore and never married unto the said Dowdarra, or that the other moiety of the lands descended and came to complt. as son and heir to Teig Mally, son and heir to John

O'Mally, son and heir to Cormacke, son and heir to be one of the sons and coheirs (according the custom of gavelkind then used in Connaght) to Melaghlin O'Mally of Mogher as in the said bill is untruly suggested …

Source: Chancery Bills (Parcels R-2 no. R.63 p.11), National Archives of Ireland
Deciphered from the original by the author

APPENDIX 1.XII

Abstract of the will, dated 13 April 1626, of Morrogh-na-Moyre O'Flaherty of Bunowen

In the name of god, Amen, I Morrogh-Na-Moyre O'Flahertie of Bunowen in the baronie of Ballinahinch within the County of Galway, Esquire ... do make my last will and Testament in manner and form followinge: First, I bequeathe my soule to God Almightie, and my bodie to the grave to be buried amongst my ancestors in St. Frances' Abbey neere Galway. I bequeath, and my said will is, that all my castles, manors and lands heretofore estated to my eldest sonne and heire Murrogh-na-Mart O'Flahertie, shall be absolutelie in the said Murrogh, his heirs and assigns for ever; and all the castles and lands heretofore estated to my second sonne Edmond O'Flahertie, shall be absolutelie to him and his heirs and assigns for ever. Item, that my third sonne Bryen O'Flahertie and his heirs shall have the Cleggan, excepting only the Aiery and hawks upon Barnanoran reserved to the said Morrogh-na-Mart. Item, that my married wife Onora Flahertie alias Bourke shall have three quarters and a half of (the lands of) Ballindoone whereupon the Castle and town of Bunowen stands, and the half quarter of Bally mc Enilly (Ballyconnelly) thereinto adjoining, without rente, and after her decease (the said lands) to be and remaine to the said Morrogh-na-Mart. Item, that mee fourthe sonne Teige O'Flahertie shall have to him and his heires the quarter of Kilkieran and Iwniscrevar out of the lands allotted to Morrogh, and that Teige shall have no power to alienate or mortgadge the said lands without the license of the said Morrogh-na-Mart. Item that my second sonne Edmond shall pass an estate into my sixth sonne Huegh and his heires of the quarter of Ballinikille with a provisio that the said Hugh shall not alienate or mortgage or sell without the license of Edmond or his heires. My will is that my said children, Edmond, Brian, Teige and Hugh and their heires shall yearly pay to Morrogh-na-Mart and his heires 3 shillings out of every quarter for ever, and that they and their heires shall answer all suits and services due to the manors of Bunowen and Ballinahinse, and from henceforth shall be obedient to the said Morrogh. Item, that my said sonne and heir Morrogh and the rest of my sonnes Edmond and Bryan, and my said wife Onora, shall in one entire payment paie to my fifth sonne Patricke who is become a scholler £20 when he is ready and determined to go beyond seas to studie, together with £10, everie yeare during his continuance beyond the seas. Item, that my daughters Soragh O'Flahertie and Owna ne Flahertie shall have such portions for their preferment in marriadge out of all the lands allotted to my said three eldest sonnes, proportionately as to the discretion of Sir Tybbot Bourke Knt. or his sonne and heire Myles Bourke and Sir John Bourke Knt. Calling to their assistance two or more of my nearest friends in Galway as shall be thought fit ... Item, I give to my said wife Onara all my plate, cowes, garrans and sheep with my household stuffe, besides her third of all my lands. In witness I have hereinto putt me hand and seale on the 13th day of April in the year of Our Lord God 1626.

Morrogh-Na-Moyre O'Flahertie
Source: Galway Archaeological and Historical Society, Vol. II, App. A, p. 54

APPENDIX 1.XIII

Extract from Letters Patent of Charles I conferring the title Viscount Mayo on Tibbott-ne-Long

As we are aware that our beloved Kingdom of Ireland has won very great renown both in the time of our father of very happy memory and in our own; and more than in proceeding ages has advanced both in civilisation and in wealth; while we acknowledge (this) singular blessing of God, so we are very pleased that such an opportunity has been given us whereby a tribute of a distinguished Chief may be made to his own subjects; especially as among other things which are of much importance to the State for our own and our subjects welfare from that (State). Very few men have sprung to fame who could suffer (more) in proportion to extent of their possessions, and could merit greater marks of distinction in accordance with the nobility of their birth and the fame of their heroic virtue. Wherefore, as Theobaldus Burke a gilded Knight, sprung from a sometime illustrious stock in England has won fame not only by reason of his broad acres (Late fundiis) and the nobility of his origin, but especially by reason of his sincere fidelity towards us and our predecessors, and by reason of his warlike valour; the one of which was revealed in his immovable constancy of mind, even when the Kingdom was ablaze with internal conflagration; the other by his daring exploits against the Spaniards when they landed not so very long ago; we think it right and that on a double title we should bring back the reward of a worthy subject and one who has ever deserved right well of his chief.

Now as there can be found nothing more noble and distinguished than Titles of Honour by which Chiefs can and are wont both to reward their subjects who have deserved well for previous exploits, and to urge them on to higher things – because too they remain for future ages an indelible mark of Kingly favour and of a subject's valour, we of our Kingly favour and munificence have decided to enrol the said Theobaldus among the number of the Peers of our Kingdom of Ireland and to promote him to the rank of a hereditary Viscount. Let ye know therefore, that we, by virtue of (these) aforesaid (i.e. dispatches) attending the said Theobaldus with our continued favour, wishing to compensate and glorify with a title of honour his favours and good works in this our said Kingdom of Ireland, of our special favour ....

Translated from Latin
Source: Lodge's Peerage, Vol. IV, p. 236

APPENDIX 2

Poems and Songs

Granuaile

There stands a tower by the Atlantic side
A grey old tower, by storm and sea-waves beat
Perch'd on a cliff, beneath it yawneth wide
A lofty cavern of yore a fit retreat
For pirates galleys; altho', now, you'll meet
Nought but the seal and wild gull; from that cave
A hundred steps do upwards lead your feet
Unto a lonely chamber!—Bold and brave
Is he who climbs that stair, all slippery from the wave.

I sat there on an evening. In the west,
Amid the waters, sank the setting sun:
While clouds, like parting friends, about him prest,
Clad in their fleecy garbs, of gold and dun;
And silence was around me—save the hum,
Of the lone and wild bee, or the curlew's cry.
And lo! Upon me did a vision come,
Of her who built that tower, in days gone by;
And in that dream, behold! I saw a building high.

A stately hull—lofty and carved the roof—
Was deck'd with silken banners fair to see.
The hanging velvet, from Genoa's woof,
And wrought with Tudor roses curiously;
At its far end did stand a canopy,
Shading a chair of state, on which was seen
A ladye fair, with look of majesty,
Amid a throng, 'yclad in costly sheen—
Nobles and gallant Knights proclaim her England's Queen.

The sage Elizabeth; and by her side
Were group'd her counsellors, with calm, grave air,
Burleigh and Walsingham, with others, tried
In wisdom and in war, and sparkling there,
Like Summer butterflies, were damsels fair,
Beautiful and young: behind a trusty band
Of stalwart yeomanry, with watchful care,
The portal guard, while nigher to its stand
Usher and page, ready to ape with willing hand.

A Tucket sounds, and lo! There enters now
A strange group, in saffron tunics drest:
A female at their head, whose step and brow
Herald her rank, and, calm and self possest,
Onward she came, alone through England's best,
With careless look, and bearing free yet high,
Tho' gentle dames their titterings scarce represt,
Noting her garments as she passed them by;
None laughed again who met that stern and flashing eye.

Restless and dark, its sharp and rapid look
Show'd a fierce spirit, prone a wrong to feel,
And quicker to revenge it. As a book,
That sun-burnt brow did fearless thoughts reveal;
And in her girdle was a skeyne of steel;
Her crimson mantle, a gold brooch did bind;
Her flowing garments reached unto her heel;
Her hair-part fell in tresses unconfined,
And part, a silver bodkin did fasten up behind.

'Twas not her garb that caught the gazer's eye—
Tho' strange, 'twas rich, and, after its fashion, good—
But the wild grandeur of her mien—erect and high.
Before the English Queen she dauntless stood,
And none her bearing there could scorn as rude;
She seemed as one well used to power—one that hath

Dominion over men of savage mood,
And dared the tempest in its midnight wrath,
And thro' opposing billows cleft her fearless path.

And courteous greeting Elizabeth then pays,
And bids her welcome to her English land
And humble hall. Each looked with curious gaze
Upon the other's face, and felt they stand
Before a spirit like their own. Her hand
The stranger raised—and pointing where all pale,
Thro' the high casement, came the sunlight bland,
Gilding the scene and group with rich avail;
Thus, to the English Sov'reign, spoke proud 'Grana Wale'.

Queen of the Saxons! From the distant west
I come; from Achill steep and Island Clare,
Where the wild eagle builds 'mid clouds, his nest,
And Ocean flings its billows in the air.
I come to greet you in your dwelling fair.
Led by your fame—lone sitting in my cave.
In sea-beat Donna—it hath reached me there,
Theme of the minstrel's song; and then I gave
My galley to the wind, and crossed the dark green wave.

'Health to thee, ladye!'—let your answer be
Health to our Irish land; for evil men
Do vex her sorely, and have buklar'd thee
Abettor of their deeds; lyeing train,
That cheat their mistress for the love of gain,
And wrong their trust—aught else I little reck,
Alike to me, the mountain and the glen—
The castle's rampart or the galley's deck;
But thou my country spare—your foot is on her neck.

Thus brief and bold, outspake that ladye stern,
And all stood silent thro' that crowded hall;

While proudly glared each proud and manly kern
Attendant on their mistress. Then courtly all,
Elizabeth replies, and soothing fall
Her words, and pleasing to the Irish ear—
Fair promises—that she would soon recall
Her evil servants. Were these words sincere?
That promise kept? Let Erin answer with a tear!

O'Hart: *Irish Pedigrees*, vol. ii, p. 675 (from the Irish)

Grana Weal

O thou that are sprung from the flow'r of the land,
Whose virtues endear and whose talents command;
When our foemen are banished, how then wilt thou feel
That the King of the right shall espouse Grana Weal!

O'er the high hills of Erin what bonfires shall blaze,
What libations be pour'd forth!—What festival days!—
What minstrels and monks with one heart-pulse of zeal,
Sing and pray for the King and his own Grana Weal!

The monarch of millions is riding the sea,
His revenge cannot sleep, and his guards will not flee;
No cloud shall the pride of our nobles conceal,
When the foes are dispersed that benight Grana Weal.

The mighty in thousands are pouring from Spain,
The Scots, the true Scots shall come back again;
To far-distant exile no more shall they steal,
But waft the right King to his fond Grana Weal.

Raise your hearts and exult, my beloved at my words,
Your eyes to your King, and your hand to your swords!—

The Highlands shall send forth the bonneted Gael,
To grace the glad nuptials of Grana Weal.

And Louis, and Charles and the heaven-guided Pope,
And the King of the Spaniards shall strengthen our hope;
One religion—one kindred—one soul shall they feel,
For our heart enthroned Exile and Grana Weal.

With weeping and wailing, and sorrow and shame—
And anguish of heart that no pity dare claim;
The craven English churls shall all powerless kneal
To the home-restored Stuart and Grana Weal.

Our halls will rejoice with friendship and cheer,
And our hearts be as free from reproach as from fear;
The hungry adventurer shall pine from the meal,
He long lapped from the life-stream of Grana Weal.

Ah! Knowest thou the maiden all beauteous and fair,
Whom her merciless foes have left plundered and bare?
The force of my emblem too well cant thou feel,
For that suffering lorn one is our Grana Weal.

But the nobles shall bring back the true king again
And justice long slighted will come in his train;
The bullets shall fly—and the cannons shall peal—
And our Charles victorious espouse Grana Weal.

James Hardiman: *Irish Minstrelsy*, vol. ii, p. 65

Grace O'Malley

She left the close-air'd land of trees,
And proud MacWilliam's palace,
For clear, bare Clare's health-salted breeze,
Her oarsmen and her galleys
And where, beside the bending strand
The rock and billow wrestle
Between the deep sea and the land
She built her island Castle.

The Spanish captain, sailing by
For Newport, with amazement
Beheld the cannon'd longship lie
Moor'd to the lady's casement,
And, covering coin and cup of gold
In haste their hatches under,
They whisper'd "Tis a pirate's hold;
She sails the seas for plunder.'

But no: 'twas not for sordid spoil
Of barque or sea-board borough
She plough'd, with unfatiguing toil,
The fluent-rolling furrow;
Delighting, on the broad back'd deep,
To feel the quivering galley
Strain up the opposing hill, and sweep
Down the withdrawing valley:

Or, sped before a driving blast,
By following seas uplifted,
Catch, from the huge heaps heaving past,
And from the spray they drifted
And from the winds that toss'd the crest
Of each wide-shouldering giant,
The smack of freedom and the zest
Of rapturous life defiant.

For, oh the mainland time was pent
In close constraint and striving,
So many aims together bent
On winning and on thriving;
There was no room for generous case,
No sympathy for candour:—
And so she left Burke's buzzing trees,
And all his stony splendour.

For Erin yet had fields to spare
Where Clew her cincture gathers
Isle-gemmed; and kindly clans were there,
The fosterers of her fathers:
Room there for careless feet to roam
Secure from minions' peeping
For fearless mirth to find a home
And sympathetic weeping;

And generous ire and frank disdain
To speak the mind, nor ponder
How this in England, that in Spain,
Might suit to tell; as yonder,
Where daily on the slippery dais
By thwarting interests chequer'd
State gamesters played the social chess
Of politic Clanrickard.

Nor wanting quite the lovely isle
In civic life's adornings:
The Brehon's Court, might well beguile
A learned lady's mornings.
Quaint through the clamorous claim, and rude
The pleading that convy'd it,
Right conscience made the judgment good,
And loyal love obey'd it.

And music was sweeter far
For ears of native nurture,
Than virginals at Castlebar
To tinkling touch of courtier,
Where harpers good in hall struck up
The planxty's gay commotion,
Or pipers scream'd from pennon'd poop
Their piobrach over ocean.

And sweet, to see, their ruddy bloom
Whom ocean's friendly distance
Preserved still unenslaved; for whom
No tasking if existence
Made this one rich and that one poor,
In gold's illusive treasure,
But all, of easy life secure,
Were rich in wealth of leisure.

Rich in the Muse's pensive hour,
In genial hour for neighbour,
Rich in young mankind's happy power
To live with little labour;
The wise, free way of life, indeed,
That still, with charm adaptive,
Reclaims and tames the alien greed,
And takes the conqueror captive.

Nor only life's unclouded looks
To compensate its rudeness;
Amends there were in holy books,
In offices of goodness,
In cares above the transient scene
Of little gains and honours,
That well repaid the Island Queen
Her loss of urban manners.

Sweet, when crimson sunsets glow'd,
As earth and sky grow grander,
Adown the grass'd, unechoing road
Atlantic ward to wander,
Some Kinsman's humbler hearth to seek,
Some sick-bed side, it may be,
Or, onward reach, with footsteps meek,
The low, grey, lovely, abbey:

And, where stories stone beneath
The guise of plant and creature,
Had fused the harder lines of faith
In easy forms of nature;
Such forms, or tell the master's pains
'Mong Roslin's carven glories,
Or hint the faith of Pictish Thanes
On standing stones of Forres;

The Branch; the weird cherubic Beasts;
The Hart by hounds o'ertaken;
Or, intimating mystic feasts,
The self-resorbent Dragon;—
Mute symbols, though with power endow'd
For finer dogmas' teaching,
Than clerk might tell to carnal crowd
In homily or preaching;—

Sit; and while heaven's refulgent show
Grew airier and more tender,
And ocean gleaming floor below
Reflected loftier splendour,
Suffused with light, of lingering faith
And ritual lights reflection,
Discourse of birth, and life, and death,
And of the resurrection.

But chiefly sweet from morn to eve,
From eve to clear-eyed morning,
The presence of the felt reprieve,
From strangers' note and scorning:
No prying, proud, intrusive foes
To pity and offend her:—
Such was the life the lady chose,
Such choosing, we commend her.

Sir Samuel Ferguson

The following song originated in Co. Leitrim around Ballinamuck about 1798 with the survivors from Mayo in the Battle of Ballinamuck fought between the Franco-Irish forces and the English.

Granuaile
As the sunlight in its glory
Ever shines on fair Clew Bay
And Croagh Patrick old and hoary
Rises o'er the ruins grey
As the streamlets in the meadows
In their pride come dancing down
Nestled close among the mountains
Stands pleasant Newport Town.

Just a mile from where the turrets
Of the ancient town uprise
And the frowning peak of Nephin
Soars in grandeur to the skies
Lie a massive heap of ruins
In their loneliness sublime
Though scattered and dismantled now
By tyranny and time.

'Twas a proud and stately castle
In the years of long ago
When the dauntless Grace O'Malley
Ruled a queen in fair Mayo.
And from Bernham's lofty summit
To the waves of Galway Bay
And from Castlebar to Ballintra
Her unconquered flag held sway.

She had strongholds on her headlands
And brave galleys on the sea
And no warlike chief or viking
E'er had bolder heart than she.
She unfurled her country's banner
High o'er battlement and mast
And 'gainst all the might of England
Kept it flying 'til the last.

The armies of Elizabeth
Invaded her on land
Her warships followed on her track
And watched by many a stand
But she swept her foes before her
On the land and on the sea
And the flag of Grace O'Malley
Waved defiant, proud and free.

On the walls of Carrick Clooney
As the Summer sun went down
And its last bright rays were fading
On the spires of Newport town.
To the watchmen on the ramparts
There appeared in long array
A band of English spearmen
By the waters of Clew Bay.

To the walls flew Grace O'Malley
With her clansmen at her side
Who had often met the foemen
On the land and on the tide.
But she saw the marshalled strength
Of the English coming on
And the colour of their armour
That in polished brightness shone.

Soon before the frowning battlements
The English columns came
Whilst on the walls before them
Stood many a bristling gun.
Then forwards towards the barbican
A herald quickly came
And demanded free admittance
In the English monarch's name.

He said 'My Royal Mistress
Sends her men-at-arms and me
With greetings good to all her friends
Who true and loyal be.
Her liegeman, Lord Hal Sydney,
With all his spears awaits
For you to open wide to him
The Barbican and gates!'

'So tell your Royal mistress,'
The dauntless Grace replied,
'That she and all her men-at-arms
Are scornfully defied.
She may own the fertile valley
Where the Foyle and Liffey flow
But tell her Grace O'Malley
Is unconquered in Mayo.

'Our flag upon the battlements
Is to the breeze out-thrown
And with God's grace we'll keep it there
In spite of Queen and throne.
There's many a brave O'Malley here
With me to man the walls
And rally round the flag we love
Until the last man falls!

'We want no English hirelings here
No soldiers of the Crown
We falter not before their spears
Nor cower beneath their frown.
No! Clansmen, let your warcry ring
Defiance on the gale
And greet those braggart Saxons
With a shower of Irish hail.'

Then sprang upon the Britons
With many a loud hurrah
A band of fierce and rugged men
Well brazed in many a fray.
On every tower and battlement
The Irish kern appears
And fiercely flash their guns upon
The foe's advancing spears.

The dauntless Grace with Spartan soul
Stands on the outer wall.
Regardless of the shower of balls
That fast around them fall.
The English come with marshalled strength
And nerved with deadly hate
They fiercely clash through friends and foes
And gain the foremost gate.

But right before them face to face
The clansmen of Mayo
Start up and greet those robbers well
With thrust and sabre blow.
And rushing fierce as mountain stream
Through dark and flooded glen
Leaps to the gate, the dauntless Grace
And all her fearless men.

Hurrah! Their spears are backward borne
Their blood-red flag is down
And Sydney vanquished and pursued
Spurs hard to Newport Town.
This lesson taught the Saxon churl
To dread a Free-man's blow
When the dauntless Grace O'Malley
Ruled a Queen in fair Mayo.

The walls of Carrick Clooney
Now lie crumbling and low
Its battlements dismantled are
All moss o'er every stone.
But the rebel youth in Westport
Feel their Irish hearts aglow
When they tell how Grace O'Malley
Fought and conquered in Mayo.

There's many a fearless rebel
In Westport and Clew Bay
Who watch with longing eagerness
For Freedom's dawning day.
There's many a brawny mountaineer
Prepared to strike a blow
For the old Green Flag and Freedom
On the soil of brave Mayo.

James Hardiman: *Irish Minstrelsy*, vol. II

Oró, Sé do Bheatha 'bhaile

I

Sé do bheatha! a bhean dá léanmhar!
B'é ár gceach tú bheith i ngéibhinn,
Do dhúiche bhrea í seilbh méirleach
'S tú díolta leis na Gallaibh.

Oró! Sé do bheatha 'bhaile!
Oró! Sé do bheatha 'bhaile!
Oró! Sé do bheatha 'bhaile!
Anois ar theacht an tSamhraidh.

II

Tá Gráinne Mhaol ag teacht thar sáile,
Óglaigh armtha léi mar gharda;
Gaeil iad féin 's ní Gaill ná Spainnigh
'S cuirfid ruaig ar Gallaibh.

III

A bhuí le Rí na bhfeart go bhfeiceam,
Muna mbeam beo 'na dhiaidh ach seachtain,
Gráinne Mhaol agus míle gaiscíoch
Ag fógairt fáin ar Gallaibh.

Pádraig Mac Phiarais

Oró and Welcome Home

I

Welcome, O woman who was sorrowful
We were desolate while you were imprisoned.
Your lovely country in the hands of vandals
And you yourself—sold to the English.

Chorus:
Oró—and welcome home,
Oró—and welcome home,
Oró—and welcome home,
Would that the Summer is here.

II

Gráinne Mhaol is coming over the sea,
With a guard of young soldiers,
They are Irish, not English or Spanish
And they will rout the English.

III

Thanks be to God that I'm seeing
(Even if I only live for a week after!)
Gráinne Mhaol and a thousand warriors
Announcing ruin on the English.

Pádraig Pearse (translated)

Granuweal—An old song

I

A courtier call'd Dorset, from Parkgate did fail,
In his Majesty's yacht, for to court Granuweal;
With great entertainment the thought to prevail,
And rifle the charms of Granuweal.

Chorus:
Sing Budderoo, didderoo, Granuweal,
The Fox in the Trap we have caught by the tail
Sing success to the sons of brave Granuweal.

II

Says the courtier to Granu, if you will be true,
I will bring you to London, and do for you too;
Where you shall have pleasure that never will fail,
I'll laurel your Shamrock, sweet Granuweal.

III

Says Granu to Dorset, if that I would do,
Bring my fortune to London, my children would rue;
We would be like Highlanders eating of keal,
And cursing the union, says Granuweal.

IV

Says Granu, I always was true to my king;
When in war, I supply'd him with money and men.
Our love to King George with our blood we did seal,
At Dettingen battle, says Granuweal.

V

Says Granu, I always still lov'd to be free;
No foe shall invade me in my liberty.
While I've Limerick, Derry and the fort of Kinsale,
I'll love and not marry, says Granuweal.

VI

Says Granu, you see there's a large stone put in,
To the heart of the church, by the leave of the King.
The works of this stone shall be weigh'd in a scale,
With balance of justice, says Granuweal.

VII

I hope our brave Harrington, likewise Kildare,
Our trade and our commerce once more will repair,
Our lives we will venture with greatest affail,
Against French and Spaniards, says Granuweal.

VIII

Now, my dear boys, we've got shut of those bugs,
I charge you my children, lie close in your rugs,
They'll hide like a snake, but will bite I'll be bail,
I'll give them shillelagh, says Granuweal.

Poor Old Granuaile

My dream to some with joy will come and comes with grief to more,
As it did to me, my country, that dear old Erin's shore;
I dreamt I stood upon a hill beside a lovely vale,
And it's there I spied a comely maid and her name was Granuaile.

Her lovely hair hung down so fair and she was dressed in green,
I thought she was the fairest soul that e'er my eyes had seen;
As I drew near I then could hear by the pleasant morning gale,
As she went along she sang her song saying 'I'm poor old Granuaile'.

In O'Connell's time in '29 we had no braver men,
They struggled hard both day and night to gain our rights again;
Still, by coercion we were bound and our sons were sent to jail,
'You need not fret, we'll Home Rule get,' says poor old Granuaile.

I thought she had a splendid harp by her side she let it fall,
She played the tunes called Brian Boru, Garryowen, and Tara's Hall.
Then God Save Ireland was the next, and Our Martyrs Who Died in
Jail,
'You need not fret, we'll have freedom yet,' says poor old Granuaile.

When I wakened from my slumber and excited by my fight,
I thought it was the clear daylight, and I found that it was night;
I looked all round and could see naught but the walls of a lonely jail.
And that was the last I ever saw of poor old Granuaile.

Irish Street Ballads, collected and annotated by Colm Ó Loughlainn,
London 1928

A New Song Called Granuaile

All through the north as I walked forth to view the shamrock plain
I stood a while where nature smiled amid the rocks and streams
On a matron mild I fixed my eyes beneath a fertile vale
As she sang her song it was on the wrongs of poor old Granuaile.

Her head was bare and her grey hair over her eyes hung down
Her waist and neck, her hands and feet, with iron chains were bound
Her pensive strain and plaintive wail mingled with the evening gale
And the song she sung with mournful tongue was Poor Old Granuaile.

The gown she wore was stained with gore all by a ruffian band
Her lips so sweet the monarchs kissed are now grown pale and wan
The tears of grief fell from her eyes each tear as large as hail
None could express the deep distress of poor old Granuaile.

On her harp she leaned and thus exclaimed 'My royal Brian is gone
Who in his day did drive away the tyrants every one
On Clontarf's plains against the Danes his faction did prepare.
Brave Brian Boru cut their lines in two and freed old Granuaile.

'But now, alas, I must confess, avengers I have none
There's no brave Lord to wave his sword in my defence—not one
My enemies just when they please with blows they do assail
The flesh they tore clean off the bones of poor old Granuaile.

Six hundred years the briny tears have flowed down from my eyes
I curse the day that Henry made of me proud Albion's prize
From that day down with chains I'm bound, no wonder I look pale
The blood they drained from every vein of poor old Granuaile.'

There was a lord came from the south he wore a laurel crown
Saying 'Grania dear, be of good cheer, no longer you'll be bound
I am the man they call great Dan, who never yet did fail
I have got the bill for to fulfil your wishes, Granuaile.'

With blood besmeared and bathed in tears her harp she sweetly strung
And oh the change, her mournful air from one last chord she wrung
Her voice so clear fell on my ear, at length my strength did fail
I went away and thus did say, 'God help you, Granuaile'.

APPENDIX 3

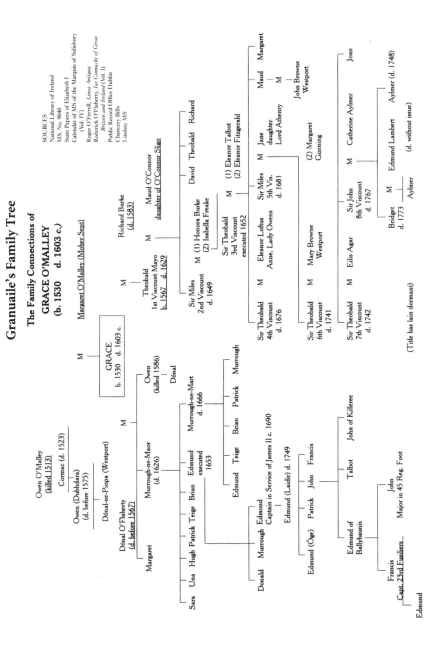

Granuaile's Family Tree

The Family Connections of
GRACE O'MALLEY
(b. 1530   d. 1603 c.)

SOURCES
National Library of Ireland
MS. No. 9040
State Papers of Elizabeth 1
Calendar of MS of the Marquis of Salisbury
(Vol. IV)
Roger O'Ferrell, *Linea Antiqua*
Roderick O'Flaherty, *Iar Connacht or Great
Britain and Ireland* (Vol. 1)
Public Record Office Dublin
Chancery Bills
Lindsay MS

Descendants of Maude Bourke and John Browne
Descendants of Maud Bourke and John Browne

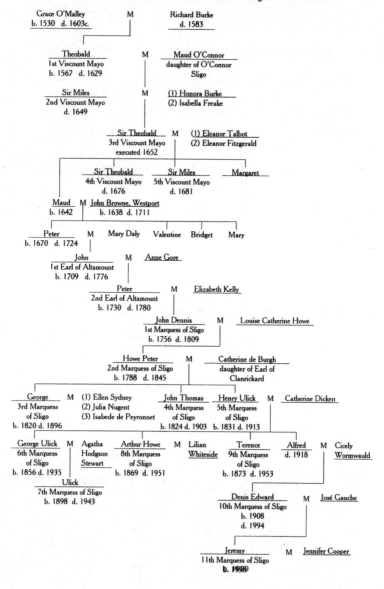

REFERENCES

Chapter 1 Powerful by Land and Sea (pages 1–17)

1. MS 1440, TCD.
2. Ordnance Survey Letters, Mayo, vol. II, p. 97.
3. *The Stranger in Ireland*, p. 304.
4. *A Chorographical Description of West Connaught*, p. 140.
5. Ibid.
6. *History of the County Mayo*, p. 189.
7. *Revue Celtique*, vol. XLIX, p. 174.
8. *Annals of the Four Masters*, vol. II, p. 1019.
9. Ibid., vol. 4, p. 815.
10. *Revue Celtique*, vol. XLIX, p. 175.
11. *History of the Town and County of Galway*, p. 83.
12. Ibid., p. 64.
13. Ibid., p. 201.
14. *Annals of Ulster*, vol. 3, p. 69.
15. SPI 63/19/56.
16. *Bold in Her Breeches*, p. 21.
17. Calendar of State Papers (Elizabeth I), vol. CCVI, p. 335.
18. Ibid., vol. CCVI, p. 335.
19. Lord of the Isles Voyage brochure.
20. Calendar of State Papers (Elizabeth I), vol. CCVI, p. 89.
21. Calendar of State Papers (Elizabeth I), vol. CCVI, p. 335.

Chapter 2 The World of Granuaile (pages 18–32)

1. Ordnance Survey Letters, Mayo, vol. II.
2. The Discourses, Book III, ch. 26.
3. Discourse of Ireland, p. 357.
4. Chancery Bill, no. R.63.
5. Calendar State Papers (Edward VI), vol. CLXX, p. 132.
6. *The Beginnings of Modern Ireland*, p. 30.
7. *A Chorographical Description of West Connaught*, p. 58.
8. Royal Irish Academy, MS no. AV2, Folio 53A.
9. *The Buccaneer Queen*, p. 24.
10. *Irish Life in the 17th Century*, p. 338.
11. *Social History of Ancient Ireland*, p. 284.
12. Ibid.
13. *A Chorographical Description of West Connaught*, p. 383.

Chapter 3 *Fortuna Favet Fortibus* (pages 33–48)

1. *Irish Life in the 17th Century*, p. 338.
2. Ordnance Survey Letters, Mayo, vol. II, p. 97.
3. SPI 63/170/63.
4. Ibid.
5. Lambeth Palace Library, MS no. 601, p. 111.
6. Calendar State Papers (Elizabeth I) vol. CCVII, p. 5.
7. Dept Celtic Studies, MS 532.
8. *A Chorographical Description of West Connaught*, p. 385.
9. SPI 63/170/63.
10. Ibid.
11. SPI 63/170/19.

Chapter 4 The Pirate Queen (pages 45–59)

1. SPI 63/170/204.
2. SPI 63/171/18.
3. Lambeth Palace Library, MS no. 601, p. 111.
4. Calendar State Papers (James I) 1623, no. 997.
5. Ordnance Survey Letters, Mayo, vol. II.
6. Dept Celtic Studies, Folklore Collection, MS no. 1134.
7. *The Way That I Went*, p. 184.
8. *Great Book of Genealogies*, p. 3259.
9. Gaisford St Lawrence Papers, Howth Castle.
10. *Howth and Its Owners*, p. 182.
11. Ordnance Survey Letters, Mayo, vol. II.

Chapter 5 'A Most Famous Feminine Sea Captain' (pages 60–76)

1. Calendar State Papers (Elizabeth I), vol. 72, no. 39.
2. *Gaelic and Gaelicised Ireland*, p. 73.
3. Lambeth Palace Library, MS no. 601, p. 111.
4. Ibid.
5. SPI 63/170/63.
6. *Hibernia Dominicana*, p. 319.
7. Ordnance Survey Letters, Mayo, vol. I, p. 1.
8. Royal Irish Academy, MS no. AV2, Folio 53A.
9. *Filí agus Filídheacht Chonnacht*, p. 267.
10. *Gaelic and Gaelicised Ireland*, p. 79.
11. *History of the County Mayo*, p. 181.
12. Calendar Carew MSS, vol. II, p. 38.
13. *Ulster Journal of Archaeology*, vol. V, p. 299.
14. Lambeth Palace Library, MS no. 601, p. 101.
15. Ibid.
16. SPI 63/60/56.
17. Ibid.

18. Ibid.
19. SPI 63/19/78.
20. *History of the Town and County of Galway*, p. 86.
21. *The Geraldines*, p. 279.
22. *Eleanor, Countess of Desmond*, p. 133.
23. Calendar of State Papers (Elizabeth I), vol. CXXII, no. 39.
24. Ibid.
25. Calendar of Carew MSS, vol. II, no. 322.
26. SPI 63/172/63.
27. Ibid.
28. *Shadow Lord*, p. 43.
29. Westport House MSS.
30. Ibid.
31. Ibid.

Chapter 6 'Nurse to All Rebellions' (pages 77–91)

1. SPI 63/96/37.
2. Ordnance Survey Letters, Mayo, vol. II.
3. Ibid.
4. Westport House MSS.
5. Ibid.
6. *Analecta Hibernia*, p. 133.
7. Calendar State Papers (Elizabeth I), vol. XCIX, p. 425.
8. Ibid.
9. Ibid.
10. *Annals of the Four Masters*, vol. V, p. 1805.
11. Ibid.
12. SPI 63/170/63.
13. *Annals of Loch Cé*, vol. II, p. 459.
14. Westport House MSS.
15. Ibid.
16. *Anecdotes and Traditions*, p. 18.
17. Calendar State Papers (Elizabeth I), vol. CLXX, p. 128.
18. *Political Works of Edmund Spenser*, p. 67.
19. Royal Irish Academy, MS no. AVI, Folio 53A.
20. Titus BXIII, p. 410.
21. SPI 63/170/63.
22. SPI 63/170/63.
23. Titus BXIII, p. 236.
24. SPI 63/170/63.
25. SPI 63/158/37.
26. Ibid.
27. SPI 63/170/63.
28. *The Elizabethan Epic*, p. 182.

29. Calendar of Fiants (Elizabeth I), no. 5173.
30. SPI 63/170/63.

Chapter 7 'A Notable Traitoress' (pages 92–105)

1. Westport House MSS.
2. Ibid.
3. SPI 63/145/6.
4. Calendar State Papers (Elizabeth I), vol. CLXV, no. 6.
5. Titus BXIII, p. 446.
6. SPI 63/147/35.
7. SPI 63/146/35.
8. Calendar State Papers, vol. 1588–92, no. 83.
9. Ibid., no. 81.
10. SPI 63/171/18.
11. Ibid.
12. SPI 63/158/62.
13. *The Celtic Peoples and Renaissance Europe*, p. 42.
14. Calendar State Papers (Elizabeth I), vol. CLXXI, p. 141.
15. SPI 63/206/92.
16. *History of the County Mayo*, p. 250.
17. Ibid.
18. *Irish Pedigrees*, vol. II, p. 675.

Chapter 8 The Meeting of the Two Queens (pages 106–24)

1. SPI 63/170/204.
2. Ibid.
3. SPI 63/171/62.
4. SPI 63/170/44.
5. Dept of Celtic Studies, Folklore, Schools MS no. 4, p. 512.
6. SPI 63/171/37.
7. SPI 63/172/34i.
8. *The Elizabethan Epic*, p. 74.
9. SPI 63/171/44.
10. SPI 63/170/63.
11. Calendar State Papers (Elizabeth I), vol. CLXX, p. 132.
12. Ibid.
13. SPI 63/171/62.
14. *The Elizabethan Epic*, p. 203.
15. Ibid., p. 73.
16. Ibid., p. 142.
17. *Irish Pedigrees*, vol. II, p. 675.
18. *The Elizabethan Epic*, p. 71.
19. Hatfield House, MSS Marquis of Salisbury, no. CP 169/128.
20. SPI 63/171/44.

21. Hatfield House, no. CP 169/128.
22. SPI 63/170/204.
23. Hatfield House, no. CP 169/128.
24. Ibid.
25. SPI 63/171/62.
26. Ibid.
27. Ibid.
28. SPI 63/171/44.
29. Hatfield House, no. CP 169/128.
30. Ibid.

Chapter 9 End of an Era (pages 125–36)

1. SPI 63/172/26.
2. Ibid.
3. SPI 63/179/81.
4. Calendar State Papers (Elizabeth I), vol. CCVI, no. 92.
5. SPI 63/179/36.
6. Ibid.
7. Ibid.
8. SPI 63/179/35.
9. Ibid.
10. SPI 63/179/70.
11. Ibid.
12. Ibid.
13. Ibid.
14. Calendar of Fiants, Elizabeth, no. 5948.
15. *New History of Ireland*, vol. III, p. 122.
16. Calendar State Papers (Elizabeth I), 1592–96, preface XXVI.
17. *Life of Hugh Roe O'Donnell*, p. 111.
18. *Scots Mercenary Forces in Ireland*, p. 142.
19. *Annals of the Four Masters*, vol. IV, p. 2013.
20. Ibid.
21. Calendar State Papers (Elizabeth I), vol. CC, p. 376.
22. Ibid., vol. CCVIII, p. 436.
23. SPI 63/237/12.

Chapter 10 The Descendants of Granuaile (pages 137–43)

1. *Shadow Lord*, p. 11.
2. Calendar of Carew MSS, vol. III, p. 490.
3. Ibid., vol. VIII, p. 136.
4. *Funeral Entries Books*, vol. V, p. 147.
5. *Galway Archaeological and Historical Society*, vol. II, p. 54.
6. Lindsay MSS, PRO.

BIBLIOGRAPHY

1. MANUSCRIPT SOURCES
British Library
Cotton Titus BXIII, XVIII, Papers on Irish affairs, 1559–1602

Department of Celtic Studies, UCD
MSS nos 86, 202, A229, 693, 838, 1134, 1181, 1206, 1238, 1838, 4844

Howth Castle, Co. Dublin
Gaisford St Lawrence Papers

Genealogical Office, Dublin
MSS nos 482–5, 699, 165, 155,
Funeral Entries Books, vol. 2

Hatfield House, Hertfordshire
Cecil Papers no. 169/128

Lambeth Palace Library
MSS 601, 619

National Library of Ireland
State Papers relating to Ireland (on microfilm, originals in the Public Record Office, London)
SP 63/19/ 56, 186, 63/61/ 74, 63/72/ 63, 63/88/34, 63/96/37, 63/145/6, 164, 63/146/35, 43i, 43ii, 43iii, 431V, 148, 63/147/18iii, 62, 63/158/37, 62, 63/170/44, 168, 204, 63/171/18, 37, 44,62,65, 81; 63/172/26, 34i, 63/173/1, 63, 63/179/35, 36, 36i, 38, 70, 75 77, 62-66, 63/199/66v, 66vi, 63/200/356, 63/206/20, 63/237/12.
MSS NOS D3375, D3650-3,

Public Record Office, Ireland
Chancery Bills nos 1.209, R.63, R.65, A.A.150

Genelogical Office, Dublin
MSS NOS 159, 165, 168, 169
Lindsay MS. NO. 6
Funeral Entries Book, VOL. 6

Royal Irish Academy, Dublin
MSS nos. AV2 f.53A

Westport House, Co. Mayo, Manuscript Collection (now in the National Library of Ireland).

2. CONTEMPORARY SOURCES

Analecta Hibernia nos 8, 24, 26

Annála Ríoghachta Éireann. Annals of the Kingdom of Ireland by the Four Masters, from the ealiest period to the year 1616, ed. and trans. J. O'Donovan, 7 vols (Dublin 1851)

Annals of Loch Cé. A Chronicle of Irish Affairs, 1014–1590, ed. W.M. Hennessy, 2 vols (London 1871).

Annals of Ulster, ed. B. MacCarthy (Dublin 1893)

Books of Survey and Distribution, Mayo 1636–1703 (Dublin 1956)

Camden, W., *Britannia* (London 1695)

Davis, Sir John, *A Discovery of the True Causes Why Ireland Was Never Entirely Subdued ...* (London 1612). Facsimile reprint (Shannon 1969)

Derricke, J., *The Image of Ireland* (London 1581). Facsimile reprint (Belfast 1985)

Hogan, E. ed., *Description of Ireland* (Dublin 1878)

Hogan, E. and N. MacNeill, eds, *The Walsingham Letterbook*, May 1576 to December 1579 (Dublin 1959)

Holinshed, R., *Chronicles of England, Scotland and Ireland*, ed J. Johnson (London 1807–8)

Moryson, F., *An Itinerary* (London 1617). Facsimile edition (Glasgow 1907–8)

Sidney State Papers, 1565–1570, ed. T Ó Laidhin (Dublin 1962)

O'Cleary, L., *The Life of Hugh Roe O'Donnell, Prince of Tirconail, 1586–1602* (Dublin 1893)

O'Donovan, J. ed and trans., *Leabhar na gCeart*. The Book of Rights (Dublin 1847)

O'Flaherty, R., *A Chorographical Description of West Connaught 1684* (Dublin 1846)

Perrot, J., *The Chronicle of Ireland 1584–1608*, ed. H. Wood (Dublin 1933)

Spenser, E., *A View of the Present State of Ireland ... in 1596*, ed. W.l. Renwick (Oxford 1970)

Stafford, T., *Pacata Hibernia* (London 1633); ed. S. H. O'Grady (London 1896)

Calendars and Printed Manuscript Sources

Calendar of the Carew Manuscripts, ed J.S. Brewer and W. Bullen, 6 vols (London 1867–73)

Calendar of Cecil Manuscripts, 8 vols (London 1883–99)

Calendar of Fiants of the Reign of Elizabeth (Dublin 1877–94)

Calendar of Patent and Close Rolls of Chancery, Elizabeth, ed. J. C. Morrin (Dublin 1862)

Calendar of the Manuscripts of the Marquis of Salisbury (London 1883–1973)

Calendar of State Papers Relating to Ireland (London 1860–1912)

Compossicion Booke of Connaught, ed. A Freeman (Dublin 1936)

Sidney, Letters and Memorials of State, written and collected by Sir Henry Sidney, Sir Philip Sidney and his brother, Sir Robert Sidney, ed. A. Collins (London 1746)

Secondary Sources

Anthologia Hibernica, vol. II (Dublin 1793)

Bagwell, R., *Ireland under the Tudors*, 3 vols (London 1885–90)

Bagwell, R., *Ireland under the Stuarts*, 3 vols (London 1909–16)

Ball, F., *Howth and its Owners* (Dublin 1917)

Beckett, J.C., *The Making of Modern Ireland* (London 1966)

Black, C., *Pirates of the West Indies* (Cambridge 1989)

Black, J.B., *The Reign of Elizabeth, 1558–1603* (Oxford 1959)

Blackwell, M., *Ships in Early Irish History* (Co. Clare 1992)

Butler, W.F.T., *Confiscation in Irish History* (1917)

Byrne, M., *Ireland Under Elizabeth* (Dublin 1903)

Callwell, J., *Old Irish Life* (London 1912)

Canny, N., *The Elizabethan Conquest. A Pattern Established, 1565–76* (1976)

Chambers, A., *Shadow Lord: Theobold Bourke—Tibbott-ne-Long: Son of the Pirate Queen* (Dublin 2007)

Chambers, A., *Eleanor Countess of Desmond, 1545–1638* (Dublin 1989)

Chambers, A., *At Arms Length: Aristocrats in the Republic of Ireland* (Dublin 2004)

Cordingly, D., *Life Among the Pirates* (UK 1995)

Corkery, D., *The Hidden Ireland* (Dublin 1979)

Dutton, R., *English Court Life* (London 1963)

Ellis, S.G., *Tudor Ireland* (London 1985)

Fallon, N., *The Armada in Ireland* (London 1978)

Falls, C., *Elizabeth's Irish Wars* (London 1950)

FitzGerald, B., *The Geraldines, 1169–1601* (London 1951)

Hardiman, J., *History of the Town and County of Galway* (Dublin 1920)

Hardiman, J., *Irish Minstrelsy*, vol. II (London 1831)

Ireland, J. de Courcy, *Ireland and the Irish in Maritime History* (Dublin 1986)

Joyce, P., *Social History of Ancient Ireland* (Dublin 1913)

Knox, H.T., *History of the County Mayo* (Dublin 1908)

Leask, H.G., *Irish Castles and Castellated Houses* (Dundalk 1972)

Loades, D., *The Tudor Court* (London 1992)

McCalmont, R.F., *Memoirs of the Binghams* (London 1915)

McClintock, H., *Irish and Highland Dress* (Dundalk 1950)

McClintock, H., *Handbook of the Old Irish Dress* (Dundalk 1958)

McCoy, G. Hayes, *Scots Mercenary Forces in Ireland, 1565–1607* (1937)

MacCurtain, M., *Tudor and Stuart Ireland* (Dublin 1972)

MacCurtain, M. O'Dowd, M., eds, *Women in Early Modern Ireland* (Dublin 1991)

Mac Lysaght, E., *Irish Life in the 17th Century* (Cork 1939)

Mason, T., *The Islands of Ireland* (London 1936)

Maxwell, C., *The Stranger in Ireland* (London 1934)

Moody, T., F.X. Martin and F.J. Byrne, eds. *A New History of Ireland*, vol. III (Oxford 1976)

Neale, J., *Elizabeth I and her Parliaments, 1584–1601* (London 1958)

Nicholls, K., *Gaelic and Gaelicised Ireland in the Middle Ages* (Dublin 1972)

O'Brien, G., *Economic History of Ireland in the 17th Century* (Dublin 1919)

O'Faolain, S., *The Great O'Neill* (London 1950)

O'Hart, J., *Irish Pedigrees* (New York 1915)

Ó Raghallaigh, T., *Filí agus Filidheacht Chonnacht* (Dublin 1938)

Otway, C., *A Tour of Connaught* (Dublin 1839)

Praeger, R.L., *The Way That I Went* (1937)

Prockter, A. and R. Taylor, *The A to Z of Elizabethan London* (London 1979)

Ridley, J., *Henry VIII* (London 1984)

Smith, L.B., *The Elizabethan Epic* (London 1966)

Stanley, J., ed., *Bold in Her Breeches* (London 1995)

Thackeray, W. M., *The Irish Sketch Book* (London 1902)

Thomas, D.A., *The Illustrated Armada Handbook* (London 1988)

Townsend, J.H., *Buccaneer Queen* (1902)

Walsh, M. Kerney, *Destruction by Peace* (Armagh 1986)

Westropp, T., *Clare Island Survey* (Dublin 1911)

Wilson, P., *The Beginnings of Modern Ireland* (Dublin 1912)

Journals and Articles

Dublin University Magazine, vol. LIII (1959)

Folklore, vol. XXVIII no. 4

Galway Archaeological and Historical Society, vols I–II, XVIII

Irish Genealogist, vol. I

Irish Sword, vol. I

Kerry Archaeological Society, vol. VIII (1975)

Lord of the Isles Voyage Brochure (1993)

Nichols, K., Land, *Law and Society in Sixteenth-Century Ireland* (Dublin 1976)

Ó Móráin, P., *Five Hundred Years in the History of Murrisk Abbey* (*Mayo News*, 7 & 14 September, 1957)

Ordnance Survey. *Letters Relating to the County of Mayo*, vols I, II, ed. John O'Donovan (Dublin 1862)

Ordnance Survey. *Letters relating to the County of Galway*, ed. John O'Donovan (Dublin 1862)

Proceedings of the Royal Irish Academy, vol. 36 XLIX

Ulster Journal of Archaeology, vols II, IV, V, VIII

INDEX

abbeys, 16–17
Achill Island, 5, 6, 158
  Castle, 15, 52
  dwellings, 28
  shipwreck, 52–3
Achill Sound, 15, 52–3
Affane, battle of, 56
Algerian pirates, 64
Anglo-Normans, 6, 23–4
Annals of the Four Masters, 3–4, 8–9, 81, 133
Aoife (warrior princess), 19
Aquila, Don Juan del, 139
Aran Islands, 52
  Granuaile attacks, 96, 100
Ardnaree, battle of, 91
Askeaton Castle, 68, 69, 71
Athenry, Lord, 45, 61, 72
Augustinians, 16

Ball, E., 55
Ballinahinch Castle, 47
Ballinrobe Castle, 75
Ballymote Castle, 86, 87, 111
bardic schools, 35
baronies, 65
Barra, Isle of, 132
Belcarra Castle, 138
Belclare Castle, 15, 28, 38, 52
betagh (*biatach*), 26–7
Bingham, Sir George, 86, 87, 98, 111
Bingham, John, 88, 89, 100, 155
Bingham, Sir Richard, 83–4, 131
  captures and releases Granuaile, 89–90
  character and career, 83–4, 92, 108

  Granuaile's meeting with Queen Elizabeth, 113, 117–19, 122–4, 160–63
  Granuaile's petition against, 97–8
  imprisons Granuaile's youngest son, 86, 87, 111–12, 123–4, 126, 165
  murders Granuaile's eldest son, 88, 118, 155
  Queen Elizabeth overrules, 123–4, 125–6, 165–6
  subjugates Connaught, 83–4, 86, 87–91, 94–104, 110–12, 130
  thwarts Granuaile's activities, 126–9
boats, 12–14
Boazio, Baptista, 125
Bonny, Ann, 11, 37
booleying, 30
Bourke, Catherine, 61
Bourke, David (Granuaile's father-in-law), 42, 60, 159
Bourke, David (9th Viscount Mayo), 142
Bourke, Edmund (Granuaile's stepson), 61, 82
  rebellion, 97, 100, 101, 104
Bourke, Edmund (of Castlebar), 86, 87, 88, 91, 98
Bourke, Finola, 42–3
Bourke, Honora, 155
Bourke, John (Granuaile's stepson), 61
Bourke, John (Viscount Mayo), 142
Bourke, Katherine, 155
Bourke, Maude, 142–3, 198
Bourke, Michael, 142
Bourke, Miles, 141

Bourke, Moyler, 89
Bourke, Richard ('Devil's Hook'),
    87–8, 89–90, 95, 127, 157
Bourke, Richard (Granuaile's
    grandson), 96, 127, 132, 133, 138
Bourke, Richard (10th Viscount
    Mayo), 142
Bourke, Richard-an-Iarainn
    (Granuaile's husband), 17, 33,
    42–3, 45, 54, 58, 79–82
    accedes to MacWilliamship, 71,
        72–6, 77, 79–81
    death, 81–2
    marriage to Granuaile, 60–67, 156
    petitions, 146, 147–8
Bourke, Shane MacOliverus, 65–7,
    72, 73
Bourke, Theobald (Tibbott-ne-Long,
    1st Viscount Mayo), 63–5, 82,
    137–41
    born at sea, 63–4
    campaign against Bourkes, 127
    character and expertise, 65, 78, 137
    chastised for cowardice, 78
    chieftain of Mayo Bourkes, 65,
        132–4, 137–41
    death, 140
    English alliance, 129, 133–4, 137–8,
        130–40
    fosterage, 65, 77, 78–9
    imprisoned by Bingham, 86, 87,
        111–12, 123–4, 126, 165
    imprisoned by O'Donnell, 132
    Kinsale, battle of, 139
    land dispute, 22, 78–9, 140, 149–50,
        170–71
    marriage, 86–7
    Murrisk Abbey and, 16
    poems in honour of, 26, 64–5
    rebellions, 88, 91, 97, 100, 101, 102–4
    source of nickname, 63–4
    treason charge and release, 111–12,
        115, 123–4, 126, 165

Ulster Confederacy and, 137–8
Viscount Mayo, 140
Bourke, Theobald (3rd Viscount
    Mayo), 141–2
Bourke, Theobald (4th Viscount
    Mayo), 142
Bourke, Thomas, 60
Bourke, Tibbot Reagh, 89, 113
Bourke, Ulick, 89, 98, 113, 158–9
Bourke, Walter, 61, 82, 158–9
Bourke, Walter (Fada), 42–3, 60, 158
Bourke, William ('Blind Abbot'), 97,
    99, 101
Bourkes, 6, 45, 50, 61, 130, 131
    Granuaile pressed into service
        against, 127
    rebellions, 85, 87–8, 89, 95–104
    Viscount Mayos, 140, 141–2
Brabourne, John, 143
Brehon law, 20, 24–5, 40, 46, 133
brehons, 27
Browne, Jeremy, 143
Browne, John (sheriff of Mayo), 83,
    89, 95–6
Browne, John (Westport House),
    142–3, 198
Bunowen Castle, 41, 43, 141
Burghley, Lord (William Cecil), 3, 89,
    98, 100, 106, 116–19, 123, 126
Burghley, Lord (William Cecil), contd
    articles of interrogatory to
        Granuaile, 117, 153–9
    career and power, 116–17
    Granuaile petitions, 129–30, 164,
        167–9
Burgos, de, 6, 77
Burkes, 6, 39 see also Bourkes
Burrishoole, 5, 6, 60, 61, 62, 65–6, 73,
    82, 99, 103, 109, 127
Burtonport, 52
Butler, Eleanor, Countess of Desmond,
    20, 26, 34, 115–16
Butler, Joan, Countess of Ormond, 34

Butler, 'Black' Tom, Earl of Ormond,
    56, 57, 94, 109, 116, 128, 129
Butlers, 6

Caher Island, 53
Caisleán-an-Circa, 43, 46–7
Carew, Sir George, 138
Carew, Sir Peter, 16, 57
Carra, 61, 77–9, 140
Carraigahowley Castle, 60, 62–3, 71, 82,
    96, 100, 103, 105, 135
Carrick-on-Suir, 128
Carrowmore, 15, 52
Castleaffy, 65
Castlebar, 99
Castlebourke (Kilboynell Castle), 77,
    78, 141, 142
Castlecarra, 78
castles, 14–15, 28, 62–3
Cathair-na-Mart, 15, 52, 81, 112
Catholicism, 27–8, 56
cattle, 31
    grazing, 30
Cecil, Robert, 3
Cecil, William *see* Burghley, Lord
ceithearn, 27
'cess' custom, 82, 85
Charles I, King, 140
chieftaincy, 24–5, 33
    women debarred, 20, 25, 47
children in Gaelic society, 33–5, 65
    fosterage, 33, 65, 77, 78–9
Christianity, 19–20, 24
Clandonnells, 12, 50, 96, 99, 102
Clangibbons, 87, 96, 103
Clanmorris, 97
Clanrickard, Earl of, 39, 45, 46, 58, 61,
    74, 99
Clare Island, 7, 30, 38
    Abbey, 16–17
    Castle, 15, 135
    Granuaile's piracy base, 48, 49–50
    Granuaile's tomb, 17, 135

Spanish Armada shipwreck, 93–5
Clew Bay, 5, 7, 12, 15, 50, 52, 60, 73,
    93–5, 103
clientship (*célsine*), 25, 66–7, 85
Clifford, Sir Conyers, 131, 132–3, 133–4,
    138
Cloonagashal Castle, 100, 102–3
colonisation, 2–3, 45, 46, 57–8, 65–6,
    70, 81, 85, 107–8, 139
Composition of Connaught, 85–6, 87,
    109, 156–7
Cormick, Charles, 56
crannóg, 15
Croagh Patrick, 6–7
Cúchulainn, 19
cuddy (*cuid oíche*), 25
Curradh Castle, 44, 52

Dana (goddess), 18
descendants of Granuaile, 137–43, 193–4
Desmond, Eleanor Butler, Countess of,
    20, 26, 34, 115–16
Desmond, Gerald Fitzgerald, Earl of,
    52, 56, 57, 83, 108
    imprisons Granuaile, 68–70
    rebellion, 71–2, 83, 108, 110
Desmond rebellion, 71–4, 83, 85, 108, 110
diet, 29–31
Dillon, Theobald, 80–81
divorce customs, 27, 41
Docwra, Sir Henry, 138
Donamona Castle, 72
Doona Castle, 52, 53
dowries, 26, 41–2, 63, 82, 157
Drake, Sir Francis, 11
Drury, Lord Justice, 69
Dublin Castle, Granuaile imprisoned
    in, 69–70
Dudley, Robert, 121
Dunton, John, 30–31
dwellings, 28, 30
education, 33–6, 65
Éire (goddess), 18

El Gran Grin, 93–5
Elizabeth I, Queen, 44–5, 68, 119–21
　colonisation policies, 2–3, 45, 46,
　　57–8, 85
　comparisons with Granuaile, 112,
　　120–21
　description of, 119–21
　Granuaile's petitions, 97–8, 106–10,
　　112, 122, 151–2
　meeting with Granuaile, 3, 35, 106,
　　112–24
　rebellion appeasement policy, 97, 99
Erris, 95, 99, 101
Essex, Earl of, 68, 138

falconry, 31
family trees, 193–4
Fenian cycle, 19
Ferguson, Sir Samuel, 185
filí (poets), 27, 33, 34, 35
Fionn mac Cúmhal, 18
fishing, 10–11, 31
Fitton, Sir Edward, 57–8
Fitzgerald, Gerald *see* Desmond, Earl of
FitzGerald, James FitzMaurice, 71, 84
FitzGerald, Margaret, Countess of
　　Ormond, 20, 26
FitzWilliam, Sir William, 92–3, 95,
　　97, 99
food, 29–31
fosterage, 33, 65, 77, 78–9
Fowle, Robert, 95
Frobisher, Martin, 68

Gaelic society, 23–32
galleys, 13–14
gallowglass (mercenaries), 12, 27, 50,
　　74, 88, 89, 90
Galway city, 10, 45, 46, 67, 72, 97
　Granuaile's piracy, 43–4
gambling, 38, 51
Garvey, James, 16

goddesses, 18
Gormflaith, 20
'Grace O'Malley' (song), 177–81
'Grana Weal' (song), 175–6
Granuaile *see* O'Malley, Grace
'Granuaile' (songs), 172–5, 181–5
'Granuweal—An old song', 192–3
Greenwich Palace, 115, 121
Gunning, Maria and Elizabeth, 142

Hardiman, James, 180, 189
Hatton, Sir Christopher, 116
Hely, Bishop, 102
Henry II, King of France, 116
Henry VIII, King of England, 39–40
Hen's Castle, 43, 46–7
housing, 28, 30
Howth Castle, 54–5
hunting, 31

Iar-Chonnacht, 41, 43, 45–6
Inishbofin, 52
Iniskea, 127
Invernan Castle, 42
Irwin, John, 55

James I, King, 140
Joyces, 43, 46–7, 87

kern (*ceithearn*), 27
Kilboynell Castle (Castlebourke), 78,
　　78, 141, 142
Kildawnet, 15, 52
Killybegs, 11, 13, 52
Kilmaine, 97
Kinlough, 75
Kinsale, battle of, 135, 139
Kinturk Castle, 78–9, 140, 141
　　MacEvilly's deed, 149–50
Knights of Ulster, 19
Knockmoy, 16

labourers, 26–7
Lacy, Hugh de, 53
landscape of Ireland, 23
land tenure, 25
Leabhar na gCeart, 7
legal system, 19–20, 24–6, 40, 46, 83,
    85, 133
legend of Granuaile, 1–4, 21, 55–6, 78,
    135–6
    songs and poems, 172–92
LeStrange, Sir Thomas, 96–7
lifestyles in Gaelic society, 28–31
Limerick goal, Granuaile imprisoned
    in, 69
literacy, 33
London, 114–15
Lough Corrib, 96
    Hen's Castle, 43, 46–7
Lough Mask Castle, 75, 77, 87, 99
Lough Swilly, 52
Louisburgh, 15

Mac Conchobhair, Conchobhar Óg, 21
MacConroys, 50
MacCormacks, 50
MacDonald, James, 90
Mac Donnell, Fionnula, 20
MacEvilly, Myles, 78, 129, 141
    deed of land to Tibbott-ne-Long
        Bourke, 149–50
MacEvillys, 77–9, 140
MacFirbis, Duald, 54–5
MacGibbon, Tibbot, 103
Machiavelli, Niccolo, 20
MacJordans, 132
MacMahons, 52, 53, 111
MacMaurices, 45, 61
MacNallys, 50, 51
MacOliverus, Richard, 79–80, 81
MacOliverus, Shane, 65–7, 72, 73
Mac Phiarais, Pádraig, 190
MacSweeneys, 52

MacTibbot, Edmund, 65, 103
MacWilliams, 6, 39, 58, 60, 61, 73–4, 87
MacWilliamship, 42–3, 60, 65–7, 68, 81,
    85–6, 97, 99, 131, 138–9
    Granuaile's husband accedes to, 71,
        72–6, 77, 79–81
Maeve of Connaught, 19
Maguires, 111, 127
Malby, Sir Nicholas, 70, 71, 72–4, 77,
    79–80, 81
    governorship of Connaught, 82–3
Manulla Castle, 78, 141
mapping of Ireland, 23, 125
marriage customs, 26, 27, 41–2
    trial marriages, 61–2
Mary, Queen of Scots, 45
Mayo, Viscounts, 140, 141–2
mead, 29
meals, 29–31
Mendoza, Don Pedro de, 93
mercenaries, 12, 27, 50, 74, 88, 89, 90
Moher Lake, 15
monks, 16–17
Mountbatten, Lord Louis, 143
Mountjoy, Lord, 139
Moycullen, 42
Mudie, Colin, 14
Muirisc, 18
Murrisk, 5, 7, 18, 29, 158
    Abbey, 16
    Castle, 15, 52

'A New Song Called Granuaile', 195–6

O'Boyle, Bishop, 102
O'Boyles, 52
O'Brien, Murrough, Earl of Thomond,
    39, 99, 132
O'Connor Sligo, Sir Donough, 86, 115,
    132
O'Connor Sligo, Maeve, 86–7
O'Donnell, Elizabeth, 56

O'Donnell, Finola, 90
O'Donnell, Hugh Dubh, 90–91
O'Donnell, 'Red' Hugh, 90, 102, 110,
    130–32, 134, 135, 137–8, 139
O'Donnell, Niall Garv, 138
O'Donnells, 87, 88–9, 130
O'Donovan, John, 56
O'Dugan, 5, 36
O'Flaherty, Dónal (*Dónal-an-
    Chogaidh*; Granuaile's husband),
    40–43, 46–7, 67, 154
O'Flaherty, Dónal (Granuaile's
    grandson), 129
O'Flaherty, Margaret, 42, 87–8, 91, 141
O'Flaherty, Murrough-na-dTuadh,
    45–6, 47
O'Flaherty, Murrough-na-Mart, 30–31,
    141
O'Flaherty, Murrough-ne-Doe, 88, 95,
    96, 100, 113, 123
O'Flaherty, Murrough-ne-Maor
    (Granuaile's son), 42, 47, 91,
    137–8, 141, 155–6
    character and expertise, 137
    chastised for treachery by
        Granuaile, 100, 122
    English alliance, 129, 133, 137–8,
        139–40
O'Flaherty, Owen, 42, 47, 98, 129, 141
    killed by Bingham, 88, 118, 155
O'Flaherty, Patrick, 141
O'Flahertys, 40–42, 43–4, 50, 58, 72
O'Hart, J., 175
Ó hEoghusa, Eochaidh, 64–5
Ó hUigínn, Mathgamháin, 64
O'Kellys, 72
O'Loughlin Castle, 52
O'Malley, Dermot, 129
O'Malley, Dónal (*Dónal-ne-Píopa*), 22,
    40, 129, 133, 143
    treason charge, 112, 123–4, 126, 165
O'Malley, Dubhdara (Owen), 21, 22–3,
    24, 28, 30, 36, 41, 154

O'Malley, Dubhdara Rua, 93–4
O'Malley, Elizabeth, 55
O'Malley, Eoghan, 11, 13
O'Malley, Grace (Granuaile)
    CHARACTER AND SKILLS
    ambition and role as wife, 42, 43–4
    bravery and prowess, 4, 44, 47, 51–4,
        64, 71, 78, 105, 132
    charisma, 2, 44, 51, 120
    comparisons with Queen Elizabeth,
        112, 120–21
    determination in adversity, 100,
        104–5, 114
    gambling, 38, 51
    gives birth at sea, 37, 63–4
    'Granuaile' name, 38
    language skills, 35–6
    leadership, 3, 43–4, 51–2, 71, 72
    legendary status, 1–4, 21, 55–6, 78,
        135–6
        songs and poems, 172–92
    political acumen, 3, 34, 68, 75–6, 91,
        109–10, 118, 126, 128–9
    political significance, 3, 106, 112, 125
    pride, 80–81
    seafaring skills, 21, 36–8
    sexual exploits, 51, 53
    son's cowardice, 78
    son's treachery, 100, 122
    suffering, 104–5, 107
    vengeful nature, 52–5, 100, 101
    wealth amassed, 52, 82
    LIFE EVENTS
    background and family, 5–17, 21–3,
        154, 197
    birth, 2, 5
    childhood and education, 33–6, 38
    'career' path, 36, 40, 43–4
    piracy, 11–14, 36–8, 43–4, 48–56, 68,
        126, 132, 134
    marriage, first, 40–43, 154
    death of first husband, 46–7
    defends Hen's Castle, 47

Clare Island piracy base, 48, 49–50
size of army, 1, 50–51
avenges lover's murderers, 52–5
abducts heir of Howth, 54–5
colonisation policy and, 2–3, 58–9,
    67, 81
marriage, second, 60–64, 81–2, 156
offers army to Sidney, 1, 13, 67–8
imprisoned by Desmond, 68–70
defends Carraigahowley Castle, 71
husband accedes to
    MacWilliamship, 72–6, 77,
    79–81
attacks Kinturk Castle, 78
refuses to pay Crown rent, 80–81
death of second husband, 81–2
son (youngest) imprisoned by
    Bingham, 86, 87, 111–12, 115,
    123–4, 126
son (eldest) killed by Bingham, 88,
    118, 155
rebels against Bingham, 88–91,
    96–105
captured and released, 89–90
pardoned, 91
Spanish Armada survivors, 95
attacks son's treachery, 100
petitions Queen Elizabeth, 97–8,
    106–10, 112, 122, 151–2
son charged with treason, 111–12,
    115, 123–4, 126, 165
meets Queen Elizabeth, 3, 35, 106,
    112–24
ageing, 107, 113, 120, 126, 132, 134
Burghley's interrogatory articles,
    117, 153–9
rebuilds pirate fleet, 126, 132, 134
Bingham thwarts activities, 126–9
pressed into service against
    Bourkes, 127
forced to Munster, 128
offers army to Queen Elizabeth,
    128–9

petitions Burghley, 129–30, 164, 167–9
O'Donnell raids Mayo, 130–32, 134
death, 135
resting place, 17, 135
descendants, 137–43, 197–8
songs and poems on, 172–92
neglected by historians, 3–4, 55, 106
O'Malley, Margaret, 21–2, 49, 154
O'Malley, Owen 'Dubhdara', 21, 22–3,
    24, 28, 30, 36, 41, 154
O'Malley, Thady, 16
O'Malley, Tuathal, 8–9, 13
O'Malleys, 5–17, 21–3, 24, 30, 39, 40,
    43–4, 50, 132
    rebellions, 72, 87, 96
Omey Island, 88
O'Neill, Art, 130
O'Neill, Hugh, Earl of Tyrone, 90–91,
    110, 119, 127, 130, 134, 135, 139
O'Neill, Shane, 45, 115
O'Neills, 39
Ormond, Joan Butler, Countess of, 34
Ormond, 'Black' Tom Butler, Earl of,
    56, 57, 94–5, 109, 116, 128, 129
Ormond, Margaret FitzGerald,
    Countess of, 20, 26
'Oró and Welcome Home' (song), 191
'Oró, Sé do Bheatha 'bhaile' (song), 190
O'Rourke, Dervogilla, 20, 26

Patrick, Saint, 6–7, 20
Pearse, Pádraig, 191
Pellam, William, 73
Perrot, Sir John, 3, 58, 83, 85, 86, 87,
    88–9, 91, 92, 107, 108, 118
Philip II, King of Spain, 56, 90–91, 92,
    116, 130
piracy, 11–14, 20, 37
    Algerian, 64
    Granuaile, 11–14, 36–8, 43–4, 48–56,
        68, 126, 132, 134
    ships, 12–14
    women pirates, 11, 37

poems and songs, 172–92
poets (*filí*), 27, 33, 34, 35
'Poor Old Granuaile' (song), 194
Praeger, Robert Lloyd, 53
Protestantism, 56

Raleigh, Sir Walter, 116
Rausakeera, 75
Read, Mary, 11, 37
Red Branch cycle, 19
religion, 27–8
Renvyle Castle, 44, 52
Rockfleet *see* Carraigahowley Castle

St Lawrence, Earl of Howth, 54–5
St Leger, Warham, 116
salic code, 2, 20, 25
San Nicholas Prodaneli, 94–5
Scathach, 19
seafaring, 7–15
    Granuaile's skills, 21, 36–8
    women and, 20–21, 36–7
Severin, Tim, 14
ships, 12–14
Sidney, Sir Henry, 35, 50, 63, 107, 108
    Granuaile offers army to, 1, 13, 67–8
    MacWilliams submission, 66
Sidney, Sir Philip, 35, 67, 68
Sligo Castle, 130, 132
society, 23–32
Somerled, Lord of the Isles, 14
songs and poems, 172–92
Spanish Armada, 13, 90–91, 92–5
Spenser, Edmund, 84, 116
Stornoway, 14
sublords, 25
surrender and regrant policy, 39–40,
    45, 85

tanistry, 25, 41, 46, 67, 81, 87
Thackeray, William Makepeace, 7
Thomond, Murrough O'Brien, Earl of,
    39, 99, 131–2

Tirawley, 99, 133
Toorglass, 94
Trá Bán, battle of, 46
trade, 10
Tuatha de Danaan, 18
Tyrenmore Castle, 6
Tyrone, Earl of *see* O'Neill, Hugh

Uí Máille, Gráinne (Granuaile's
    namesake), 60
Uí Mháille *see* O'Malleys
Ulick sept, 39, 60, 87–8, 100
Ulster, 110–11
Ulster Confederacy, 119, 133, 135, 137–8,
    139
Umhalls, 5–7

Viking ships, 13

Walsingham, Sir Francis, 68, 69, 80, 88
Wentworth, Sir Thomas, 141
West Indies, 37
Westport House, 15, 143
Wilton, Sir Grey de, 74, 84
women, 18–22, 25–6
    debarred from chieftaincy, 20, 25,
        47
    description of Gaelic women, 22
    education, 33–5
    Irish heroines, 1, 20, 26
    life expectancy, 60
    marriage customs, 26, 27, 41–2, 61–2
    pirates, 11, 37
    poetesses, 34
    seafaring and, 20–21, 36–7
    society's negative attitude towards,
        19–20
    warriors in legend, 18–19

Yellow Ford, battle of, 134